www.wadsworth.com

wadsworth.com is the World Wide Web site for Wadsworth and is your direct source to dozens of online resources.

At *wadsworth.com* you can find out about supplements, demonstration software, and student resources. You can also send email to many of our authors and preview new publications and exciting new technologies.

wadsworth.com
Changing the way the world learns®

The Wadsworth SERIES IN CRIMINOLOGICAL THEORY

2001

Bohm: *A Primer on Crime and Delinquency Theory,* Second Edition

Fishbein: *Biobehavioral Perspectives in Criminology*

Messner/Rosenfeld: *Crime and the American Dream,* Third Edition

Piquero/Mazerolle: *Life-Course Criminology: Contemporary and Classic Readings*

2002

Sacco/Kennedy: *The Criminal Event: Perspectives in Space and Time,* Second Edition

THE CRIMINAL EVENT

Perspectives in Space and Time

Second Edition

Vincent F. Sacco
Queen's University

Leslie W. Kennedy
Rutgers University

WADSWORTH

THOMSON LEARNING

Australia • Canada • Mexico • Singapore • Spain
United Kingdom • United States

To Tiia, Daniel, Katherin, and Ema,
Ilona, Alexis, Andrea, and Grandparents

Executive Editor, Criminal Justice: Sabra Horne
Criminal Justice Editor: Shelley Murphy
Development Editor: Terri Edwards
Assistant Editor: Dawn Mesa
Editorial Assistant: Lee McCracken
Technology Project Manager: Susan DeVanna
Marketing Manager: Beverly Dunn
Marketing Assistant: Neena Chandra
Advertising Project Manager: Bryan Vann
Project Manager, Editorial Production:
  Matt Ballantyne

Print/Media Buyer: Robert King
Permissions Editor: Bob Kauser
Production Service: G&S Typesetters, Inc.
Copy Editor: Rosemary Wetherold
Illustrator: Glenda Hassinger/G&S Typesetters, Inc.
Cover Designer: Laurie Anderson
Cover Images: main image and man on street ©
  Mel Curtis, PhotoDisc; hand and fingerprint
  images provided by Getty Images
Compositor: G&S Typesetters, Inc.
Text and Cover Printer: Webcom, Limited

Printed in Canada
1 2 3 4 5 6 7 05 04 03 02 01

For more information about our
products, contact us at:
**Thomson Learning Academic
Resource Center
1-800-423-0563**

For permission to use material from this
text, contact us by:
Phone: 1-800-730-2214
Fax: 1-800-730-2215
Web: http://www.thomsonrights.com

ISBN 0-534-52456-7

Wadsworth / Thomson Learning
10 Davis Drive
Belmont, CA 94002-3098
USA

Asia
Thomson Learning
60 Albert Street, #15-01
Albert Complex
Singapore 189969

Australia
Nelson Thomson Learning
102 Dodds Street
South Melbourne, Victoria 3205
Australia

Canada
Nelson Thomson Learning
1120 Birchmount Road
Toronto, Ontario M1K 5G4
Canada

Europe / Middle East / Africa
Thomson Learning
Berkshire House
168-173 High Holborn
London WC1V 7AA
United Kingdom

Latin America
Thomson Learning
Seneca, 53
Colonia Polanco
11560 Mexico D.F.
Mexico

Spain
Paraninfo Thomson Learning
Calle/Magallanes, 25
28015 Madrid, Spain

Contents

Preface

In this edition of *The Criminal Event,* we have radically revised the way in which we present the idea of crime occurrence, putting singular focus on the elements of space and time that influence the formation of crime places. In the previous edition, we presented discussion of a wide range of theoretical applications to the study of the event. In this edition, we have pared away this review to allow us to discuss more directly how events can be understood and analyzed. We have reordered the discussion and introduced the concept of the criminal event in Chapter 1. It is here that we develop a model that helps us understand the ways in which events transpire; we introduce methodological approaches, including new spatial applications, that we can use to study these events.

In Chapter 2, we discuss separately the actors (offenders, victims, and guardians) who are present in events and how these actors interact to bring about criminal outcomes. The context in which the events occur is presented in Chapter 3. Two models are examined: the ecological, or social disorganization, model; and the opportunity, or lifestyle, model. We review the contributions that these models make to our understanding of the roles physical and social factors play in creating conditions under which criminal events can occur.

In Chapters 4 through 6, we introduce the importance of social domains in creating qualitative differences in the context in which crime occurs. These domains provide an overlay of criminal events that highlights the differences in crimes that occur in public versus private locations, and between strangers versus intimates. Closely connected to the perspectives that emphasize exposure related to certain lifestyles, the domain structure allows us to encapsulate this analysis in an easy-to-understand typology. We have chosen to highlight three major domains: the household, work, and leisure. Although these categories may not completely encapsulate all crime or account for crime that goes beyond these boundaries, they represent important differences in context that help us make sense of crime patterns.

Chapter 4 presents a review of crimes that occur in the household. Increasingly, violent crime is common in intimate locations among family members. Because of privacy issues, this type of crime is hard to detect and to deter, although important strides have been made in recent years to battle the reluctance of participants to report these events. The household is also a target for property crime, because the routine activities that people follow in daily living can enhance vulnerability.

Chapter 5 examines the second context, work, which may have both a private and a public component. The risks that come with some jobs dealing with clients or handling money or precious goods create special circumstances for companies who need employees to fill these positions. Furthermore, workplaces provide opportunity for crime or may become criminogenic if the work itself is part of a criminal enterprise. Chapter 6 reviews the context of activity that more often occurs in public areas in the pursuit of leisure. We are particularly interested in the exposure that comes from activities that put young people on the street or in bars, where violence is common.

In the final chapter, we examine how criminal event analysis can be used in the study of current theories about controlling crime. We focus on three areas that could provide a basis for analysis: opportunity reduction, community policing, and crime prevention through social development. Each of these applications requires that we look at crime as a dynamic process that takes place in space and time. They also are areas in which the greatest amount of innovation has been applied to manage crime places.

The backdrop for this edition of *The Criminal Event* is the dramatic reductions in crime that have occurred in the last half of the twentieth century, a trend that was only just beginning to be recognized when the first edition of this book was published. Some criminologists have sought to explain these crime drops, but traditional approaches have come up short, prompting one commentator to suggest that such things as prison building or mandatory sentencing practices have had a limited impact on crime rate declines (Rosenfeld, 2000). The suggestion is that the declines in crime are due not to any single factor but to a combination of factors, although how to isolate one from the others is not clear. This combination, or interaction, effect is exactly what we are addressing in this book. The importance of our approach is that the factors that we look at, such as opportunity and lifestyles, can be discussed only in terms of how they interact with one another in place and time. We believe that the search for the reasons for crime rate increases and drops should begin with this contextualized approach, which provides a much more powerful analytical framework and policy base for understanding the etiology of crime.

Les Kennedy would like to thank the staff and faculty at the School of Criminal Justice at Rutgers University, specifically Shirley Parker and Edith Laurencin, for their help in scheduling time for this all-consuming job of writing. He also thanks Marcus Felson for providing excellent feedback on our ideas, and Erika Poulsen for her help with the maps. To all his current and former students, thanks are due for providing the intellectual stimulation to continue to study these ideas. And, as always, thanks to his family—Ilona, Alexis, and Andrea—who fill his days with new and interesting adventures!

Vince Sacco would like to thank his friends and colleagues for their help and support. In particular, he owes a special debt to his students (graduate and undergraduate) at Queen's University who continue to ask hard questions about the character of crime and the relative value of particular approaches to its study. As always, Tiia, Katherin, and Daniel deserve his gratitude for the many ways (often unbeknownst to them) in which they contribute to his work.

We are especially grateful for the participation of the following reviewers, who read and reviewed portions of our manuscript throughout its development: Don Bradel, Bemidji State University; Sandra Wachholz, University of Southern Maine; Bruce A. Arrigo, California School of Professional Psychology, Fresno; Agnes Baro, Grand Valley State University; Alexander Alvarez, Northern Arizona University; Susan Smith-Cunnien, University of St. Thomas; Gregg Barak, Eastern Michigan University; David Kauzlarich, Southern Illinois University; Michael R. Norris, Franklin College; Ross Macmillan, University of Minnesota; David Luckenbill, Northern Illinois University; Gai Berlage, Iona College; Dana Britton, Kansas State Univesity; Richard Janikowski, University of Memphis.

Also, we appreciate the staff at Wadsworth, in particular Shelley Murphy and Sabra Horne, for the confidence they have shown in our ideas and in the worthiness of this project.

1

The Criminal Event

The victim's wife wept. She called the decision unbelievable. Her husband was dead, and she thought she knew who was responsible. Twenty-six other men were dead as well, and their relatives, too, had hoped for a murder conviction for the people they held responsible. However, the court had ruled that the evidence was insufficient to support the allegations and therefore had dismissed the case. The families of the victims were not to find out why the men died or who was to blame, compounding their grief and frustration.

This case did not involve a mass murderer wielding an assault weapon and mowing down innocent bystanders in a shopping mall or targeted victims in a factory. The men died in an explosion at the Westray coal mine in Nova Scotia. Murder charges alleging failure to enforce proper safety standards in the workplace had been brought against Westray's mine manager and underground manager ("Westray Charges Thrown Out," 1993).

In the Cicero area of Chicago, on the same day, one teenager was killed and four other people were wounded when gunfire, apparently triggered by gang rivalries, broke out at a crowded public swimming pool on Cicero's northeast side ("Driveby Shooting," 1993). Meanwhile, in Los Angeles, a former Bank of America branch manager was sentenced to twenty-four years in prison for her role in a drug and money-laundering operation. According to the U.S. attorney, the woman worked for a major drug trafficking ring that distributed cocaine, marijuana, and methamphetamines. Prosecutors claimed that members of the operation hid large amounts of cocaine in the roofs of tour buses traveling from Mexico and unloaded the cocaine in Fontana, where it was repackaged and sold ("Ex Bank Manager," 1993).

These three events appear to be very different from one another. However, we can approach these—and other actions that might be deemed criminal—in consistent ways that allow us to make sense of what happened and to put it into a broader context. Although we may not always be able to understand why people do certain things, we can search for the motivations behind crime by examining such factors as circumstances, characteristics of offenders and victims, and their relationships to one another. What events led up to the act? Who else was involved? Where did the event take place? What did the police do? We also want to know what was done afterward to deal with the consequences of the event. What punishment was handed down to ensure that similar events would not happen again? Although the examples presented here may seem to be unique social events, they share many characteristics that allow us to make sense of them as a singular type of behavior. Before we examine the contexts in which crime takes place, we need first to address how behavior comes to be defined as criminal.

CONCEPTUALIZING CRIME

Criminology, like all of the social (and other) sciences, is built upon three foundations: theories, research, and concepts. Theories attempt to explain the relationships among categories of phenomena. Research includes all of the kinds of studies that criminologists undertake in the "real world" to test their theories or to generate new ones. The nature of criminological theory and research is a central issue in this book. Concepts are general terms that name a class of objects, persons, relationships, or events. In other words, concepts are the linguistic categories that we use to classify those aspects of social or physical reality that interest us. A central concept within the field of criminology is, of course, crime. Although in day-to-day conversation we use this term casually, it is important for us in the present context to ask, more precisely, what its usage implies. What do criminologists mean when they use the term *crime?* As a device for classifying social reality, what kinds of acts and behaviors does crime include? What kinds does it exclude?

How crime is conceptualized is an important matter. How we conceptualize phenomena has significant implications for the ways in which we understand them. Put differently, particular conceptualizations encourage us to ask some kinds of questions and not others. It is essential, therefore, that we examine the manner in which much of modern criminology conceptualizes crime. We focus on three types of conceptualizations—crime as a legal construct, crime as normative violation, and crime as social control. Although they differ from each other in some important ways, these conceptualizations share a tendency to define crime in offender-centered terms.

Crime as Lawbreaking

The dominant way of thinking about crime is in legal terms. Thus, crime is conceptualized as a behavior that breaks the law and leaves the offender liable to public prosecution and punishment. In this conceptual scheme, crime is defined relative to the concept of law. Thus, the law may be understood as a form of social control that evaluates the moral nature of the behavior in question. When we describe an act as criminal, we imply that the act is disvalued. It is a form of wrongdoing that "good people" should avoid at the risk of punishment. One of the major functions of the law is to deter people from engaging in the behavior that it prohibits. The law comprises a set of written rules that are supported by state authority and accompanied by a standardized schedule of penalties.

Those who conceptualize crime in legal terms find it useful to distinguish between crime *mala in se* and crime *mala prohibita*. This distinction signals us that not all crimes resonate to the same degree with popular morality. Crimes *mala in se* are crimes that are seen as wrong in and of themselves. They are acts that most people would see as wrong even if they were not against the law and that have been widely condemned both historically and cross-culturally. Murder, robbery, and other predatory crimes are examples of crimes *mala in se*. In contrast, some types of behaviors are not as widely or as consistently condemned. Crimes *mala prohibita* are acts that are wrong not in and of themselves but by prohibition. Alcohol consumption and certain sexual activities, for instance, are viewed as criminal only in some societies and only at some points in history.

That someone behaves in a way that seems to be inconsistent with the requirements of the law does not mean that he or she has committed a crime. To be criminal in a legal sense, an act must be intentional (Boyd, 2000). The mere physical act—known legally as the *actus reus*—is not enough. The act must also have a willful quality—what the law refers to as *mens rea*. Moreover, to be criminal, an act must be committed in the absence of a legally recognized defense or justification (Boyd, 2000). For example, although the law in the United States defines assaultive behavior as a crime, a particular assaultive act may not be criminal if it was accidental (rather than intentional) or was committed in self-defense (and is therefore legally justifiable).

Individual Accountability All criminal law derives from a model of behavior that accounts for individual psychology. Individuals must employ judgments in controlling their acts so that accidents do not occur. The law traditionally has sought to hold able but negligent people accountable for their actions. To do this, it has included the concept of constructive intent. The penalties for doing damage through negligence are usually lighter than those for being deliberately criminal, yet the term *crime* applies to both. A criminal intention *(mens rea)* without the action *(actus reus)* is not a crime. Because intent is part of the definition of *crime,* prosecutors must establish such purpose in the perpetrator. They sometimes try to do this by constructing the motive, asking, "Why would the person act as he or she did?" Establishing a motive does not establish guilt, however; intent and action together are required to obtain a criminal conviction.

Courts can also define the criteria used in judging guilt. Felony murders are a case in point. Under the law, an accidental (and nonnegligent) death that occurs in the context of the commission of any other felony would nevertheless be defined as a murder. Thus, the law defines as "murder" an action that would otherwise not be considered as such, based solely on its connection with the commission of another felony (Rush, 1994).

In some cases, individuals may commit acts that are beyond their control to prevent. This situation is covered by a judgment of competence, which may be restricted because of age, duress, self-defense, or insanity. With respect to age, all criminal behaviors of youths are handled not in the criminal justice system but rather in the juvenile system. The philosophy and organization of the juvenile court system are notably different from those of the adult, or criminal, system in many ways. For example, the juvenile system has as its primary mission the well-being of children, whereas the criminal courts are primarily designed to punish crimes. Although the legal definition of *juvenile* varies somewhat from state to state, most juvenile courts set the minimum age of jurisdiction somewhere between 6 and 10, and the maximum age of jurisdiction is most likely to be 18. (There are exceptions to this. Connecticut, New York, North Carolina, and Vermont, for example, set the maximum age of jurisdiction for the juvenile court at 16.)

Individuals operating under duress may also claim that they did not intend to commit a crime and therefore are not guilty of an offense. In these cases, it must be proved that some unlawful constraint of influence was used to force an individual to commit an act that he or she would otherwise not have committed (Rush, 1994). The idea that a person is under duress when committing a crime is often difficult to prove. The degree of force used must be commensurate with the degree of harm the individual perceived was being directed his or her way. Duress, however, is never a defense against murder.

Self-Defense Self-defense involves actions taken to protect oneself or one's property in the face of a threat involving reasonable force. These cases are not always straightforward, and the view of self-defense is evolving. Originally, the doctrine of self-defense held that the danger must be immediate and severe in order to justify criminal actions. More recently, in delineating situations in which self-defense claims may be made, the law has begun to recognize issues such as power differentials between victims and offenders and/or the presence of a long-term pattern of abuse and the fear that might be associated with it. An example of such a pattern can be found in the "battered-woman syndrome." A battered woman who killed her abuser may claim self-defense if she had a reasonable cause to think that her life was in danger, regardless of whether she was actually physically abused in the immediate incident.

Legal and Social Controls The legal system plays an important role in managing criminal events. Legal definitions of crime may appear to be immutable, determined by clear-cut rules of evidence in establishing guilt or innocence, but in reality, this is not the case. Legal responses can be and are heavily influenced by circumstance, public tolerance, and judicial discretion. Police and courts apply the law not only to prevent crime and punish criminals but also to reduce social conflict. Any study of crime needs to account for behavior that is disorderly or dangerous but not yet unlawful. Alternative or informal legal responses set the outside limits of criminality by redefining responses of the criminal justice system to misbehavior.

Law is only one form of social control (Black, 1976). Social life is also regulated by informal expectations about how people should and should not behave. Whether we call these expectations etiquette, professionalism, or simply good taste, people evaluate the morality of each other's behavior and respond accordingly through a variety of means. Gossip, ridicule, and ostracism are forms of social control that involve fewer formal social processes than do legal forms. When actions are classified as crimes, much more is implied than the mere condemnation of the behavior. Calling an act a crime implies that the problem will be processed in a particular way and that specific state agencies will assume responsibility for solving it. In other words, to label a particular deed a crime is to confer "ownership" of the problem in question to the police, the courts, and other criminal justice agencies (Gilsinan, 1990).

If a problem is defined as one that involves an uninformed public acting on the basis of incomplete or incorrect information, then educational experts might be expected to provide a solution. If a problem is defined as one that results from some medical condition, then mental or physical health professionals will dominate efforts at problem amelioration. However, when behavior is deemed criminal, the issue will likely be surrendered to law enforcement and crime prevention specialists. Evidently, these alternative views of a behavior are associated with dramatically different consequences. As Gusfield (1989) notes, it makes a real difference whether we see social problems as involving people who are troubled or people who are troublesome.

Crime, Politics, and the Law

Our interest of legal conceptualizations of crime necessitates some discussion of the concept of the law. Where do the criminal laws come from in the first place? Two theoretical explanations have been advanced to answer this question (Grattet, Jenness, and Curry, 1998). One explanation argues that the law emerges out of and reflects a social consensus about morality and about the need to respond to particular types of events in particular ways. The other view suggests that reactions to crime have more to do with power, conflict, and inequality than with social consensus.

At a broad level, these approaches may be distinguished with respect to the ways in which they conceptualize the role of social interests (Bockman, 1991). According to some theorists, the members of a society have many interests in common, and their reactions to crime may be said to serve these collective interests. Laws are written and enforced to meet the needs of the majority.

Deviation from these laws is generally accepted as reason for punishment. Others argue that, in a complex society, social groups may pursue different interests and that the degree of success with which they do so depends on how powerful they are. In this framework, reactions to crime can be understood as reflecting particular class, cultural, or other social interests rather than more broadly defined collective interests.

In the study of law, the concept of social consensus is meant to alert us to the apparently broad-based agreement in society about what kinds of acts are serious crimes that warrant direct and immediate intervention and what types are not. This concept suggests that, even in a complex, highly differentiated society like that of the United States, people who differ from one another in terms of gender, age, ethnicity, and social class are likely to agree about certain basic moral standards.

Punishment is directed toward a commonly agreed-upon set of behaviors that offend social mores. We punish murderers more severely than we punish other criminals, because of the general social consensus that murder is among the most serious infractions that a person can commit. We "criminalize," through the passage of laws, behaviors that are widely understood as threatening to our shared values, and we attach the most severe penalties to those crimes that offend our sense of collective morality most deeply.

Consistent with this view, a large body of public opinion research indicates that, by and large, legal responses to crime reflect widespread social sentiments (Goff and Nason-Clark, 1989; Johnson and Sigler, 2000). The view that laws emerge out of and reflect special interests seems to be contradicted by the commonsense observation that some laws, at least, appear to reflect the interests of everyone in society. For example, laws against murder, robbery, or sexual assault would seem to be in everyone's interest, not just in the interests of those who have the most power.

However, the late British sociologist Steven Box (1981) argued that it is not really correct to say that the law prohibits murder, sexual assault, and robbery. Rather, it prohibits certain types of such behaviors while at the same time not prohibiting equally or more destructive behaviors committed by more powerful people.

With respect to murder, for instance, Box wrote,

> The criminal code defines only some types of killing as murder; it excludes, for example, deaths which result from negligence such as employers' failure to maintain safe working conditions in factories or mines or deaths which result from government agencies' giving environmental health risks a low priority or death resulting from drug manufacturers' failure to conduct adequate research on new chemical compounds before conducting aggressive marketing campaigns. [Therefore,] criminal laws against murder, rape, robbery and assault do protect us all, but they do not protect the less powerful from being killed, sexually exploited, deprived of their property, or physically or psychologically damaged through the greed, apathy, negligence and the accountability of the relatively more powerful. (48–49)

As one critic of the consensus position has noted, "Laws do not simply appear miraculously on our law books and do not reflect 'society's' values. Instead, the acts and people we call 'criminal' and our concern with crime at any given time reflect the activity of groups in this society seeking legal support for economic, ideological and status interest" (Sheley, 1991: 39). From this standpoint, definitions of crime must be seen as part of a larger struggle among groups attempting to use the law, or legal control, in the pursuit of their interests.

There is little agreement among scholars as to what might constitute such competing groups in society. Some scholars, for instance, locate attempts to control the mechanisms for reacting to crime in the conflicts between social classes (Chambliss, 1986; Reiman, 1998). Such scholars encourage us to recognize that industries that pollute the environment and victimize consumers are generally treated less harshly than the street criminal who robs a convenience store (Michalowski and Bohlander, 1976). From this perspective, the fact that the average person might agree that the cold-blooded killer of a convenience store night clerk should be treated more harshly than the CEO of a corporation that sells defective—and potentially dangerous or even lethal—products does not demonstrate evidence of a spontaneous consensus about what types of crimes are more serious. It merely demonstrates the ability of powerful interests to manipulate the consciousness of the members of a capitalist society.

Others argue that laws and other aspects of the legal machinery do not merely reflect class conflict but may involve a variety of other interests as well (Bernard, 1981; Gusfield, 1989). Conflicts arise among cultural, lifestyle, or ethnic groups, and the factors that propel groups to use the legal machinery in the service of their interests may be diverse. The conflicts in which social groups are involved are not necessarily fought on a level playing field. Groups have different degrees of access to resources that allow them to influence the outcome of the conflict. From this perspective, the machinery of legal control can be thought of as one such resource. Groups may wish to see laws passed in order to have their values officially recognized by society, or they may wish to see the law used to control a group that threatens their values or social position.

The preceding discussion illustrates that crime is more than a legal construct, and its definition is heavily influenced by social context and competing views of various interest groups in society. When we talk about social behavior as crime, we need to understand that the legal definition is not always applied and that authorities or individuals do not always interpret social behavior as criminal. Crime occurs in context. That fundamental observation serves as the basis for our discussion of the criminal event.

CRIME IN CONTEXT:
INTRODUCING THE CRIMINAL EVENT

Throughout most of the history of criminology, researchers have attempted to understand crime largely in terms of the actions of criminal offenders (Cohen and Felson, 1979). The simple implication of this approach is that crimes represent little more than the enactment of the will of people who are motivated to behave criminally. If this view is valid, the task of the criminologist is to explain why some people behave criminally, whereas the task of the police and other criminal justice agencies is to prevent offenders from behaving criminally or to capture and reform them after they have done so. As is the case in defining crime, analyzing criminal events solely on the basis of the actions of the offender is problematic.

Although we cannot hope to understand crime in society without reference to the lawbreaker, it is also true that there is much more to crime than the offender. Crimes also involve, in many cases, victims who resist their victimization and in so doing affect the course of action. Further, crimes may involve bystanders and witnesses whose presence can deter an offender or whose apparent tacit approval of the offender's actions can facilitate the commission of the crime. Bystanders or victims may also summon the police, whose appearance at the scene may affect the response of offenders.

Crime cannot be separated from the physical and social settings in which it occurs. Many forms of crime are intricately linked to the routine activities in which both victims and offenders engage as well as to the places in which these activities occur. More generally, crime involves the members of the public whose response to perceived increases in criminal levels results in pressure on police to pursue some categories of offenders more aggressively. On an even broader scale, crimes involve the actions of lawmakers and the social groups to whom they are responsive.

The concept of the criminal event encourages us to conceptualize crime in terms that encompass but also extend beyond the study of offenders. In other words, rather than being individual events, crimes are social events (Gould, 1989). To characterize crimes as events is to recognize them as incidents that occur at particular times and in particular places. Like any other type of social event—a dinner party, a corporate board meeting, or a car accident—criminal events are more likely to happen under specific circumstances and to involve specific types of people. This conceptualization of crime runs counter to our tendency to think about criminal events as merely the by-product of chance. We speak of the crime victim as having been "unlucky." We maintain that crimes occur because some people are "in the wrong place at the wrong time." If such events are accidents, however, they are systematic accidents (Felson, 1987). Like many other surprises in life, the likelihood of criminal events is influenced by the choices people make about how and where they spend their time, energy, and money.

The term *event* also conveys an episodic quality. Criminal events, like all forms of social events, have a beginning and an end. The participants in the event may have had a prior association or, in the case of a homicide, for instance, some form of conflict may have predated the event (Luckenbill, 1977), but the criminal event also has its own dimensions, which are both related to and distinct from what went on before it. In a similar way, we can speak of the aftermath of criminal events, in which other social processes are set in motion. Much of the daily business of the criminal justice system is relevant in this respect. Offenders are accused and tried, court dispositions are carried out, and victims must learn to cope with the pains of victimization. In addition, members of the public who learn about criminal events through mass media reports or conversations with neighbors may become more concerned about their personal safety or about the crime problem and its effect on society.

The systematic nature of crime is reflected in the debates that surround "random violence." But what is random violence exactly, and how accurate are the claims made about it in popular culture? An informative answer to such questions is provided by sociologist Joel Best in *Random Violence: How We Talk about New Crimes and Victims* (1999). According to Best, the concern about random violence reflects three assumptions—that such violence is patternless, that it is pointless, and that it is on the rise. Best argues, however, all three assumptions invite critical scrutiny.

Patternless. If by the term *random* we mean "without pattern," then clearly violence is not random. Given the social scientific evidence, to assume that all the members of this society face equal risks of becoming crime victims is completely incorrect. Instead, the research tells us that risks vary dramatically by age, gender, social class, and a range of lifestyle indicators. Although we might think, based on horror stories in the mass media, that we are all equally likely to be murdered, the research evidence suggests that young socially disadvantaged males are much more likely to be killed than other Americans.

Pointless. Often the violent crimes that we read about in the newspaper seem to make no sense. Why would one youth beat up another youth over a pair of gym shoes? Why would a child "out of the blue" attack his classmates with a firearm? Whether an act is pointless is very much a matter of perspective. Violent offenders often believe that they have valid reasons for doing what they do. They may say that they were angry or "tired of being pushed around." Of course, we might not see these as valid reasons and so we assert that the acts are pointless. But this circular reasoning implies that they are pointless by definition. From the point of view of the participants, the criminal acts in which they engage may seem sensible.

On the rise. A big part of the concern about random violence is that the problem is getting worse. Indeed, many people are likely to believe that crime rates are climbing even when the statistical evidence reveals strong trends in the opposite direction. Moreover, assertions about whether violence is getting worse or getting better assume some point of historical reference against which the comparison is made. For example, rates of many kinds of crime now are higher than they were in the 1950s but lower than they were a few years ago. In short, glib overall statements about how random violence is spiraling out of control are surely exaggerated.

The social character of criminal events derives from the fact that they involve interactions between people in particular locations. If the event has several offenders, these offenders interact with one another as well as with victims or bystanders. The police interact with these and other event participants. Even an act of vandalism involving a lone youthful offender and an unoccupied school building has social dimensions. A sticker on the door advising that the property is patrolled by security guards may encourage the offender to weigh the risks associated with the offense. Conversely, a run-down building with broken windows may be read by the offender as announcing that no one cares about the appearance of the property (Kelling and Coles, 1996; Wilson and Kelling, 1982). In either case, the offender reads and, using past experience as a guide, interprets the signs and then acts accordingly. The vandalism itself may be intended as a message to other youths or to unpopular teachers.

The behavior of any one participant in the criminal event, then, intersects with and influences the behavior of other participants. This interaction plays a key role in shaping the course of the event, determining the stages through which it proceeds and the extent to which it will be judged a serious one. In order to fully appreciate the complexity of criminal events, we must understand their behavioral and situational elements.

To summarize the above discussion, as criminologists, we are interested in more than just the motivation of the offender, the actions of the victims that led up to the criminal act, or the role of the police in responding to the crime. These elements come together in a transaction that influences the likelihood that crime will take place. Such transactions have temporal and spatial characteristics.

The effects of social conditions and social domains are mediated through a "criminal event place" that combines factors that generally increase the potential of crime. How these factors are similar to or different from normal behavior needs to be specified. Criminal event places can be seen as parallel to what Barker and Schoggen (1973) call behavior settings, environments in which one could expect prescribed forms of behavior to occur. These places have been discussed in terms of high-risk neighborhoods or areas such as "zones of transition" where crime incidence is higher than in other areas. Crime places also include drug markets and prostitution strolls. Criminal event places are mutations or alterations of general event spaces. How things combine to create these event places becomes the focus of this analysis. In addition, we can consider certain locations where crimes occur repeatedly—also known as hot spots.

Criminal events are also influenced by the social domains in which they occur. We will use, as a basis of comparison, categories based on the extent to which these domains can be seen as private or public. First applied by Oscar Newman (when he discussed the extent to which we can implement crime prevention in public versus private spaces), the notions of territoriality, intimacy, and restricted access have been used in distinguishing behavior settings or crime places. We find the continuum that runs between private and public places to be useful in illustrating the different kinds of criminal events that can occur depending on social context. We will divide our discussion of social domains around this distinction.

Events occur over time in a sequential fashion. The major components are (1) the precursors of the event, including the locational and situational factors

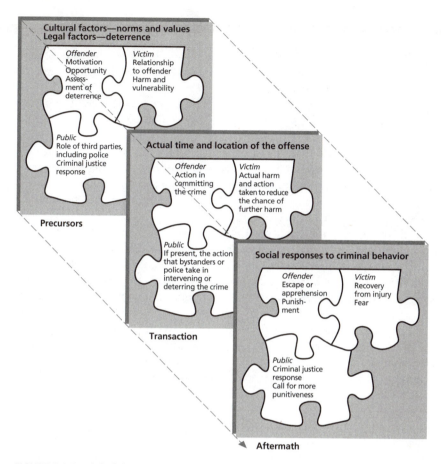

Cultural factors—norms and values
Legal factors—deterrence

Offender
Motivation
Opportunity
Assess-
ment of
deterrence

Victim
Relationship
to offender
Harm and
vulnerability

Public
Role of third parties,
including police
Criminal justice
response

Precursors

Actual time and location of the offense

Offender
Action in
committing
the crime

Victim
Actual harm
and action
taken to reduce
the chance of
further harm

Public
If present, the action
that bystanders or
police take in
intervening or
deterring the crime

Transaction

Social responses to criminal behavior

Offender
Escape or
apprehension
Punish-
ment

Victim
Recovery
from injury
Fear

Public
Criminal justice
response
Call for more
punitiveness

Aftermath

FIGURE 1.1 Model of the Criminal Event

that bring people together in time and space; (2) the transactions that indicate how the interactions among participants define the outcomes of their actions; and (3) the aftermath of the event, including the report to the police, their response, the harm done and the redress required, and the long-term consequences of the event in terms of public reactions and the changing of laws. Figure 1.1 shows a model of the criminal event and its key components.

Precursors

Understanding criminal events as deriving from predisposing conditions helps us separate the social behavior that is criminogenic from that which is not. Studying the precursors of criminal events also allows us to see that, depending on circumstances, behavior that is defined as or evolves into criminality in one situation may not have the same consequences in other situations. As will be discussed in Chapter 2, the main actors in the criminal event come to the setting with different expectations. Criminologists have conducted a great deal of research seeking to understand who offends, their perceptions, and the factors that they see as conducive to their criminal actions. In this context, we address the relationships among participants, the interpretation of the harmfulness of the acts, and the anticipated responses to certain behavior.

The event conceptualization of crime stresses the importance of opportunity in elucidating where and when crimes occur. Only when people who are ready, willing, and able to offend encounter conditions favorable to offending are criminal events likely to develop. From a policy standpoint, therefore, actions that control the appearance or accessibility of opportunities to engage in crime may help to prevent much crime. The important implication of this approach is that the risks of crime can be managed by improving neighborhoods, without changing the character of offenders.

Of course, understanding preconditions will not necessarily allow us to predict criminal outcomes with greater accuracy. The difficulties of prediction are illustrated in the recent debate over the extent to which spousal homicide could have been anticipated on the basis of previous behaviors (Sherman et al., 1991). Although the predictive capability of police is low with respect to spousal homicide, it is likely quite high with respect to repeated interpersonal violence. In determining the precursors of crime, we must reconstruct criminal events by using information that may be distorted by faulty memories, rationalizations, and other restrictions. But the courts use exactly this process to establish guilt or innocence. An example of crime dynamics that considers precursors can be drawn from the research on victims, the second key set of actors in criminal events.

In an early and influential study of 588 criminal homicides in the city of Philadelphia, sociologist Marvin Wolfgang (1958) reported that, in about one quarter of these cases, the victims could be said to have precipitated their own murder. In such cases, Wolfgang noted, the eventual victim, frequently under the influence of alcohol, was the first to brandish a weapon or to threaten deadly force. The eventual offender, fearing for his or her own safety, either intentionally or unintentionally reacted to the threat in a way that proved fatal for the victim. In a stereotypical case, an altercation between two individuals at a bar escalates to the point at which one of the parties produces a gun, a knife, or a broken bottle and says to the other party, "I'm going to kill you." The other party responds with haste and force, and suddenly the person who uttered the threat is lying dead on the barroom floor.

The concept of victim precipitation encourages us to understand the outcome of a crime situation as the joint product of the behaviors of the offender and the victim rather than simply the offender's motivation. In the case of the barroom encounter, the killing can be said to result not from the killer's actions but from the killer-killed interaction. It is important to point out that what people might intend by their words or actions in cases of this type is much less important than how those words or actions are interpreted by others in the interaction. The person who brandishes a broken beer bottle and threatens death to a disputant may be expressing mere bravado rather than serious intent to harm the other party. To the disputant, however, whose judgment is clouded by alcohol and who believes the threat to be real, other interpretations of the situation are well out of reach. With respect to such cases, we have little trouble understanding the explanatory value of the concept of victim precipitation. The homicide would probably not have occurred, we can conclude, if the victim had not initially behaved in an aggressive fashion; thus, the victim was an active contributor to his or her own violent demise.

Problematic from a theoretical standpoint is the degree to which the explanatory logic of victim precipitation is generalizable to other types of events. Is it reasonable, for instance, to argue that crimes such as robbery, theft, or sexual assault can also be victim precipitated? In these types of events, does it make sense to argue that victims actively contribute to their own victimization? Amir (1971) concluded from a study of more than 600 rape cases in Philadelphia that about 1 case in 5 was victim precipitated. Amir classified rapes as victim precipitated if the victim "actually, or so it was deemed, agreed to sexual relations but retracted before the actual act or did not react strongly enough when the suggestion was made to the offender" (266).

Although we might be inclined to agree that victims who initially threaten their offenders in some sense precipitate a homicide, we authors would not agree that victims who initially consent to sexual relations precipitate rape if they subsequently change their minds. For one thing, the assumption in the latter case seems to be that the female rather than the male is responsible for the level of male sexual arousal and that, if that arousal is not satisfied, the female must bear the violent consequences. In addition, it seems to imply that a subsequent decision not to engage in sex, after some initial agreement to do so, is appropriately understood as precipitous of violence. Finally, homicide and sexual assault differ in a fundamental way that is obscured by the haphazard application of the concept of victim precipitation. The types of homicides described by Wolfgang involve events in which victims threaten their offenders with deadly force and are repaid in kind. In the cases of rape described by Amir, the victim is not behaving in a threatening or aggressive fashion, and the violence exhibited by the offender cannot be understood as "payment in kind."

Amir's study illustrates a serious concern that many people have with the concept of victim precipitation: that it is difficult to separate the moral dimensions of the concept from its explanatory dimensions. The assertion that victims precipitate victimization seems uncomfortably close to the suggestion that victims should be blamed for their victimization. For many criminologists, victim blaming should be avoided at all costs (Timmer and Norman, 1984). At the same time, most people can express some degree of empathy for the battered wife who, after years of being subjected to violence, kills her abusive husband. To call a killing of this type victim precipitated does not usually elicit a charge of victim blaming.

For some criminologists, the solution is to recognize that crude attempts to sort crimes into precipitated and unprecipitated categories are doomed to failure. Victims and offenders may contribute to the unfolding of a criminal event in a variety of ways, and thus a broader taxonomy of victim and offender roles is necessary (Fattah, 1991). Another solution involves recognizing that, in many cases, to speak only of victim or offender roles is inappropriate, because doing so minimizes our understanding of the ways in which the circumstances of the events themselves determine who shall bear what label. In other words, there is a need to move beyond the study of victim precipitation to "the full round of interaction," which involves not only the eventual victims and offenders but also other event participants (Luckenbill, 1984).

Other groups that are important in influencing the precursors to crime are bystanders and witnesses and the police. Bystanders may affect the ways in which the behavior occurs through deterring offenders from acting criminally or by acting as witnesses to the action. Bystanders also call the police and play an important role in surveillance in dealing with both private and public events, although, as we will discuss, respect for privacy can influence the actions that bystanders take in reporting criminal behavior. Bystanders can also contribute to a crime's occurrence by assisting the offender or encouraging the offender's actions.

The role of the police in the precursors to criminal events goes beyond active presence in areas to arrest offenders. Police officers believe that patrolling provides deterrence to offenders, but increasingly, the police understand that they must also help community members develop strategies that prevent crime from occurring. The police certify that a crime has occurred, but even with restrictions that have been imposed on the discretion of police agencies in the recent years, the police apply their own interpretation to situations that may lead them to see events as not requiring legal sanctioning.

Transactions

When we study the transaction of an event itself, we move into an assessment of the circumstances, incidence, and frequency of certain types of crimes. Within this context we are able to examine the changes in offender behavior and the extent of victimization. We are particularly interested in viewing the criminal event not in isolation but rather in relation to social events as well as to other criminal events. Interaction can be affected by the location of the event (for example, private versus public), by the presence or absence of drugs or alcohol, and by the availability of weapons.

Discerning trends in these events helps us understand the extent to which we need to respond to them. We also want to understand how trends in crime patterns coincide with shifts in social and economic conditions, resources for policing, and so on. The explanations provided by these types of analysis throw light on the vulnerability of certain groups to social change and the extent to which legal intervention can deter or alter criminal behavior.

Defining (or not defining) certain events as criminal may be problematic. Victims may not immediately appreciate that they have been subject to a crime, and offenders may rationalize their behavior as something other than criminal. As was said above, the strict definition of criminality derives from the actions of the police, who certify criminality through the enactment of legal process, either by naming an event as criminal or by arresting an offender.

But what about events that do not come to the attention of the police but that could nevertheless be defined as criminal? This hidden dimension of crime has important implications for how we define criminal events, as well as for the processes by which the police target certain victims or offenders. Criminal events, then, are dynamic not only in terms of their responsiveness to interactional factors in the environment but also in terms of the claims that are made about them by interested parties. These claims are continuously changing in response to changing political and cultural values.

Goffman (1959) suggested that human behavior is acted out as though part of a theatrical performance, or a "situated transaction." What's important in the interaction is the impression that the actor gives to others. If we are to understand criminal events as situated transactions, we need to emphasize the study of what goes on among the participants rather than what any one of them does. Based on this impression, which generally involves the playing out of a particular role in specific situations, individuals extract information about others in the interaction and about the context (social and spatial) in which the interaction takes place. When enough information is obtained for each individual to define the situation to his or her satisfaction, the roles can be correspondingly acted out (Martin, Mutchnick, and Austin, 1990: 332). With these definitions in hand, individuals are able to sustain and complete a number of transactions throughout their daily lives. These transactions do not always have positive outcomes, however.

Luckenbill (1977) used a transaction approach in analyzing seventy homicides that occurred in a California county. Like other researchers, Luckenbill reported that these murders tended to occur in informal settings and generally involved people who knew each other. What distinguishes his approach, however, is his view of homicide as a product of the situated transaction rather than as a product of the behavior of individual participants. For Luckenbill, situated transactions should be viewed as "character contests" in which efforts on the part of the disputants to "save face" result in deadly combat.

Luckenbill (1977) has argued that homicide can be understood as a situated transaction. Homicide is a transaction in that an offender, a victim, and possibly an audience engage in an interchange that leaves the victim dead, and it is situated in that the participants interact in a common physical territory (196). Based on his analysis of the seventy homicide events in California, Luckenbill argued that these incidents typically move through six stages:

Stage 1. The opening move in the transaction is an action undertaken by the (eventual) victim and defined by the (eventual) offender as an offense to face. For example, the victim says, "Get lost" or "What are you staring at?"

Stage 2. The offender interprets the victim's words or actions as personally offensive.

Stage 3. The offender makes an opening move in salvaging face or protecting honor. In short, the offender retaliates verbally or physically.

Stage 4. The victim responds in an aggressive manner, and the actions suggest a working agreement that the situation is one suited to violent resolution. By cheering or heckling, onlookers may encourage the movement toward violence. They may also block a convenient exit for one or both parties or prevent others from breaking up the fight.

Stage 5. A physical interchange occurs, typically brief and precise.

Stage 6. The brief battle is over, and at this point, the offender flees or remains at the scene, either voluntarily or as a result of force applied by bystanders.

This perspective on criminal events is not meant to imply that situated transactions are restricted to one type of crime. The kinds of transactions that result in acquaintance rapes differ from those that result in homicides. Even in the case of homicides, important differences characterize the nature of the situated transaction (Williams and Flewelling, 1988). For example, it is incorrect to argue that the victims of mass murderers or serial killers are combatants who are committed to battle, although these crimes, too, have situational dynamics.

In many cases, the complexities of transactions blur in our minds whatever a priori distinctions we might wish to make between victims and offenders. How useful is it for us to say that individuals are of a certain criminal type when we know that their behavior can be affected to such a large extent by the situations they face and the roles they believe they must play in completing the transaction? It is the course of action that, to a large degree, determines the identity of the eventual victim and offender. We look not to the victim for the causes of the violence (as we do in cases of victim precipitation) but rather to the victim-offender exchange. With respect to the homicides described by Luckenbill, up until the moment of battle either party might have pulled out of the exchange or responded differently, resulting in quite different consequences. Questions about who should have done what, and when, to prevent the violence are likely to elicit more than one answer from interested observers.

Aftermath

The extent to which we can develop an event perspective depends strongly on the types of information about behavior to which we have access. We are concerned not only with the actual event but also with the reactions by the police, victims, and others. In considering the aftermath of an event, we are interested in the degree to which the victim has been harmed and in the resources needed to aid in his or her recovery. We are also concerned with whether the offender believes that he or she can repeat the offense with impunity. With respect to punishment, has there been sufficient certainty, severity, or celerity to deter a repeat occurrence? These considerations frame a great deal of the discussion about how we are managing our crime problems. Lending focus to this debate are the responses to different types of crime. We need to understand that our responses to criminality are a function of our perspectives in interpreting the reasons for its occurrence and, moreover, that our responses will influence the types of crime that we will experience in the future.

Criminal events elicit responses from many individuals and groups in society. As we will see, the fear of crime is regarded as a pervasive problem, particularly in large urban areas. Obviously, the aftermath of criminal events must be seen, to some extent, as an outcome of the event transaction as well as of the wider social context within which these events occur. The level of injury that a victim of violence experiences, for instance, will be related to decisions by the victim to resist an offender and decisions by the offender to actively overcome that resistance (Kleck and Sayles, 1990; Ziegenhagen and Brosnan, 1985). A "random" murder that is given sensationalist treatment by the mass media will elicit more public fear than a murder involving drinking partners (Liska and Baccaglini, 1990). And an offender who is caught selling illegal drugs when society is in a state of panic about drug crimes can expect less sympathy than an offender who is apprehended during a period when the level of concern is lower.

One of the most significant effects to be associated with victimization is an increase in fear of crime. Serious crimes, especially crimes of violence, may result in a vulnerability conversion, as victims develop a sudden understanding that they are more susceptible to the dangers of life than they thought (Lejeune and Alex, 1973).

Janoff-Bulman and Frieze (1983) maintain that serious criminal victimization is stressful in large part because it is unusual, and unlike more routine stressors, it does not trigger well-developed coping mechanisms. Such events, they argue, make evident people's "psychological baggage" and suggest a need to question not only their assumptions of invulnerability but also other assumptions that underlie their day-to-day existence.

One such assumption is that the world is meaningful. Most of us prefer to go through life believing that things happen for a reason, that good things happen to good people, and that bad things happen to bad people. In general, it is comforting to think that, all things considered, the world makes sense. We can hold these beliefs because we also believe that we can exercise a certain amount of control over what happens to us. A serious, random act of crime, however, can challenge this assumption. In the aftermath of such an event, the world appears to make less sense, and we have become victims of misfortune even though we may have tried hard to keep ourselves safe.

Because of the strong negative effects of crime on public perceptions of safety, criminologists and the police have concentrated much effort on preventing crime by focusing on protecting targets—victims and property—from offenders. They have, as well, paid attention to the importance of policing in influencing crime reduction and to the role of social disorganization in reducing the extent to which informal social control can influence deviant behavior.

All three forms of prevention—situational crime prevention, community-based policing, and addressing social disorganization—address the whole event. The first, situational crime prevention, emphasizes opportunity reduction by modifying situations in which crimes occur.

Situational prevention is based on two important assumptions. The first is that crimes are most effectively prevented when we are attentive to their particular characteristics (Brantingham and Brantingham, 1990). Thus, the first step in opportunity reduction is careful crime analysis: Who commits these crimes? When are they committed? Where do they most frequently occur? What do offenders hope to achieve by committing these crimes? How might certain characteristics of the physical environment contribute to these events? Are there natural forces of guardianship that might be activated in the situations in which crimes typically occur? The answers to such questions help crime prevention planners tailor specific solutions to specific crime problems.

The second key assumption in situational prevention relates to the nature of the offender. Opportunity reduction approaches reflect the model of the rational offender. In other words, offenders' decisions are based on their assessment of the various costs and benefits associated with a particular course of action. How easily can a crime be committed? Is anyone who might take action to prevent the crime standing guard? Are there less risky ways of obtaining the rewards that the commission of the crime promises? Offenders will seek answers to such questions and behave in ways that reflect their best interests. If the opportunities conducive to crime can be made less attractive or less plentiful, many types of crimes (particularly those that are largely opportunistic in nature) may occur much less frequently. According to Clarke (1992), situational prevention involves increasing the risks and decreasing the rewards associated with crime. As offending situations become more difficult, riskier, and less rewarding, rational offenders will be discouraged from offending.

One obvious way to increase the difficulties associated with crime is through target hardening, which refers to measures that decrease the vulnerability of personal or household property. Entry into a house with locked doors and windows is more difficult than entry into a house with unlocked doors and windows. Various forms of access control, such as locked gates and entry phones, also increase the degree of effort needed to commit certain crimes.

The risks involved in the commission of crime may be increased by measures that make it more likely (or, at least, make it appear more likely) that the offender will be discovered and apprehended. A high level of surveillance by security guards, citizen patrols, and security cameras clearly is intended to serve this purpose. Perhaps less obvious is the role of other types of crime prevention measures, such as locks. As Felson (1992: 32) argues, "The strategic role of a lock is not to prevent entry! Rather, its strategic role is to force the offender to make a lot of noise, in hope that others will hear that noise. Ideally, the potential offender will take a look at the lock, note the noise it will force him to make, fear the consequences of that noise, and decide against committing the crime."

Criminal event analysis can also be important in community-based policing, the second of the three forms of crime prevention. Important initiatives that promote problem solving beyond targeting offenders have improved police performance and contributed to lowering crime rates. These police programs have succeeded where the police have taken time both to analyze the nature of the problem and to develop strategies that include community-based solutions to deviance and social disorder, rather than looking at crime incidents.

Crime event analysis can also inform the third method of crime prevention, approaching crime and disorder from a social development perspective. Social disorganization that comes from poverty, unemployment, and disadvantage can influence many parts of the crime event. The physical disorder in inner-city neighborhoods, the impact of drugs and alcohol, the differential opportunities for education and employment, and the increased danger that comes from gangs and guns all affect the ability of communities to respond to crime. In our account of criminal events, we consider the importance of social disorganization in reducing the level of social cohesion in communities and thus in reducing the informal social control that can be mobilized in these areas. In its place, we encounter policing in poor and minority communities that fails to take into account local concerns and directs suspicion at all members of the neighborhoods being policed.

CRIMINAL EVENT DOMAINS:
FROM PRIVATE TO PUBLIC

The patterned social interaction that comes from lifestyles formed by family, work, or leisure can be viewed in terms of criminal event domains. These domains may be thought of as connecting to major spheres of life, in which we invest most of our time and energy. Each domain is distinguished by a particular location and pattern of activity, thus combining the elements of social and cultural definitions of acceptable behavior with the physical characteristics that facilitate or constrain this behavior in crime places (Lynch, 1987). People differ with respect to the amount of time that they spend in each of these domains. For the elderly retired person, the time spent in the household may be of greatest importance. Children spend much of their time at home, but during the teenage years, involvement in this domain declines while involvement in the workplace and in leisure activities outside the home increases.

The distinctions we make among domains may not apply with equal force to all individuals. Some people work out of their homes; others restrict their leisure activities to the household; still others may view the workplace as a leisure setting, with a chance to gossip with coworkers. Despite these complications, the identification of distinct domains helps us clarify differences in patterns of criminal events.

The people we encounter in these domains, the relationships we have with those people, and the social activities that occur there strongly influence the kinds of criminal events that take place in a given social domain, as well as the reactions to those events. Victim surveys indicate that people who report that they frequently go out in the evening to bars also report higher rates of victimization (Sacco and Johnson, 1990). Moreover, observations of barroom behavior (Stoddart, 1991) and police data suggest that taverns are the sites of a disproportionate amount of crime (Roncek and Pravatiner, 1989). Much juvenile crime (including drug use, vandalism, and fighting) resembles leisure pursuits (Agnew and Peterson, 1989) and is most likely to occur when youths are engaged in unsupervised peer activities such as "hanging out" (Kennedy and Baron, 1993). Many forms of sexual assault, especially date rape, occur in leisure environments rather than in more structured environments (DeKeseredy, 1988; Thompson, 1986). Similarly, homicides are most likely to occur when the participants are engaged in recreational pursuits in informal settings (Luckenbill, 1977).

Other types of criminal events are more closely related to non-leisure activities. For the organized criminal, crime is a form of work. For the white-collar or corporate criminal, the offending behavior may represent little more than a simple extension of his or her legitimate business practices. In other cases, a person's employment may be related to the risk of criminal victimization (Block, Felson, and Block, 1984; Lindner and Koehler, 1992). For example, people who handle money, who work in an environment that is open to the general public, or who travel from one work site to another are especially vulnerable to many forms of victimization (Collins, Cox, and Langan, 1987; Mayhew, Elliott, and Dowds, 1989). Partially because of these factors, taxi drivers, police officers, and nurses experience relatively high rates of violence (Block, Felson, and Block, 1984).

From Family to Workplace to Leisure

The most private of all domains is the household, which is generally understood as comprising the social and physical setting within which family life is organized. Many surveys (such as those used in the census) lead us to equate families with households, but in doing so, they may distort the empirical reality of family relations. Family relations in many cases extend beyond a particular household. Husbands and wives who are separated, for instance, usually maintain separate households, although (perhaps because of dependent children) family relations may be sustained. The American family, then, has been changing. We are witnessing a move away from the conventional single-family unit to variations that include single parents, multiple singles, and lone individuals. These varying structures make social relations within families different from what we would have expected in the past. In addition, as growing numbers of households have come to be occupied by the elderly, this group's dependence on their children is increasing.

Reflecting the change in family social relations are the significant changes in the physical setting of households (Hasell and Peatross, 1990). In the layout of the typical suburban home, formal dining rooms have been replaced by family rooms or TV rooms. Master bedrooms have increased in size and have walk-in closets and attached bathrooms, both of which make it easier for couples rather than individuals to get ready for work in the morning. Similarly, kitchens are larger so that adults in a hurry can jointly engage in meal preparation. All such changes have important implications for the types of criminal events that occur in the family domain, as well as for the rate at which they occur. In still other cases, an absence of activity is related to the occurrence of criminal events. With respect to breaking and entering, for instance, households that are unoccupied for long periods of time are at greater risk of victimization than are households that have higher and more regular occupancy rates (Cohen and Cantor, 1981).

The cultural tendency to idealize the family as the most intimate and nurturing of social groups has discouraged research into the extent to which violence is a part of family life (Miller, 1990). Consequently, the recognition of family violence as a social problem has occurred only gradually and in distinct stages. In the 1960s, the problem of child abuse emerged as a policy and research issue (Best, 1990). In the 1970s, wife abuse moved onto the agendas of researchers and criminal justice professionals (Loseke, 1989). In the 1980s, elder abuse came to be recognized as a form of family violence requiring attention. Criminologists have begun to research and theorize about other forms of family violence as well, including sibling violence (Pagelow, 1989) and adolescent violence toward parents (Agnew and Huguley, 1989).

Until recently, it was widely believed that the police could do little about the problem of violence within the family. However, revelations about the pervasiveness of family violence have focused attention on the structure and dynamics of family life and on the need for involvement by criminal justice and other social agencies. Interpersonal conflict theory has been used to shed light on how families run into the kinds of problems that lead to interpersonal violence. The following proposals draw on the insights provided by Gelles and Straus (1988).

First, family life provides the social setting for omnipresent conflict. Family members spend a great deal of time with one another, and their interactions cut across a wide number of dimensions, ranging from decisions about how money will be spent to who will spend it; from where vacations will be spent to how to pay for them; from who will prepare dinner to what that dinner will consist of. The frequency of those interactions, coupled with their intense nature, sets the stage for conflict. In addition, because the family is a heterogeneous social grouping—including within it males and females and people of different ages—it also provides the context for the playing out of gender or generational conflicts that have societal origins. Because family members usually know one another so well, they are aware of each other's weaknesses and vulnerabilities. Such intimate knowledge facilitates the escalation of conflicts into violent exchanges.

Second, family life is private life. What happens between family members frequently takes place behind closed doors. The private character of family life reflects a consensus view that families are different from other social groupings. The privacy of the family has structured the ways in which the police and the courts have responded to intrafamily violence. Neighbors, friends, or coworkers may not know about violence that occurs between family members, and even if they do know about it, they may regard it as none of their business. Moreover, the view that violence in the home is a family matter may be shared by the victims of violence. All such factors reinforce the low visibility of violent conflict in the home and suggest the extent to which it is immune to many of the informal social controls that regulate such behavior among nonintimates. Some scholars argue that concerns for the privacy of the home simply shield the abuser from the sanctions of the criminal justice system. Such concerns, they argue, reflect a bias toward maintaining power relationships in families that favor men while ignoring the injustices perpetrated against women and children.

Third, cultural attitudes toward family violence are highly ambivalent. In the family, unlike in the workplace or other more formal settings, physical violence continues to be tolerated. This is most evident with respect to the spanking of children (Steinmetz, 1986). A majority of parents believe that under certain conditions it is perfectly appropriate for one family member to use physical force against another family member. This is not to suggest that spanking is necessarily abusive (although it well may be), but rather that rules about violence in the home differ from rules about violence in other social domains. Nor does the tolerance of physical violence extend to dependent children alone. In the recent past, violent behavior by husbands against wives was tolerated in much the way that parental violence toward children currently is viewed. Most people still continue to regard violence among siblings as normal and natural and, despite obvious physical consequences, not really a form of violence at all.

Fourth, the family is a hierarchical institution. This means that some family members have more power than others. Obviously, parents are more powerful than children. In traditional patriarchal family structures, which are characterized by the presence of an adult male authority figure, the husband is assumed to have the right to make decisions that are binding on other family members (Hagan, Gillis, and Simpson, 1985). Such authority relations, which are recognized by law, create a situation that allows those with more power to behave with relative impunity toward those who have less power. In addition, the widespread support for existing authority relations encourages those with power to believe that they have a right to expect compliance from those who are less powerful. Violence may be understood as one effective way in which such compliance is gained.

The workplace is the social domain that combines private with public transactions. We will examine the workplace from the point of view of how individuals engaged in legitimate work fall victim to crime while pursuing this activity. Also, what opportunities for crime does legitimate work afford offenders?

The second area of the workplace domain that we will investigate is enterprise crime, which involves the exploitation of opportunities for the development of criminal business. We will chronicle the major changes in the workplace over the years, investigating how they have affected crime patterns. We will explore a number of work situations where crime might occur, either as a part of regular work patterns or as work itself, to follow how this domain supports these outcomes. Many believe that, as unemployment increases or decreases, crime rates follow. We consider the important effects of unemployment on participation in crime.

People "at leisure" have been looked at as being highly likely to be involved in crime, both as offenders and victims. Over the years, the perception of youth crime has been formed by the belief that it stems from idleness, which is often equated with youth at leisure. Some crimes have even been connected to leisure participation, as in the case of "recreational drug use." Suspicion has been directed, as well, at the corrupting influence of leisure activities, including violent television, videogames, and activities in which youth simply hang around on the street.

The street is also a likely location for crime and victimization, as we adopt lifestyles that take us away from our homes and into public areas in search of leisure pursuits. Leisure may be defined in a variety of ways. Frequently, we use the term in an objective way to describe the "spare time" or "free time" that is left over after paid work or other obligations (such as child care) have been taken care of (Iso-Ahola, 1980). However, leisure has a subjective as well as an objective character. In other words, leisure is not just free time but rather free time that is used in a particular way—usually for play or recreation. Leisure activity may be regarded as intrinsically satisfying in that it contains its own rewards. In addition, we usually assume that leisure activities are freely chosen and that leisure interaction occurs among peers. By contrast, family- or work-related activities tend to be less voluntaristic and to be characterized by authority relations that are enforced by law or custom.

Like other scarce resources, leisure time is unequally distributed (Wilson, 1980). Teenagers and the elderly tend to have more leisure time than young parents or middle-aged individuals. And because household tasks and child-care responsibilities reduce free time, men generally have more leisure time than women have. People also differ with respect to their leisure preferences and the resources they have to pursue them. Those in higher-income groups are more likely to frequent restaurants, whereas young people are more likely to go to bars, movies, or video arcades (Provenzo, 1991). The elderly are less likely to go out in the evening for leisure of any kind (Golant, 1984); elderly people who do engage in leisure outside the home tend to visit friends or to go to a shopping mall.

Often the concern about juveniles comes from the view that their leisure activities free them from social control of parents or other adults. The popular view is that delinquency follows from this lack of supervision. Also, the influence of other peers reinforces the propensity toward delinquent behavior.

The role of leisure in the development or the lessening of delinquent motivation may have more to do with the behavior of males than of females (Riley, 1987). In part, this is because female adolescents have traditionally been subject to higher levels of control, which restrict their leisure options (Singer and Levine, 1988). These gender differences may be rooted in patterns of family socialization. Whereas risk-taking behavior is encouraged in male children, female children are generally subjected to significantly greater degrees of parental control. Gender differences in delinquent leisure may reflect these patterned gender differences in risk taking and control.

For many youths, the street is itself a leisure setting. For others, it is the route that they take from one setting to another or from these settings to their homes. Criminal events in the street seem to support the argument of opportunity theorists that people are victims of routines that leave them vulnerable to offenders. In fact, research indicates that, despite the horror stories from inner-city areas where people of all ages are vulnerable to crime, the group that is most likely to be involved in these "risky" routines on the street are young males. Their behavior tends to be more public than that of most other groups, and they frequent the street to a greater degree than others.

MEASURING CRIMINAL EVENTS

Much of what we know about criminal events is based on the reports provided by offenders, victims, and the police. In addressing the limitations of these data, two issues require consideration: the type of event that is captured by each method of data collection, and the perspective brought to bear on those events that are captured. Research data are indispensable to the understanding of criminal events. They allow for the testing of theoretical ideas, they help us chart the dimensions of criminal events for policy purposes, and they provide us with indicators of the quality of life. Although data about criminal events may derive from many different sources, they tend to be generated by one of two basic investigative strategies: observations and reports.

Criminal events may be directly observed either in naturalistic settings or in the context of field or laboratory experimentation. Though much can be learned about criminal events by waiting for them to happen (as in the former case) or by making them happen (as in the latter case), most contemporary research depends on information revealed by reports about crime.

Uniform Crime Reports (UCR)

The reports most widely used in crime research come from those who are most active in criminal events: police officers, victims, and offenders. The data collected by the police through the Uniform Crime Reporting system describe a wide range of crimes and provide a continuous national record. Recent revisions to the UCR survey are likely to increase the value of these data for both academic and policy purposes. The major limitation of these data is that any police-based information system can tell us only about crimes that come to the attention of the police. In the case of the UCR system, the organizational perspective of policing agencies determines the rules for data collection. Administrative or political pressure may dictate that the policing of certain kinds of criminal events (for example, impaired driving) be emphasized over others (for example, soft drug use) (Jackson, 1990; O'Brien, 1985). Police practices, public tolerance for particular kinds of behavior, and the needs of the agency for particular kinds of data all influence the ways in which data are collected.

The police reports that form the basis of the UCR are in some ways the most comprehensive data source. The UCR includes crimes without direct victims, as well as crimes committed against businesses, the community, and individuals who are unlikely to appear in surveys (Reiss, 1986b).

A recent experiment with incident-based police accounting, the National Incident-Based Reporting System (NIBRS), offers an improvement over summary-based UCR systems by providing reports on more than 50 types of crime (the UCR's accounting is limited to less than 30 types). Maxfield (1999) notes that these data sets also provide a great deal of detail about incidents, including characteristics of offenders and victims, their relationships, circumstances of the event, and information about the arrest. From this data set, we are able to characterize the event location and the types of activity taking place there. We can follow our interest in different domains by using these data in ways that are not possible using the summary-based UCR numbers.

NIBRS also provides other information that is not easily gained from the UCR. Missing populations, ranging from the homeless and businesses, can be identified and analyzed in a way that is not possible by using summary statistics or victimization surveys. In addition, NIBRS allows us to identify and examine the effects of crime on those under 12 years old, a group that cannot be identified using the UCR data sets.

With this more complete data set, we are able to conduct criminal event analysis not previously possible using official data. Although the data set is limited in coverage (only eighteen states are participating, and many reporting jurisdictions provide incomplete data), complicated in its record structure, and hard to use, the incident information can nevertheless be used to look at an event-based structure of crime occurrence.

Snyder (2000) has examined the NIBRS data to do just that in his study of sexual assault of young children. As he points out, although law enforcement, child protective services, and legislatures work hard to reduce the incidence of sexual crimes against children, little empirically based information about these crimes is available. The National Crime Victimization Survey (NCVS), described below, provides the only existing national data on these crimes. According to the NCVS, 197,000 incidents of forcible rape and 110,000 incidents of other sexual assault involving victims ages 12 or older were recorded in the United States in 1996. Snyder points out that in less than a third of the cases (about 94,000 cases) victims reported sexual assaults to law enforcement agencies. Beyond the difference in volume, little is known about the victims, their offenders, and other characteristics of these crimes.

However, using the NIBRS, we can look at detailed descriptions of sexual assaults reported by participating law enforcement agencies. According to Snyder,

> NIBRS captures a wide range of information on each incident of sexual assault reported to law enforcement. This information includes demographic information on all victims; the levels of victim injury; victims' perceptions of offenders' ages, gender, race, and Hispanic ethnicity; and the victim-offender relationships. NIBRS also collects information on all offenses involved in the incident; the types of weapons used; the locations

of the incident; the dates and times of the incident; the demographics of arrestees (if any); and the methods of clearance, such as arrest or victim refusal to cooperate with the investigation. (1)

These are all data that contribute to a criminal event analysis.

In an effort to connect the characteristics of the victims and offenders to the aftermath of the offense, specifically whether or not the event led to an arrest, Snyder examined the NIBRS data set for trends in the statistics. He found that the probability that an offender is arrested appears to be largely unrelated to the offender's age. Snyder was able to establish that the only age-related difference that appeared was for very young offenders, who were not likely to be arrested.

In further analysis, Snyder (2000) established that the factors that had the largest influence on the probability of arrest were as follows:

- The number of victims in the incident—where there was more than one victim, arrest probabilities increased.
- The number of offenders in the incident—where there was just one offender, arrest probabilities increased.
- The age of the victim—juvenile victims increased arrest probabilities.
- The sex of the victim—male victims tended to decrease arrest probabilities.
- The relationship of the victim and the offender—offenders who were strangers had decreased arrest probabilities.
- The location of the incident—incidents that happened outside of residences decreased arrest probabilities.
- The injury to the victim—incidents in which the victim was injured decreased arrest probabilities.

The connections between transactions and aftermath of events are clearly evidenced in this analysis, which illustrates how the NIBRS data can provide important new insights into the criminal event. With increasing coverage and more developed analytical strategies, this data set will become an important tool in criminal event analysis.

Calls for Service Data

In recent years a new opportunity for crime analysis has appeared with innovations in the ways in which police respond to calls for service. With the advent of computer-assisted dispatch (CAD) systems, police are able to create machine-readable records of their activity, using the calls for service data as a basic reference for information about crime occurrences. Although calls for service data include many noncriminal events, the CAD system provides a tool for managing incident-based information about those events that are criminal, including whether or not arrest resulted. This information has traditionally been guarded closely by police agencies as constituting strategic data that should not be shared with the public. More recently, police agencies have recognized a value in providing these data—properly screened to protect confidentiality—to the public through placement on Internet sites or in newspapers (see, for example, block-by-block crime data for Houston at *http://www.ci.houston.tx.us/department/ police*). This openness provides crime researchers with a new opportunity to study criminal events by using individual-based data. This increased availability of data is particularly valuable in the search for criminal places, because these incidents can be studied in terms of spatial and temporal patterns.

Incident-based data are ideal for use in combination with geographic information systems (GIS), which can be used to map crime occurrences. With the increasing sophistication of these analytical tools, we are able to identify crime hot spots by looking at the density of crime patterns. We can search for boundaries that define these crime places and examine the relationship between crime patterns and urban structure. GIS applications allow for layering of urban data provided by transportation agencies, planning departments, census bureaus, and utility companies. We can now perform geographic analysis not previously possible. Police agencies and planners have come to understand the value of these approaches in their efforts to prevent crime and promote safer environments. Underlying these approaches is the knowledge that crime and crime prevention depend on a clear understanding of the dynamics of place.

National Crime Victimization Survey (NCVS)

Each year, data are obtained from a survey of a nationally representative sample of approximately 50,000 households comprising nearly 100,000 persons. Surveys of victims and offenders are intended to illuminate crimes that are not recorded by the police. Despite the valuable information they provide, these surveys are subject to all of the problems that characterize any type of survey. Victims and offenders are not always as accessible as we would like them to be, and we cannot always be sure that they will not, intentionally or unintentionally, distort the truth in response to questions about their involvement in criminal events.

Victimization surveys usually ask respondents only about those events that have a direct and immediate victim (Reiss, 1986b). Because they are household surveys, they tend to exclude crimes that victimize businesses or the wider community (for example, vandalism of public property). Victimization surveys also exclude victims to whom access is limited, including children, the homeless, and residents of psychiatric or other institutions (Weis, 1989).

Two general strategies can be used to investigate the ways in which victims are affected by crime. First, survey respondents can be asked directly about the losses that they experienced. Responses to these questions, like all responses when people are asked to report on past events, are subject to errors as a result of faulty memory, dishonesty, and misunderstanding (Skogan, 1986). Usually, the questions focus on the most obvious losses to the victim, such as injury or stolen or damaged goods. Although such questions are useful, they focus attention only on what happens during or immediately after the event but reveal little about what happens to the victim over the longer term. In the case of the NCVS, for example, respondents are asked about victimization events that occurred during the six-month period preceding the survey; therefore, knowledge gained from these surveys about victimization problems that emerge later is minimal.

The NCVS provides a great deal of information about the crime incident, including characteristics of victims, offenders, the circumstances of the event, and the aftermath. The structure of the survey focuses attention on the temporal and spatial aspects of the victimization, providing information that can be used in criminal event analysis. Of particular interest in recent surveys have been the efforts on the part of analysts at the Bureau of Justice Statistics in the U.S. Department of Justice to produce tables that describe the crime event (U.S. Department of Justice, 2000). These tables present results on a range of circumstances that individuals report that are connected to the crime they experienced. For example, we are able to identify crime type by the victim's activity at the time of incident (such as on the way to or from work, shopping, or attending school). Further, we are able to examine the actual interaction that took place between the victim and the offender. For example, survey respondents are asked to report whether or not they used self-protective measures in warding off attack by offenders. They are also asked to discuss the extent of their injury and whether or not they sought out medical assistance. The individual record count of each victimization provides the analyst with the ability to track victimization through the event stages and to make comparisons across crime type, victim type, and characteristics of offenders.

Victimization data rely on victims' perceptions of criminal events. As such, their quality is subject to whatever distortions, intentional or unintentional, characterize these perceptions. The accuracy of respondents' reports also is subject to numerous compromises. For example, respondents may fail to disclose experiences in which the researcher is interested (Skogan, 1986). If someone is victimized during the course of an illegal activity, he or she may not want to tell the researcher about it. If the event is of minor significance, it may be forgotten by the time of the interview; this may be a particular problem when the reference period about which the respondent is asked is long. The opposite problem involves what is called telescoping (Skogan, 1986). In this case, crimes that the victim regards as significant life events may be reported as having occurred during the reference period when, in fact, they actually occurred earlier. Telescoping is most likely to be a problem in the study of serious violent crimes.

In many cases of serious victimization, the victim may be discouraged from reporting the event to a researcher. For instance, in cases of family violence, the victim may feel ashamed or embarrassed or may believe that reporting the event may put him or her at risk. This problem may occur particularly with sexual assaults or crimes involving strangers.

Victims' perspectives are limited in other ways as well. If respondents cannot or do not define an event as a crime, they are unlikely to tell a researcher about it (Block and Block, 1984). In some cases, people may be victimized but not realize it—many forms of fraud are intended to accomplish precisely this outcome. Similarly, if a purse is stolen but the victim believes that she lost it, she will not report it to a researcher who asks her a question about theft. Much of the criminal harm that is perpetrated by corporations and governments is not readily apparent, even to those who are directly affected; as a result, victims may have no idea that they have been victimized (Walklate, 1989).

Self-Report

Interviews with offenders can give us important insights into their behavior, attitudes, and motivations. We might learn why they commit the type of offenses that they commit, how they feel about their victims, and how they assess their risk of being apprehended by the criminal justice system (Bennett and Wright, 1984). Perhaps the most obvious form of offender reports is obtained from samples of known offenders such as prison inmates or those who have been convicted of an offense and are awaiting sentence (Baunach, 1990). Surveys of this type can shed light on a range of subjects, including the use of weapons by offenders (Wright and Rossi, 1986) and the characteristics of offenders' victims (Innes and Greenfeld, 1990). Such information can lead to useful insights into how offenders regard their own actions as well as the actions of other event participants.

One major concern with surveys of known offenders relates to the generalizability of the findings (Flowers, 1989). Given that many offenders are not captured and that many of those who are captured are not convicted or sentenced, what we learn in interviews with convicted offenders may not be representative of the larger offender population.

Self-report studies have been used primarily to obtain information about the common delinquencies of youth. They have been criticized for excluding the more serious, but less frequently occurring, types of delinquency (such as extreme forms of violence) while emphasizing nonserious forms of behavior (such as cutting classes or disobeying parents) (Braithwaite, 1981). When students in criminology classes are asked to demonstrate with a show of hands whether they have committed any of the crimes listed in the self-report questionnaires, a large number always respond in the affirmative. Even political leaders have admitted to experimenting with marijuana as youths. A loose interpretation of these data, then, can make everyone a criminal (Figlio, 1990).

The issue of perspective is central to any attempt to make proper use of crime report data. Each method offers a limited perspective because it elicits information from only some types of event participants. Event participants' understanding of criminal events may also differ quite markedly. We expect, therefore, that their reports will reflect these differences.

Respondents are also likely to differ in their views as to what level of violation constitutes a crime (Gove, Hughes, and Geerkan, 1985). Some studies show, for instance, that highly educated people are more likely to report assault victimization. Such a finding is most reasonably interpreted in terms of class differences in the definition of injury or in the willingness to tolerate violence rather than in terms of the greater threats of criminal violence faced by more highly educated respondents (Skogan, 1990b).

Self-report studies help us understand criminal events from the perspective of the offender. Yet offenders who have the most to hide may be least willing to participate in the research (O'Brien, 1985). Moreover, some offenders may exaggerate their wrongdoing (perhaps as a show of bravado), whereas others may be reluctant to admit to involvement in criminal activity (Wright and Bennett,

1990). When the latter do report, they may be more willing to admit to trivial rather than serious offenses (Jupp, 1989).

Ethnographic Research

Ethnographic research is another means by which information can be gathered from known offenders. As a research strategy, ethnography moves beyond the use of a structured interview as the researcher attempts not only to speak with but also to directly observe and interact with the people being studied (Wright and Bennett, 1990). The researcher gathers offender accounts by informally participating in and developing some intimate knowledge of the social world of the offender (Fleisher, 1995).

This approach rests on the assumption that formal interviews with offenders yield very limited research data. Researchers may find it difficult to gain access to members of "outlaw" motorcycle gangs (Wolff, 1991), organized-crime groups, and professional thieves through conventional means (Ianni and Reuss-Ianni, 1972; Wolff, 1991). However, if researchers are able to cultivate informal relationships with offenders, they may be able to penetrate their social world and thereby learn much that would be invisible to an outside researcher. Ethnographic studies of street gangs (Baron, 1997; Kennedy and Baron, 1993; Sullivan and Miller, 1999), violent criminals (Fleisher, 1995), and male prostitutes (Calhoun and Weaver, 1996) provide insights that could not be gleaned in police statistics or victim surveys. Chambliss (1975), a proponent of this method of urban ethnography, argues that data on organized crime and professional theft, as well as other presumably difficult-to-study types of criminals and crime, are much more available than we usually think: "All we really have to do is get out of our offices and onto the streets. The data are there; the problem is that too often the sociologist is not" (39).

Comparing Data Types

Reiss (1986a) argues that the perspective implicit in police data offers a distinct advantage over self-report and victimization data. Whereas the latter two data sources reflect the view of highly self-interested parties, police data allow for a more balanced picture. Police reports of criminal events are based on a wider variety of information sources, including victims, offenders, bystanders, and witnesses. In addition, police data normally are collected closer in time to the actual event than is the case with victim or offender surveys. As a result, police data are less likely to be influenced by the selective effects of memory.

In a similar vein, Gove, Hughes, and Geerken (1985) suggest that, in comparison with other data sources, official statistics provide more rigorous criteria for the definition of criminal events. The authors argue that victimization surveys give only the victim's perspective, which is insufficient in determining whether a crime has in fact occurred. In order to make this judgment, we also need to know the offender's intention, the circumstances surrounding the event, and the condition of the victim (Mayhew, Elliott, and Dowds, 1989).

Criminal events that are recorded in official statistics have passed through two filters. First, they have been judged sufficiently serious to be worth reporting to the police. Second, they have been certified by the police as serious events deserving of criminal justice intervention. According to Gove, Hughes, and Geerken (1985), UCRs data provide a good indicator of the extent to which citizens feel injured, frightened, and financially harmed by a criminal act.

These different perspectives have important implications for how criminal events are understood. If, for example, an individual gets into a fistfight with a drinking companion, the event might be understood differently within the context of different data collection systems. If the individual is asked in a victimization survey whether anyone has hit him or threatened to hit him, and he responds honestly, he is likely to be counted as a victim. If he is asked in a self-report survey whether he has hit anyone, and he answers honestly, he is likely to be counted as an offender. If the police are summoned, they may, because of the circumstances and the relationship between the parties, screen the event out so that it never enters the official record.

We do not necessarily expect reports from different event participants to tell us the same things. Victimization surveys and UCR data may disagree because they employ different criteria in determining the types of events that are to be included (Blumstein, Cohen, and Rosenfeld, 1992). Thus, if researchers undertook a victimization survey in a given community and then compared the survey rates to the UCR rates for that same community, several sources of variation would be apparent. While the UCR measures would encompass crimes committed against businesses, institutionalized persons, and individuals who do not have a permanent residence, the victim survey would probably omit such crimes. The UCR rates would include crimes committed within the policing jurisdiction, irrespective of victims' place of residence. Thus, the UCR might include crimes committed against tourists who were visiting the community as well as crimes against commuters who work in the community but live elsewhere. By contrast, the victimization study, because it usually involves a household survey, would restrict attention to crimes committed against community residents, regardless of whether the crime occurred in the local community or elsewhere. Similarly, the descriptions of offenders that emerge from police reports of crimes serious enough to have passed through citizen and police filters cannot be expected to concur with offender profiles that emerge from self-report studies that focus on nonserious delinquency (Hindelang, Hirschi, and Weis, 1981; West and Farrington, 1977).

Although for decades criminologists have engaged in an intense debate about the relative value of specific crime measures, clearly no single data source is sufficient to answer all of the questions we might have about criminal events (Jackson, 1990; Menard and Covey, 1988). Because our data sources tell us different things, it does not really make sense to think about one data source as better than another. Subsequent chapters of this book will make extensive use of data derived from these sources, but it is important that these data always be approached cautiously and critically.

The problems associated with these major sources of crime data—police, victim, and offender reports—do not suggest a lack of knowledge or awareness on the part of those who collect the data. Rather, they remind us that any attempt to investigate complex social phenomena is fraught with inherent difficulties.

We have also seen that no single data source is likely to answer all of the questions that we have about criminal events. Our major data sources tell us quite different things, because they are likely to capture different types of events and to bring different perspectives to bear on these events. For this reason, it is unproductive to engage in endless debates about the superiority of one data source over another. To a considerable extent, the usefulness of any data source varies, depending on how well it helps us address particular questions.

We should not dismiss crime data just because our data sources are flawed and less comprehensive than we would like. A great deal can be learned from a judicious use of crime data. Although we know that our data are problematic, in many cases we also know how they are problematic. Frequently, the errors that characterize our efforts at data collection are not random but systematic. Knowing the sources and consequences of these systematic errors makes data more valuable than they might otherwise be.

The Crime Funnel

The data most frequently used by criminologists interested in the study of criminal events, then, come not from direct observation but from the reports of those who have direct knowledge of the event, principally the police, victims, and offenders. Criminal justice system agencies besides the police, such as courts and prisons, can also be important sources of information about criminal events. After all, such agencies are in the "crime business" and keep records of people who are arrested, cases that go to trial, and the number of people incarcerated.

If our interest centers on the criminal event, the data made available by the various criminal agencies differ in terms of their value. In part, this is because different agencies have different needs and therefore do not all collect the same type of information. Of equal importance is that criminal justice agencies are connected to one another in a "volume-reducing system" (Reiss, 1986a). In other words, cases traveling through the various stages of the criminal justice system have a high rate of attrition. Not all criminal events that come to the attention of the police result in an arrest, not all arrests result in a trial, and not all trials result in a conviction. Some writers have described this attrition process as a "crime funnel." For example, according to government estimates, in the early 1990s:

- About 54 percent of all burglaries were reported to the police (U.S. Department of Justice, 1994b).
- Of the burglaries that were reported to police, about 13 percent were cleared by an arrest (U.S. Department of Justice, 1994a).
- Of the burglary cases that were brought to trial, about 68 percent resulted in a conviction (U.S. Department of Justice, 1993).

In a similar vein, Dutton (1987) argues that, as cases of wife assault move through the criminal justice system, a "winnowing process" occurs. The probability of wife assault's being detected by the justice system is about 6.5 percent. Once detected, the probability of arrest is about 21.2 percent. Given these contingencies, offenders in the cases of wife assault that Dutton studied had only a 0.38 percent chance of being punished by the courts. Of course, with mandatory arrest instituted in family violence cases, this number has increased in recent years. Still, some studies have shown that family violence incidents still result in conviction in less than half of the cases that are reported.

SUMMARY

When crimes occur, they have a dynamic character that involves choices by offenders, victims, and others, all of which affect the outcome. Crimes can thus be said to have an interactional character—what any one participant does depends on what others do. An important consideration in this equation is the role of the victim, who, together with the offender and other main players, comes to be involved in what is called a situated transaction. In such transactions, the characteristics of the individuals involved come to define the direction that a crime will take. In the early stages of these interactions, it is often difficult to predict the eventual victim and offender. The actions that occur during the interaction more clearly define these roles. Depending on the actions of third parties, harm and guilt are, in many cases, clearly worked out only after the fact.

Interactional approaches suggest, then, that crimes are the outcome of social exchanges between people who find themselves in specific circumstances and who must make quick decisions about how to respond to one another's behavior. Their responses determine the outcomes. These outcomes are not always predictable in that they can be affected by many factors in the situation. Interactional approaches help us determine the effectiveness of various strategies that are used by victims or the police in deterring or preventing crime.

Crime is, strictly speaking, the breaking of the law. But laws and their interpretation are an embodiment of social morality. As such, they are subject to change, as is our understanding of criminal events. Crime is a social construct that varies according to definition and response by legal authorities. Criminologists have the job of assessing how legal and moral definitions of crime coincide with the circumstances that people face and how that combination of factors evolves into events that demand enforcement and result in labeling individuals as criminals.

The criminal event is a social event. Like all other social events, it has a beginning and an end. It takes place in space and time. Criminal events appear to occur according to some systematic pattern, operating according to the routines followed by actors in social environments and based on opportunities that emerge in those environments. Criminal events are social in that they involve patterned interaction between human beings. The nature and form of this interaction shape the course of the event, determine the stages through which it proceeds, and define how serious it is judged to be in terms of harm done. Several types of actors are involved in these events.

One other important aspect of criminal events relates to the conditions under which they occur. The different dimensions of people's lives, ranging from the privacy of family interaction to the semiprivate arenas of work to public leisure activities, all invite different types of behavior and offer circumstances that may or may not give rise to criminal events. Criminal events, like all forms of social events, are complicated affairs. This chapter has discussed their basic dimensions and, in so doing, has raised questions about who participates in these events, when and where the events occur, and why they elicit particular forms of societal reaction. In order to understand a criminal event, we need to understand how each of its elements combines and interacts with the others.

2

The Main Actors
in the Criminal Event

We begin our discussion of the criminal event by looking in detail at the roles that main actors play in influencing the precursors, transactions, and aftermath of crime. The major players include offenders, victims, bystanders or witnesses, and police officers. Each actor brings to the event different perspectives and motivations. We are interested in looking at each group in terms of their characteristics, but further, we examine how they come together and influence one another's behavior. As was discussed in Chapter 1, criminologists have focused most of their attention over the years on the actions and motivations of offenders. We will begin our discussion with an examination of current theories relating to offenders before we turn our attention to the other actors in the event.

OFFENDERS

According to the general theory of crime presented by Gottfredson and Hirschi (1990), offering distinct explanations for distinct types of criminal conduct is unnecessary. The reasoning behind this argument is that crimes of many sorts, despite their differences, may be defined as "acts of force or fraud undertaken in pursuit of self-interest" (Gottfredson and Hirschi, 1990: 15).

Moreover, Gottfredson and Hirschi suggest that the acts we call crimes share many common elements:

- They provide immediate gratification of desires.
- They are exciting, risky, or thrilling.
- They provide few or meager long-term benefits.
- They require little skill or planning.
- They result in pain or discomfort for the victim.

In short, the researchers argue, crime as a type of activity appeals to people who are impulsive, shortsighted, physical, risk-taking, and nonverbal. Gottfredson and Hirschi use the term *low self-control* to describe this propensity, and they maintain that people who are attracted to crime will also be versatile in their behavior and attracted to other activities (such as alcohol or drug use) that share similar elements.

The characteristics that motivate offenders, in Gottfredson and Hirschi's view, are most likely to influence the behavior of those in late adolescence and early adulthood. Offending related to property crime peaks at a somewhat earlier age than does violent offending (Flowers, 1989). Property crime arrests peak at age 16 and drop by one-half by age 20, whereas violent offending reaches a peak at age 18. In 1999 the FBI reported that the under-25 age group accounted for 44 percent of the violent crime arrests and 55 percent of the property crime offenses (FBI, 2000). Despite the assumption that criminals will be involved in all forms of crime and misbehavior, crimes such as embezzlement, fraud, and gambling appear not to conform to this general trend, for they are characterized by higher levels of involvement somewhat later in the life cycle (Steffensmeier and Allen, 1991).

Offender status is also strongly related to gender (Campbell, 1990). In 1999, for example, 78 percent of all offenders who were arrested were males, as were almost 83 percent of those arrested for an "index violent offense" (homicide, rape, robbery, or aggravated assault). Although the rate at which women are arrested has increased somewhat over the past decade (while arrests of males decreased 5 percent, arrests of women increased 18 percent, with a 37-percent rise in their arrests for violent crimes), the offending rates of males continue to be higher than those for females in virtually every category of crime (FBI, 2000). Recent evidence indicates that the gender gap in offending has been closing, but much of the rhetoric about the "new female criminal" has overstated the case. The narrowing of the gender gap has occurred primarily with respect to nonviolent property crime, for which the gender differential has always been less extreme than for violent crime (Flowers, 1989; Hartnagel, 1992). For most types of criminal events, offending is still very much a male activity.

For many so-called common varieties of crime, such as assault, burglary, robbery, and homicide, offending is associated with various measures of social and economic disadvantage (Silverman and Nielsen, 1992). These differences emerge most clearly when the most serious forms of crime are examined (Harris, 1991). Arrest data reveal that offenders tend to be unemployed, temporarily employed, or employed in part-time, unskilled, or semiskilled jobs (Flowers, 1989). Offending is also associated with minority group membership. Corporate crimes suggest a departure from this pattern in that offenders involved in such crimes tend to be "predominantly well-educated people with good jobs" (Snider, 1992: 320).

An emphasis on the social and demographic characteristics of individual offenders should not detract attention from the fact that, in the context of many criminal events, offending has collective dimensions. Most delinquent acts, for instance, are committed in groups rather than by individuals (Giordano, Cernkovich, and Pugh, 1986). Criminal events involving corporate offending or organized crime may involve several complex levels of organization (Snider, 1993). These differing levels of offender organization strongly affect the course of criminal events.

The Lives of Offenders: Life Course

Although low self-control may predict criminal activity at a given time, whether or not this self-control is invariant, as Gottfredson and Hirschi (1990) argue, has been debated. In other words, do individuals maintain a steady level of impulsiveness or need for instant gratification throughout their lives? Also, do they face an unchanging set of life circumstances that continue to promote criminal involvement? Sampson and Laub (1990) address these questions in their formulation of the life course perspective. They defined their task in terms of reconciling two contradictory sets of research findings. On the one hand, a body of research indicates that adult criminality is strongly influenced by patterns of childhood behavior (Wilson and Herrnstein, 1985). This research suggests that because people embark on criminal paths long before adulthood, the characteristics of adults' social roles (such as unemployment) are largely irrelevant as causes of crime. On the other hand, another body of research indicates that changes in people's lives (like getting or losing a job, or getting married or having children) affect the likelihood of involvement in crime. Sampson and Laub argue that because most criminological attention is focused on the study of teenagers, researchers have not really examined how the propensity to crime does in fact change or remain stable over the life course.

The life course perspective of Sampson and Laub makes an important distinction between trajectories and transitions. Trajectories are the pathways on which people are located or the directions in which their lives are moving. Transitions, however, are specific life events—like a first job or a marriage or the birth of a child—that might or might not serve to alter the trajectories. For example, a juvenile who is actively involved with delinquent peers, lives in an abusive home, and is failing at school might be on a criminal trajectory. However, suppose in the later teen years, the individual begins a romantic relationship with someone who is nurturing and supportive, and the two decide to get married and raise a family. After the individual develops a deep commitment to the relationship and begins to plan for and think about the future, the involvement in crime is diminished. In the life course framework, we would see the marriage as a transition that altered the individual's criminal trajectory.

According to Sampson and Laub, trajectories change when transitions alter the nature and number of social bonds that help ensure conformity. However, they argue that it is not simply the occurrence of particular life events that is likely to bring these changes about. Rather, it is the social investment in the institutional relationship that dictates the salience of informal social control.

Uggen (2000) provides compelling evidence that work involvement can have a direct impact in lowering criminal recidivism. This effect is most directly felt, he argues, for individuals aged 27 or older. Warr (1998) has argued that life course transitions involve much more than shifts in the amount and types of informal social control to which individuals are exposed. He shows that major life changes such as moving to a new residence or starting a new job affect relationships with delinquent peers. Of special interest, Warr suggests, is that marriage often serves to replace involvement with criminal peers with "preoccupation with one's spouse and family of procreation" (209). Warr concludes that life course theory needs to take greater account of delinquent "peer careers" in any explanation of why criminal involvement changes over the life course.

It is important to note that the interpretative value of the life course perspective extends beyond the individual. Macmillan (1995), for instance, has used life course theory to explain the increase in rates of Canadian property crime over the last several decades. During this period, Macmillan argues, young people were more likely to leave their parental homes earlier, to marry later, and to wait longer for parenthood. The implication with respect to life course theory is that young people (especially young males) were less likely to make those transitions that would have connected them to networks of informal social control. These changes may be said to have led to an increase in the pool of potential criminal offenders over the period. Macmillan's analysis shows that changes in rates of crime may be related to structural changes in the life course.

The Criminal Career

How do offenders decide to get involved in crime? How and when do they decide to give up a life of crime? The extreme differences in the rates at which individuals offend were first documented in a cohort study undertaken by Wolfgang, Figlio, and Sellin (1972). The researchers attempted to examine the offending patterns of all males born in Philadelphia in 1945 for the period up to their eighteenth birthdays in 1963. The study identified 627 career criminals who, though they constituted only 6 percent of the original cohort and 18 percent of the delinquents, were responsible for more than half of all the crime engaged in by cohort members. More important, perhaps, was that these career criminals were responsible for 71 percent of the murders, 73 percent of the rapes, and 82 percent of the robberies.

Later studies have supported the view that small numbers of offenders account for large numbers of crime. A longitudinal study in England, known as the Cambridge Study of Delinquent Development, found that about 6 percent of a sample of 411 boys accounted for about 50 percent of all criminal convictions (Farrington, 1989). In a study by the Rand Corporation of offenders in California, Michigan, and Texas prisons, the most active 10 percent of all inmates who had committed robbery reported committing at least 58 robberies per year, and the most active 10 percent of burglars reported committing 187 or more burglaries per year (Chaiken and Chaiken, 1982).

However, contrary to what we might expect, this research also shows that offenders whose careers are characterized by high rates of offending seldom specialize in only one type of crime (Visher, 1991). Instead, they tend to commit a variety of violent and property crimes (Kempf, 1987). The research into career criminals also shows a general stability in levels of offense seriousness over the course of a career. It does not appear, for instance, that the longer offenders offend, the more likely they are to move from one type of crime to another type that requires more technical skill or knowledge.

The notion that crime may be thought of in career terms is widely shared both inside and outside of criminological literature. The true-crime section of any bookstore usually carries several titles that detail the exploits of the professional thief, professional robber, or contract killer. Such books promise a look into a world of crime that, at least superficially, seems to be organized in ways that reflect the occupational structure of the legitimate work world. In some fundamental sense, these offenders view crime as their job. They have acquired the technical skills they need to perform this job, and they derive their livelihood principally from successful job performance. Just how superficial are comparisons between crime and legitimate work? Does it make sense to conceptualize criminal involvement in career terms?

A useful place to begin this discussion is with a brief consideration of the concept of career itself. In occupational terms, the concept of career denotes the sequence of movements from one position to another that any individual makes within an occupational system (Becker, 1963). This definition is consistent with popular usage. We think of a work career as beginning at some specific point in time and continuing until death, retirement, or a voluntary or forced career change. Over the course of a successful career, we can identify movement through various stages (which, in the context of formal organizations, we call promotions). Each stage brings with it new responsibilities and additional rewards and provides the individual with the skills, knowledge, or experience he or she needs to advance to successive stages.

The relative success that characterizes career movement is dependent on several career contingencies. The occupational system may, for instance, allow for little career advancement, or the individual may lack the training that would allow movement beyond a certain occupational level. Contingencies include any factors on which career success depends. Within the setting of a business or other organizational bureaucracy, a useful metaphor is a high-rise building. Each floor represents a career stage, and the career itself may be understood as the elevator that carries people upward or, in unfortunate cases, downward. Clearly, the career concept has more general applicability. Think of your college or university career as having begun when you started your postsecondary education. As your career takes you through several well-defined stages, your success will be judged in large part by the grades you receive. However, your success will depend on career contingencies such as the types of examinations used to judge performance, the restrictions placed on program enrollment, and your abilities as a student.

How valuable is the career concept in the study of crime? Although there is a long history of research and theory that attempts to link the study of offending to the study of careers (Letkemann, 1973; Miller, 1978), criminologists debate whether this exercise is worthwhile. Some criminologists maintain that the career concept is useful in understanding the relative degree of involvement of offenders in criminal activity. From this point of view, every offender may be said to have a criminal career. The use of the term *career* in this context does not necessarily mean that crime provides the offender's major source of livelihood. The individual who commits only one crime early in adolescence may have a short career in contrast to the person who engages in serious crime throughout his or her life. By focusing on criminal careers, we are encouraged to ask why offenders' careers develop as they do. Although the criminal career is not a theory in and of itself, it is seen as a useful way of organizing what we know about crime.

Moreover, it is argued, the career concept encourages us to ask questions we would not otherwise be prompted to ask (Blumstein, Cohen, and Farrington, 1988a,b). The first question has to do with entry into a criminal career, which is sometimes called the onset. Here we might ask what sorts of factors encourage movement into a criminal career. Or we might try to discover the ages at which people typically begin criminal careers. The second question has to do with the degree of career productivity, which, in the context of legitimate work, might be called the level of success. During the duration of the career, how many crimes do offenders commit, and what contingencies affect the relative success of criminal careers? Finally, we might ask about what is called desistance. How and why do offenders end their criminal careers?

Advocates of the career concept argue that, for theoretical reasons, it is important to distinguish questions about onset from questions about frequency and desistance, because factors that affect one aspect of the career may be unrelated to another (Blumstein et al., 1988a). For instance, some of the apparently confusing findings about the relationship between crime and unemployment might become more comprehensible if we recognize that unemployment may not be related to onset, productivity, and desistance in the same ways. For example, the level of unemployment might not be expected to affect the onset of criminal careers that people typically begin in their teenage years, before they are eligible to enter the adult labor force. Once a criminal career has begun, the availability of legitimate work may affect the timing of desistance. An individual may abandon a criminal career if offered more profitable legitimate work. Conversely, although most people end their criminal careers before middle age, desistance may be delayed if the rate of unemployment decreases the likelihood of securing a legitimate job. In general, the career concept suggests that trying to find simple and direct effects between familiar criminogenic concepts and rates of crime may be misguided. Factors such as employment may affect different career aspects in different ways, and a factor that is important at one point of a career may have no causal significance at a later point.

Gottfredson and Hirschi (1990) question whether anything of value is to be gained from examining criminal careers. The concept of a career, they argue, usually assumes some notion of specialization and career progress, and yet the available evidence undermines the validity of such assumptions. Gottfredson and Hirschi also contend that it is fruitless to search for the unique factors that explain desistance from criminal careers, because all offenders—irrespective of the types of offenses in which they engage or the rates at which they engage in them—become less productive as they age. To argue that different factors explain different career elements is also misleading, according to Gottfredson and Hirschi, because most of the factors in which career researchers are interested (such as unemployment) are only weakly related to crime. According to these authors, the tendency to engage in crime is highly stable for all offenders and is related to a low level of self-control.

In a somewhat different way, Luckenbill and Best (1981) also question the value of the career concept as a way of understanding crime and other types of nonconformity. They maintain that the analogy between legitimate and deviant careers is very limited, in large part because legitimate careers must be understood in the context of organizational settings, whereas criminal careers emerge in much less structured settings. Criminal careers are not formed in response to institutional requirements that "spell out the career's positions, pathways for mobility, and rewards, while authorities enforce these rules and ensure the career's security" (Luckenbill and Best, 1981: 197). By contrast, those who are involved in deviant careers are not able to draw on such institutional resources. Moreover, they risk the possibility of social control sanctions and exploitation by deviant associates, and their rewards from deviance are uncertain. Luckenbill and Best (1981) express the differences between legitimate and deviant careers as follows:

> Riding escalators between floors may be an effective metaphor for respectable organizational careers, but it fails to capture the character of deviant careers. A more appropriate image is a walk in the woods. Here some people take the pathways marked by their predecessors, while others strike out on their own. Some walk slowly, exploring before moving further, but others run, caught up in the action. Some have a destination in mind and proceed purposefully; others view the trip as an experience and enjoy it for its own sake. Even those intent on reaching a destination may stray from the path; they may try a shortcut or they may lose sight of a familiar landmark, get lost and find it necessary to backtrack. Without a rigid organizational structure, deviant careers can develop in many different ways. (201)

We acknowledge the difficulties in adhering strictly to a perspective that suggests that life circumstances or criminal careers drive criminality, but our perspective demands that we include these factors in our consideration of the ways in which offenders operate in a social context. Life circumstances change over time and space as do opportunities that come from employment, marriage, parenting, and other life events. Exposure to the social contexts that life events bring individuals into provides both the opportunities to offend and the social controls to force them to desist. Life circumstances also bring offenders into contact with potential victims.

As we said earlier, a homicide that results from a heated argument between drunken patrons of a bar may not seem as clear-cut as one that occurs in a more sedate environment. When we draw attention to the relationship between offender labels and offender characteristics, to the victim-offender relationship, or to the social setting, we are suggesting that the study of the offender is inseparable from the study of other dimensions of the criminal event, including the domain in which it occurs.

VICTIMS

Victims may be reluctant to define events in which they are involved as crimes. In some cases, even while the event is under way, it may feature ambiguous or unfamiliar elements that are not readily understood as criminal victimization. A study of mugging victims reported that many of those victimized did not immediately define the event as a predatory crime; some even thought the mugger was a neighbor in search of assistance or someone playing a joke (Lejeune and Alex, 1973).

Willingness to label an event a crime generally depends on the degree of coherence between the victim's definition of a "typical crime" and the characteristics of the event in question (Ruback, Greenberg, and Wescott, 1984). However, some types of crimes are inherently more ambiguous than others. The meaning of many forms of sexual victimization may be highly problematic with respect to the labels that victims assign to them. For instance, a study of 94 women who were sexually assaulted in a number of ways did not define the act as rape unless sexual intercourse was involved (Scheppele and Bart, 1983). Overall, however, crime definitions are generally less ambiguous when the events contain elements that imply a high degree of legal seriousness (Agnew, 1985).

The issue of family violence provides a particularly vivid illustration of the importance of victim definition processes. The reluctance of women to label violence that occurs in the context of intimate relationships as criminal or abusive has been well documented (Ferraro and Johnson, 1983; Sedlak, 1988). As in the case of sexual assault, a cultural tendency to blame women for their victimization in domestic relationships has been firmly entrenched until recently. If women remain in abusive relationships, they may be labeled "sick" or "masochistic" or they may be accused of "bringing it on themselves." If they attempt to flee the abuse or confront the abuser, such actions may increase rather than decrease the risk of future victimization. As parents, in-laws, and neighbors choose sides, many of them may blame the victim for breaking up the family and may suggest that if she really loved her children she would have "made the best of it." These factors may discourage a woman from viewing herself as a victim, because acknowledging that one's mate is an abuser is the first and hardest step in reevaluating and changing one's life circumstances, a process that might entail violent retaliation by the abusive partner. A denial of the violent character of the victimization and the victimizer may allow the abused partner to tolerate conditions an outsider would think intolerable (Ferraro and Johnson, 1983). Tjaden and Thoennes (2000) discuss important steps that have been taken to improve education and awareness in the public about the dangers of domestic abuse. They also make a special point to include more surveillance by the medical profession in their recommendations for increasing awareness about the extent of this problem.

Surveys of direct victims of crime demonstrate that involvement in criminal events as a victim, like involvement as an offender, is not a random matter. In fact, many of the social characteristics associated with offending are also associated with victimization. For one thing, like offenders, the victims of crime tend to be young. According to the 1999 National Crime Victimization Survey, the highest rates of both violent and property (theft) crimes were experienced by people between the ages of 12 and 24.* The violent crime victimization rates for young people, for example, was more than 20 times greater than the rates of violent victimization reported by people over age 65 (Rennison, 2000).

Surveys of crime victims also indicate that, for most types of crime, males have higher rates of victimization than females. For example, the 1999 NCVS found that the male rate of violent victimization was 37 per 1,000; the rate for females was 28 per 1,000 (Rennison, 2000). A notable exception to this pattern is found with rape, a crime in which the vast majority of victims are women. Note, too, that several researchers question the extent to which surveys like the NCVS accurately portray the levels of women's victimization.

The link between social disadvantage and victimization is less clear-cut than in the case of offending (Cohen, Kluegel, and Land, 1981; Fattah, 1991). To some extent, the nature of the relationship depends on the type of event. For violent crimes, data from the 1999 NCVS suggest a steady decrease in the rate of victimization as income rises, although the relationship is less apparent for property crimes (Rennison, 2000).

Finally, race and/or ethnicity also seem to be identifiable factors that increase the chances of victimization, especially for violent crime. For example, rates of violent victimizations for African Americans in 1999 were markedly higher than for white/European Americans (41.6 and 31.9 per 1,000, respectively). Of note is that these rates have dropped since 1993, when they were close to 70 per 1,000 for African Americans and close to 50 per 1,000 for whites (Rennison, 2000).

An analysis of data from the 1998 NCVS (U.S. Department of Justice, 2000) estimated that the direct cost to victims of crime was $17.056 billion. The crimes covered by the survey are rape, robbery, assault, personal and household theft, burglary, and motor vehicle theft. About 25 percent of victims of robbery and assault sustained physical injury. About 7 percent of all victims lost time from work as a result of a crime of violence, and 5.5 percent as a result of a property crime.

---

*Rates are for 1,000 persons aged 12 and over (for crimes against persons) or per 1,000 households (for property crimes).

With respect to financial loss, it is obvious that the economic costs sustained when someone steals a purse from a victim equals the replacement price of the purse and its contents. But suppose the victim reacts to the theft by deciding to install deadbolt locks and to take taxis rather than walk to evening destinations. Suppose as well that she decides that, instead of carrying cash, she will write checks for her purchases in the future. Should the costs of the locks, the taxi fares, and checking charges be considered an economic cost of the crime? The nature of the problems involved in analyzing crime data becomes even more apparent when we recognize that financial losses are perhaps the easiest to calculate, given that there is a convenient standard of measurement.

Physical Consequences

With respect to physical injury, if a victim sustains a broken bone, the injury clearly should be considered a consequence of the crime. But if stress resulting from the crime aggravates a preexisting health condition, is it correct to say that the incident resulted in physical harm, even though no apparent physical injuries resulted?

Data from the 1998 NCVS provide some indication of the levels of economic loss sustained by victims. The survey found that 68 percent of all personal crimes reported resulted in some economic loss through theft or damage. This included 90 percent of all personal crimes of theft and 15 percent of all crimes of violence. Not surprisingly, motor vehicle thefts were most likely to result in the largest losses. In addition, victims recovered none of their property in about 77 percent of the personal crimes and about 87 percent of the property crimes. Victims of motor vehicle theft were somewhat more fortunate in that about 48 percent got their vehicles back and about 25 percent got some back in the form of automobile parts (U.S. Department of Justice, 2000).

The 1998 NCVS data revealed that victims incurred medical expenses in 7 percent of all violent victimizations. Moreover, victims were not covered by health insurance or were ineligible to apply for public health benefits in 33 percent of the incidents that resulted in injury. This was most likely to be a problem for low-income victims, who would have been least able to shoulder the costs associated with their medical care.

The analysis of 1998 NCVS data shows 25 percent of the 7.5 million reported crimes of violence led to physical injury. An analysis of trends of victimization over the period of 1973 to 1991, based on data from earlier studies, revealed that, of 36.6 million people who were injured as a result of violent crime, about one in six received serious injuries (Zawitz et al., 1993). Of the victims of violent crime who were injured, 84 percent received bruises, cuts, scratches, or other minor injuries. More serious injuries occur with lesser frequency. Among those who were victimized by violent crime between 1973 and 1991, 1 percent received gunshot wounds, 4 percent received knife wounds, and 7 percent suffered broken bones or had teeth knocked out.

The findings from the 1992 NCVS provide some indication that women are more likely to be injured in robberies than are men (U.S. Department of Justice, 1994a). In addition, the survey found that assault victims were more likely to receive physical injuries from an offender who was known to them than were victims who were assaulted by a stranger. Of the injured victims who received medical care, about 6 in 10 received care in an emergency room and about 4 in 10 received inpatient care.

Emotional Consequences

Although victimization studies are quite useful in telling us about the direct injuries incurred from criminal victimization, they tell us relatively little about longer-term effects. Although not evident in surveys of this sort, the injuries that result from physical encounters can lead to a worsening of existing health problems, and when mobility is restricted, the victim may be less able or even unable to exercise or to meet nutritional requirements.

Victims can experience a variety of emotional reactions to crime, from mild to extreme. These reactions may include shock, mistrust, sleeplessness, anger, stress, depression, and a diminished capacity to enjoy life events. Victims may also express a sense of guilt because they blame themselves for what has happened (Mayhew, Maung, and Mirrlees-Black, 1993).

Victims' differing abilities to cope with the costs of criminal victimization are due to a number of factors. Victims who are isolated from supportive others may find it more difficult to manage the stresses associated with crime than will those whose families and friends are able to lend emotional or practical assistance. People with more economic resources may find it less difficult to absorb economic losses or to replace stolen or damaged property. Also important are prior psychological functioning and previous victim history. Individuals who are already suffering from depression may respond to criminal victimization more negatively, as might those who have already been victimized by crime (Sales, Baum, and Shore, 1984).

Criminal victimization may also undermine an individual's positive self-concept. Victims may develop feelings of weakness and helplessness and believe that they could have done more than they did to prevent themselves from being victimized. Traditionally, society has reinforced this view by holding victims responsible for what has happened to them.

It is not only violent interpersonal crimes that have emotional consequences. Burglary is one type of crime against property that can invite a strong response, in part because it can be viewed as a crime with the potential for violence. Even though victims are typically away from home when the offense occurs, they are forced to contemplate what might have happened had they been at home. In addition, because a burglary could threaten violence against other members of the household, each member of the household may feel concern not only for his or her own personal safety but also for the well-being of other family members. Finally, because burglary is a crime that represents an invasion of privacy and, in many cases, involves theft of or damage to objects that might have sentimental value, the emotional response may be severe (Hough, 1987).

Ironically, it has often been argued that victims' psychological distress can be magnified by social and criminal justice agencies charged with the responsibility of helping victims (Rosenbaum, 1987). In particular, the police have sometimes been accused of failing to provide victims with the emotional support they require and often expect (Skogan and Wycoff, 1987). Victims may feel that the police are not doing enough to help them or to recover stolen property. When property is recovered, they may wonder why it is not returned to them more promptly.

To some extent, victim discontent with the police reflects the routine nature of police work. Some victims of even minor crimes expect a rapid response when they telephone the police. For the dispatcher overwhelmed by calls for service, however, a minor crime may be assigned low priority. As a result, the victim feels let down by the police. In a similar way, victims who know with certainty that they have been victimized might expect that the police officer who arrives on the scene will accept their version of the story at face value and then engage in hot pursuit of the offender. For the police officer, the situation may be more ambiguous, and it may be necessary to ask questions before sense can be made of the event. In addition, the officer's experience suggests that "hot pursuit" is pointless because the offender is unlikely to be found in this way, if at all.

In general, much of the research on emotional reactions to victimization indicates that when symptoms occur, they are likely to erode slowly over time (Hough, 1987). However, some evidence also suggests that symptoms sometimes persist or even re-emerge months after the incident (Sales et al., 1984). Such findings imply that the recovery process may not be as linear as is sometimes believed.

Victims attempt to cope with the costs of victimization by engaging in a reevaluation of the event (Taylor, Wood, and Lichtman, 1983). In so doing, victims redefine the situation to make it less threatening to their self-esteem or to their future plans. In short, victims are attentive to various cultural adages that advise us to "look on the bright side." Taylor and colleagues suggest that victims achieve this end through a series of evaluative strategies. They may, for instance, compare themselves with less fortunate others. Provided that one chooses the criteria for comparison carefully, one can always find examples of people who have lost more or suffered more. Alternatively, despite suffering or loss, victims might try to discover some way in which the event was beneficial. In this respect, the victim might say, "I sure learned my lesson" or "I won't ever get myself into that situation again."

Agnew (1985) suggests that this process resembles the neutralization process that Matza and Sykes (1961) described in their explanation of why offenders commit crime. However, rather than convincing themselves, as offenders do, that a particular criminal act is not really wrong, victims try to convince themselves that particular acts of victimization are not really harmful. Victims may, for instance, invoke a "denial of injury" in order to minimize the harm caused. Or they may articulate a "denial of responsibility" to minimize the guilt or shame that accompanies self-blame. These neutralizations, claims Agnew, allow victims to avoid feelings of fear or other negative emotions that sometimes accompany criminal victimization. In a simple way, a victim's loss is often an offender's gain. A victim's loss of cash or property in a theft or loss in a physical encounter can translate into wins for the offender. Of course, the offender risks apprehension and punishment, but these risks are often slight. Proponents of punishment or rehabilitation contend that if offenders are apprehended, the criminal justice system may play an important role in discouraging further offending.

Behavioral Consequences

Some of the behavioral effects that result from victimization are directly related to physical injuries or economic losses. Victims may need to take time off from work, for instance, because medical care is required or because property must be repaired or replaced. The 1992 NCVS found that victims lost time from work in about 8 percent of violent victimizations, 4 percent of personal thefts, and 6 percent of household crimes (U.S. Department of Justice, 1994a). About 35 percent of the victims of personal crimes who lost time from work were away less than a day, and 9 percent were away for 11 days or more.

Victims exhibit a variety of behavioral reactions to crime, many of which are intended to make them safer. A common response is avoidance behavior, by which victims seek to distance themselves from the kinds of people or situations that they perceive as dangerous. In extreme cases, this may involve changing residences or neighborhoods (Burt and Katz, 1985). Victims might also try to increase home protection by installing new locks or an alarm system or to increase personal protection through the purchase of a gun or enrollment in a self-defense course. An important irony revealed in research is that although victims often engage in these behaviors, they may be less likely than others to believe that they are safer because they do so (Lurigio, 1987).

Victims also seek help from others. A common response (although less common than many think) is to contact the police. Victims appear most likely to do this when they see some practical or tangible reason to do so. However, even before they contact the police, victims often contact friends or family members in order to ask their opinions about what should be done. The victim might be unsure, in some cases, whether the event is in fact a crime or whether it is serious enough to warrant police intervention. These friends or family members can help clarify matters by reminding the victim of standards against which the event can be judged (Ruback et al., 1984).

Over the longer term, victims might engage in some form of collective participation (DuBow, McCabe, and Kaplan, 1979). The most obvious form of such participation might be membership in some community crime prevention group such as Neighborhood Watch (Rosenbaum, 1988). Alternatively, victims may get involved in one of the many generic or more specialized victims' groups that have proliferated in recent decades.

A common reaction is to tell others the story of the crime (Wachs, 1988). Lejeune and Alex (1973) reported that this reaction was nearly universal in their sample of mugging victims. They observed as well that the interest of the victim in telling the story seemed to be matched by an interest on the part of others in hearing it. Telling the story of one's victimization might have important therapeutic value. When others react in supportive ways or tell similar stories, the victim may find it easier to make sense of the event and to put it into some broader perspective.

The behavioral reactions of victims can be easily overstated because most people are familiar with someone who has responded to crime in perhaps an extreme manner. However, in general, most victims do not seem to react to the crime by making major or basic lifestyle changes (Hindelang, Gottfredson, and Garofalo, 1978). Because our lifestyles are a product of our family responsibilities and occupational commitments, they are not changed easily.

Although criminological literature addresses such changes as costs of victimization that limit behavior, some benefits may also result. As Skogan (1987) states, when people change their behavior in other circumstances in response to negative experiences, we call this "learning." To the degree that such changes do make people less vulnerable without dramatically affecting the quality of life, they may be beneficial.

Victims include people whose purses are stolen and whose homes are broken into and who are murdered in the course of the event. For other event categories, such as drug use or gambling offenses, victims cannot be said to exist in any direct and immediate way, although many would argue that to consider such offenses as victimless crimes is incorrect (Schur, 1979). The degree to which the law should be applied to victimless crimes revolves around the issue of harm. Although support for legalizing various forms of vice is widespread, great concern persists as to the potential negative effects of doing so. One view is that victimless crimes are not victimless and need to be regulated through criminal law.

Proponents for removing the legal sanctions associated with victimless crimes argue that policing these acts represents an overreach of the law and that consenting adults should have the freedom to partake in certain activities. Criminalization disproportionately affects the disadvantaged and others who cannot pursue these activities in private. Some have argued that the massive incarceration explosion that has occurred in the last decade across the United States, largely attributable to the application of strict drug enforcement, mandatory sentencing rules, and longer incarceration times has disproportionately affected minority communities. According to Beck (2000), at year end 1999, in state and federal jurisdictions, African American inmates represented an estimated 46 percent (558,700) of all inmates with sentences of more than one year, whereas white inmates accounted for 33 percent (403,700), and Hispanic inmates 18 percent (219,500). The two major areas of increases in first-time offenders were violent crime and drug crime. Overall, the increasing number of drug offenses accounted for 25 percent of the total increase among African American inmates, 18 percent of the total increase among Hispanic inmates, and 12 percent of the total increase among white inmates.

VICTIMS AND OFFENDERS TOGETHER

According to Sampson and Lauritsen (1990), the difficulties that we have in identifying offender and victim in many criminal events derive from the fact

that the likelihood of victimization increases the more frequent one's c
or association with members of demographic groups that contain a disp:
tionate share of offenders. In this matrix, the dynamics of the situation, ...g
the approach of Luckenbill (1977), make it likely that victims and offenders will
be drawn from the same group, a view consistent with the proposal of Hindelang and colleagues (1978) that those with common lifestyles are more likely to
be victimized by one another. These views suggest that elements in the place
and in the initiation of social events increase the likelihood that crime will occur. It has been suggested that certain locations are hot spots of crime, that is,
that these events recur over and over again. Further, there is evidence that individuals, once victimized, will be victimized again (Pease and Laycock, 1996).

Crimes are the outcome of social exchanges among people who find themselves in specific circumstances and must make quick decisions about how they
should respond to each other's behavior. A robbery does not occur merely because an offender with an inclination to rob encounters an opportunity conducive to robbery. The potential victim may resist in ways that turn a potential
robbery into an attempted murder. The potential victim of an attempted
breaking and entering may overreact by killing the offender. Victims of property crimes contribute to the interaction through the steps they take or don't
take to protect their property; their actions, or lack thereof, send a message to
the potential offender about the risks of trying to steal the property. Victims are
not, therefore, merely passive objects of an offender's predatory desires; nor are
they necessarily active contributors to their own victimization. They are, however, key event participants whose actions shape and constrain event outcomes.

BYSTANDERS

In many cases, criminal events involve individuals other than those who can be
described as offenders or victims. Bystanders in many events are more than passive spectators. They may by their very presence deter an offender from committing a crime, or they may prevent an event from escalating. Conversely, they
may facilitate the offender's actions. For example, a young male who is insulted
by someone in the presence of his peers may be naturally inclined to respond
in an aggressive fashion or else be encouraged to do so by his peers.

Bystanders may also call the police or offer to act as witnesses (Shotland and
Goodstein, 1984). What bystanders do, if anything, depends on several factors.
Their actions may be influenced, for example, by their view of or relationship
to the victim and/or offender (Steffensmeier and Steffensmeier, 1973), by their
assessment of the personal costs associated with intervention, and by their confidence in their ability to intervene.

Bystanders are also affected by what they perceive to be transpiring between
victim and offender. According to Shotland and Straw (1976), bystanders are
less likely to intervene in a violent assault perpetrated by a man against a woman
if they perceive them to be married rather than strangers. In a highly publicized
case that took place in New York City a number of years ago, a woman named

Kitty Genovese was attacked by a man in the courtyard of a large apartment complex (Conklin, 1975). The attack continued for a long period of time, during which Genovese's screams for help went unanswered. She finally succumbed to the attack and died on the street. Although many people in the apartment block witnessed the attack, no one called the police, much less intervened. According to those who researched the event, the apartment dwellers had interpreted the attack as a quarrel between a married couple and therefore as a private affair. Similarly, Davis (1991) suggests that when people witness an adult physically abusing a child in public, their reluctance to intervene in a "private matter" outweighs their concern for the child's welfare.

Criminal events are frequently ambiguous from the standpoint of bystanders. We do not expect to witness a crime and may be so engrossed in our own activities that an event may be well under way before it comes to our attention (Hartman, Page, and Walder, 1972). By the time we make sense of the event and think of a response, it may be too late. The presence of several bystanders tends to reduce the likelihood that any one bystander will assist a victim, particularly if the bystanders are strangers to one another and do not share a common cultural frame of reference (Shotland and Straw, 1976). One bystander among many is required to accept only part of the responsibility for not acting; he or she may rationalize that somebody else would take action were something seriously wrong.

Bystanders may be asked to perform as witnesses. How valuable are eyewitness accounts in providing accurate depictions of the activities in a criminal event? The research suggests that these eyewitness accounts are quite inaccurate, with bystanders failing to remember even key characteristics of the offender or the event (Loftus, 1979).

The study of homicide by Luckenbill (1977) revealed that the role of bystanders in situated transactions should not be minimized. He found that the presence of bystanders and the actions they took shaped the course of the transaction. In the early stages, they sometimes increased the likelihood of mortal battle by encouraging the offender to interpret an offensive remark as requiring a firm response, and in the later stages, they sometimes supplied a weapon or blocked the exit of the potential victim. Of course, just as bystanders may facilitate the occurrence of a crime, they may also prevent crimes or transform one type of crime into another. A bystander who has the presence of mind to call 911 upon witnessing an assault or who is familiar with cardiopulmonary resuscitation (CPR) may prevent an assault from becoming a murder.

POLICE PRACTICE

Police involvement in criminal events may result from either proactive or reactive mobilization. As the police engage in routine patrol work, they may encounter individuals or situations they define as criminal. Proactive policing is not in any sense a random or arbitrary process. Rather, it is heavily influenced by police priorities, prevailing community concerns, available police resources, and the styles and traditions that characterize police work in given areas (Desroches, 1991). Ericson and Haggerty (1997) report that police officers who are engaged in patrol activities use cues that structure their proactive work. For example, their attention may be attracted by individuals who appear in particular places at particular times of the day. Conversely, events that could be defined as crimes are not labeled as such because the police choose not to stop and question a suspect.

In his study of the policing of a heroin-using community, Stoddart (1991) reports that heroin users who act as police informants are less likely to be pursued by the police than are heroin users who are perceived as interfering with police work. This finding suggests that proactive police activity is influenced not only by what the police do but also by the visibility of the offenders' behavior. Stoddart argues that changes in the nature of the heroin-using community over time have increased the probability of arrest. Members of this community today are more apathetic than their predecessors are about the fate of their colleagues and less attentive to the risks associated with illegal drug use.

Citizens may decide to mobilize the police reactively as a result of police-sponsored crime prevention campaigns that encourage them to do so. Conversely, widespread public concern about specific crime problems may influence police to adopt a proactive mobilization strategy. Desroches (1991) reports on a police investigation of impersonal homosexual behavior in public washrooms, known as tearooms. Although the gathering of evidence through police surveillance techniques would appear to suggest a proactive police stance on the problem, Desroches indicates that this police involvement was largely a response to requests from citizens and businesses for more aggressive enforcement.

The type of mobilization, whether proactive or reactive, does not indicate how the police will intervene in a particular event. The actions taken by officers may depend on a variety of contingencies, including the characteristics of the incident, the behavior of the participants, and the nature of the requests being made of the police (Bayley, 1986).

Police tend to respond most emphatically to (that is, to treat officially) events that they perceive as conforming to legal definitions of serious crimes (Black, 1970). Also of importance in determining police response is the relationship between the victim and the offender. According to Black, the more distant the relationship between victim and offender, the more likely the police are to regard the incident as criminal. This observation is consistent with the frequently cited tendency of police officers to process crimes "unofficially" when the disputants are family members (Bell, 1987).

The characteristics of victims and offenders have been shown to influence police decisions. Violence between males is more likely to result in arrest than is violence between a male and a female, which tends to be resolved through less formal means, such as the physical separation of the disputants. Police decision making may also be influenced by the demeanor and preferences of the event participants (Smith, 1987). Thus, the police are more likely to label an event as a crime when the complainant is deferential to them or requests that they take official action (Black, 1970; Gove, Hughes, and Geerkin, 1985).

As we pointed out earlier, in most jurisdictions, police discretion is removed in sensitive cases, such as cases of family violence. Officers are now required to make an arrest when they have physical evidence that an assault has taken place, even if the victim is reluctant for them to do so. This practice was established, in part, in response to the findings of Sherman and Berk (1984) that arrest is the most effective way of deterring violence among intimates and that mediative techniques do not curtail repeat offenses.

For some observers, removing police discretion means reducing the chances that police bias will influence decisions about the seriousness of certain violent acts. For others, it means depriving police of the opportunity to defuse situations before they become dangerous. Recent research indicates that arrest may actually heighten rather than lower the chance of violence in domestic situations (Sherman, 1992). It has also been argued that bringing individuals into an overburdened court system that is ill equipped to handle their problems merely creates new problems.

The problems caused by discretion in policing extend to the use of labels and the identification of patterns of behavior that the police have used to identify suspects, to anticipate problems, and to intervene when they believe a crime is happening or is likely to occur. In defining precursors of crime events, police may include factors that create unfairness or demonstrate bias toward certain groups. Recent research shows that police have used race as a factor in profiling suspects (Harris, 1999). Profiling works on the assumption that those who belong to certain groups are more likely to commit crime, a dangerous and immoral assumption that breeds suspicion based on race or ethnicity rather than actual behavior. Police agencies that have been charged with this form of policing, including Maryland and New Jersey state police, have been directed by federal agencies to change their operations to eradicate this discriminatory tactic (in the mid-1990s, the New Jersey State Police, in traffic stops, reported that 89 percent of those who gave consent to be searched were minorities, a figure that is much larger than their representative proportion in the overall population). Research reported by the Maryland State Police showed that on I-95, 70 percent of the drivers who were stopped between January 1995 and December 1997 were African Americans, though they composed only 17.5 percent of the drivers (and of the speeding drivers) (Leitzel, 2001). A study conducted by Langan and colleagues (2001), which included data from interviews of 1,000 respondents nationwide, found that in 1999 half of the contacts that the public had with police in all jurisdictions (not just with state police) involved traffic stops. Although overall whites were more likely per capita to be stopped by police in traffic stops, African Americans were still twice as likely as whites to report that they had been searched.

Kennedy (1998) argues compellingly that police must be restrained from using race as a factor in identifying offenders, even when combined with other characteristics. He suggests the routine use of race in identifying suspects not only creates injustice but, further, has the damaging effect of instilling fear and distrust on the part of minority communities toward the police. This effect is reflected in attitude surveys that show that almost 60 percent of whites, but only about 40 percent of African Americans, had confidence in the police (*Sourcebook of Criminal Justice Statistics,* 1999). This distrust leads to animosity between these groups and a lack of cooperation, which the police need in providing services and protection. As the most egregious cases of profiling indicate, all members of a community are targeted when using these characteristics as markers, including large numbers of innocent people who face humiliation at the hands of the police.

SUMMARY

The main actors in criminal events are offenders, victims, and bystanders (who can be guardians or not). The most obvious participant is the offender. Offenders tend to be young, disadvantaged males. At the same time, however, we are witnessing a growth in family violence; the major offenders in these crimes frequently are older and more affluent males. Further, women are increasingly becoming involved in property crimes.

Much attention has been directed at understanding the motivations, as well as the group pressures, that influence the behavior of criminals. The study of offender perceptions is an important source of information about the pressures that direct individuals to behave in certain ways. Offenders may choose to deal with their blameworthiness by rationalizing their crimes.

Although the victims of crime, like offenders, tend to be young and male, other groups are heavily victimized in particular types of crime. Sexual assault and family violence are disproportionately directed against women. The nature of victims and of their relationship to offenders, then, is very much a function of the type of event that has occurred and is governed by location and circumstance. Like offenders, victims may redefine the event as harmless or at least not criminal. Victim definitions can be important in influencing the actions taken by criminal justice agencies in criminal events.

Bystanders and witnesses also play a role in defining and interpreting the social events that become crimes. They may defuse a violent situation or they may actually promote violence through their actions. Though bystanders can be helpful in clarifying what actually occurred during a criminal event, their accounts often prove to be inaccurate.

The police play a major role in criminal events as well. They have the power to certify an event as a crime by assessing the match between the event as they have come to understand it and their knowledge of what the law disallows. In reactive policing, the police respond to reports from citizens, who may be either victims or bystanders. In proactive policing, certain groups or communities are targeted, sometimes unfairly, for police attention as a way of preventing criminal events.

With respect to intervention, the police are heavily influenced by their perceptions of what they can do to reduce crime. Police use a great deal of discretion in their work, discretion that can be used negatively to discriminate against certain groups. Police discretion in family violence cases is increasingly being removed.

The police operate through the administration of the law, and although they use some discretion in applying it, the legal structure outlines clear expectations vis-à-vis personal behavior and the legal response to the breaking of these expectations. Law is a form of social control that defines individual actions on the basis of socially acceptable standards. Criminal events are social events and, as such, are governed by societal as well as legal tenets. Forms of control may also be socially based. Gossip, ridicule, and ostracism may combine with legal threats to discourage individuals from acting in a criminal manner.

We can study each group's makeup and response to crime in and of themselves. But in the context of the criminal event analysis, we are as interested in their interaction with one another as we are in their characteristics per se. Consistent with our stated interest in studying the behavioral consequences of actors and not the actors themselves, we can draw insights about motivations and intentions into a larger context of situational dynamics.

3

The Social Context
of Criminal Events

To suggest that a relationship exists between criminal events and the places in which these events occur is to imply that location involves something more than just happenstance. In other words, place matters (Eck and Weisburd, 1995). The current focus on crime places is summarized by Anselin et al. (2000): "Theoretical concerns focus on how place might be a factor in crime, either by influencing or shaping the types and levels of criminal behavior by the people who frequent an area, or by attracting to an area people who already share similar criminal inclinations" (215).

Something about particular types of locations increases or decreases the likelihood that criminal events will unfold. Any attempt to investigate these issues is plagued by the fact that particular types of places are intricately linked to particular types of activities. People who live in the center of a major city may structure their activities differently from the way those who live on the suburban fringe do. Those of us who do not live in the downtown core may occasionally journey there in search of "excitement," but for rest and relaxation we head for the countryside. We shop at malls, drink in taverns, perform occupational tasks at work, and read or study at the library. We might ask why some of these places host more criminal events than others do. Is it because certain types of people tend to be attracted to these settings? Does the physical character of a place make criminal events more or less likely? Are the activities associated with a particular setting more or less likely to lead to criminal events? Although these issues are discussed in greater detail in later chapters, it is useful at this point to review some of the empirical evidence about the locations of criminal events.

PLACES FOR CRIME

According to data collected by police officers and survey researchers, rates of many types of crimes tend to be higher in urban centers than in rural areas. Criminal events in general occur with greater frequency in urban areas than in rural areas. In the 1999 National Crime Victimization Survey (NCVS), rural residents reported 60 percent (per capita) of the levels of both violent and property victimization reported by urban residents. These patterns have been changing as crime rates have dropped. Although the data reveal no significant differences in rates of violent crime victimization for residents of suburban and nonmetropolitan areas in 1999 (rates of victimization were 28 and 25 per 1,000,* respectively), differences have started to appear. Residents of the central city were still more likely to experience violent criminal victimizations (40 per 1,000). Rates of property crime were also higher for residents of the central city (256 per 1,000). The suburban rates were 33 per 1,000 for violent crime and 181 per 1,000 for property crime. Those in rural areas reported experiencing the lowest rates—25 per 1,000 for violent crime and 160 per 1,000 for property crime. Over time, then, the drop in crime victimization was most strongly experienced in urban environments (Rennison, 2000).

Although urban areas are now experiencing less crime overall than just a few years ago, the rates of crime vary across neighborhoods (Sampson, Raudenbush, and Earls, 1997). Research into the factors that characterize high-crime neighborhoods sometimes produces conflicting evidence (Brantingham and Brantingham, 1984), but much of the data indicate that these areas are likely to be poor and densely populated and to have transient populations (Cater and Jones, 1989; Flowers, 1989; Roncek, 1981; Stark, 1987).

Even in cities or neighborhoods characterized by high crime rates, most areas are free of crime places. For example, although we may think of subway stations as dangerous, data collected by Normandeau (1987) in Montreal reveal that most of the city's stations have relatively low rates of crime, with only a few stations accounting for most of the crimes that occur in the subway system. This point is more generally illustrated in a study by Sherman, Gartin, and Buerger (1989) of the locations of requests for police assistance in the city of Minneapolis over a one-year period. This study revealed that relatively few "hot spots" accounted for the majority of service calls; specifically, only 3 percent of the locations in the city (addresses or street intersections) accounted for 50 percent of the 323,979 calls. With respect to predatory crimes, robberies occurred at 2.2 percent, rapes at 1.2 percent, and automobile thefts at 2.7 percent of these locations. Research by Eck, Gersh, and Taylor (2000) confirms the appearance of hot spots in drug calls. Further, Spelman and Eck (1995) report that 10 percent of the victims in the United States are involved in 40 percent of the victimizations, 10 percent of the offenders are involved in 50 percent of the crimes, and 10 percent of the places are involved in 60 percent of the crimes.

---

*Rates are for 1,000 persons aged 12 and over (for crimes against persons) or per 1,000 households (for property crimes).

As researchers have attempted to explain these crime concentrations, two types of literature have developed. The first emerged from the seminal research conducted in Chicago in the 1920s and 1930s under the general theme of human ecology. The human ecologists witnessed cities undergoing rapid population changes that were accompanied by growth in urban crime. To understand this crime problem, the ecologists argued, the ways in which communities changed, both demographically and physically, needed to be examined. The "natural areas" that emerged from the competition between different social and economic groups dictated a mosaic of social organization and disorganization that both prevented and encouraged deviance. The ecologists were fascinated with the changes that took place in urban neighborhoods over time and in the social climate of these neighborhoods. When they discussed crime, their major thrust was best exemplified in the work of Louis Wirth and, later, of Clifford Shaw and Henry McKay. In their view, the criminogenic aspects of these neighborhoods sprang from the decline in community structures that accompanied the disruption in family ties during large-scale urban in-migration. This theme was further adopted in the work of social disorganization theorists who have studied this issue in the last couple of decades (Sampson and Raudenbush, 1999).

The second major theme in the spatial analysis of crime has emerged from studies concentrating on the daily routines and interactions of people in different settings. The vulnerability to crime that accompanies these daily activities creates opportunities that offenders exploit (Felson, 1998). These opportunities are enhanced in certain places under specific conditions. The social control that is exercised over these behaviors is specific to guardianship that comes from surveillance from the police or others in the environment rather than to an emphasis on social disorganization and its consequences.

Although these perspectives are not necessarily contradictory, they have operated separately from one another in their explication of what occurs in urban settings and have emphasized different factors that would reinforce the importance of place in our analysis of crime occurrence. Both perspectives—social disorganization theory and opportunities theory—share the view that place does matter. Our examination of these two perspectives will provide an overview of how place can be studied and its relevance in our understanding of criminal events.

SOCIAL DISORGANIZATION THEORY

According to Wirth (1938), the larger, the more densely populated, and the more heterogeneous a community, the more accentuated are the characteristics associated with urbanism, including isolation and social breakdown. Urbanism brings together individuals who have no sentimental or emotional ties to one another. From this mixture emerges a spirit of competition, aggrandizement, and exploitation. To counteract this spirit, society reverts to formal controls.

People who are in frequent social contact with strangers and acquaintances also develop a reserve toward one another. The strong family and friendship ties necessary for intimate communities disappear in cities, and the result is higher levels of alienation, anomie, and delinquency. To prove the point, Wirth points out that crime rates in urban areas are higher than those in rural areas, where the informal social controls between intimates still operate.

Accompanying the increase in personal wealth in the late nineteenth and early twentieth centuries was a demand for the protection of private property. Moral crusades called for the constraint of undesirable practices such as gambling and vagrancy, a response still evident today in the calls for tough legal response to emerging youth violence (Sullivan and Miller, 1999). The response to demands for more social order included devising techniques of criminalization through the imposition of standardized and universally applied laws, uniformed policing, and incarceration (Gurr, 1980).

The fear of crime that stems from the disorder of fast-growing cities has resulted in increased calls for more police officers and for more efficient and effective courts. The view that we are moving away from the community as the major basis of social control in society is counterbalanced by evidence that the community still plays a crucial role in both generating and controlling deviance. On the one hand, then, the community has become less important as a forum of social control because the state has assumed responsibility for protecting the victim. On the other hand, the diversity of communities makes the imposition of a unitary state power difficult. This is a lesson that the police are learning in their experiments with community policing.

Researchers such as LaGrange and colleagues (1992) and Skogan (1990a) argue that public concern about disorder is usually gauged by asking survey respondents to indicate how serious they perceive several types of problems to be in their own neighborhoods. The types of disorder about which people are typically asked include the following:

- trash and litter lying around
- dogs barking loudly or being a nuisance
- inconsiderate or disruptive behavior
- graffiti on sidewalks and walls
- vacant houses and unkempt lots
- unsupervised youths
- noisy neighbors
- people drunk or high on drugs in public
- abandoned car parts lying around
- kids or adults trespassing in people's yards

If some urban neighborhoods more effectively constrain the delinquent inclinations of youths, then we might be able to explain why some parts of the city have higher rates of delinquency than do others. Theoretical arguments of this type were originally proposed by Clifford Shaw and Henry McKay (1942), two sociologists at the University of Chicago. They were interested in trying to understand why some parts of the city of Chicago had consistently high rates of crime, delinquency, and other social problems. What intrigued them was that rates of delinquency remained high even when the resident population, identified at any given point in time, moved out or died and were replaced by new groups of urban residents. In other words, regardless of changes in the ethnic or demographic mix of the population residing within an area, rates of delinquency were relatively constant. According to Shaw and McKay, urban variations in crime rates are associated with the social context of urban areas rather than with the specific characteristics of the populations who live there.

Shaw and McKay conducted a series of analyses over many years in Chicago, as part of the Chicago Area Project. Their research revealed that it was the characteristics of the neighborhoods, which concentrated negative social conditions, rather than the characteristics of the inhabitants (for example, immigrant status) that contributed to the decline into delinquency. Shaw and McKay provided extensive analysis of the physical distribution of their various indices of social breakdown, including percentage of families on government relief, percentage of foreign-born residents, and rates of dependent families. The researchers sought to examine how these factors correlated with concentrations of delinquency.

According to Shaw and McKay, high-crime areas are characterized by a high degree of social disorganization, which may be defined as an inability on the part of area residents to achieve their common values or solve their common problems (Kornhauser, 1978). Shaw and McKay argued that areas with a high level of social disorganization tend to be economically disadvantaged, to have a high rate of population turnover, and to be racially and ethnically diverse. In such areas, the informal social controls that might be expected to constrain delinquency are ineffective. As predicted by Wirth (1938), local friendship networks are less likely to develop and the level of participation in formal or voluntary organizations is low. As a result, adults in these communities may be ineffective in their attempts to supervise or control teenage groups that are likely to become involved in delinquency (Sampson and Groves, 1989).

Shaw and McKay's conclusions about social disorganization and delinquency attracted a great deal of criticism. Jonassen (1949) challenged Shaw and McKay's assumptions about the delinquency-producing factors inherent in the community. He argued that because the researchers had access only to aggregate data about neighborhoods, their analyses suffered from an ecological fallacy: they could test only the relative importance of the characteristics of communities and of residents in explaining delinquency. This limitation in the analyses of Shaw and McKay derives from their not having access to micro-level data or to the technical sophistication currently available to address what is called "spatial dependency" of the variables in their studies. Because Shaw and McKay relied on descriptive rather than analytical approaches (Bursik and Grasmick, 1993), they left themselves open to the contention that they saw behavior in communities as resulting from ecological determinism—that is, that the area characteristics controlled the behavior contained therein. Even though Shaw and McKay attempted to deny this determinism, they were unable to show how their work is not subject to this criticism.

Neighborhoods with a high degree of interaction are more likely to control crime informally through the residents' collective ability to respond to violations of the law and neighborhood norms (Unger and Wandersman, 1985). This informal control depends, however, on the neighborhood's having a consensus on values or norms, the ability to monitor behavior, and a willingness to intervene when necessary. These characteristics are generally absent in urban neighborhoods that have a high rate of residential mobility, especially in areas where the population is decreasing. As Sampson and colleagues say (1997), "Economic stratification by race and place thus fuels the neighborhood concentration of cumulative forms of disadvantage, intensifying the social isolation of lower income, minority and single parent residents from key resources supporting collective social control" (919). The disadvantages that Shaw and McKay witnessed in transient neighborhoods, then, were compounded by the destabilization that occurred by constant migration of people throughout these urban enclaves. The consequent crime outcomes arise, according to Sampson and colleagues, when this disorder results in low levels of community participation, making it difficult to mobilize local resources to maintain social control within neighborhoods. In an analysis of urban neighborhoods in Chicago by Sampson and Raudenbush (1999), the importance of community efficacy from this perspective supersedes the impact of physical or social disorder in explaining crime outcomes. However, dealing only with one part of the problem (low community participation) will not be successful if the other (social and physical decay and disorder) is not also addressed.

This recent debate about the relative importance of physical disorder and social interaction in influencing crime comes back to the historical assertion of the Chicago school (of which Wirth and Shaw and McKay were adherents) that an understanding of social life must include an understanding of the arrangements of social actors in particular social times and places. As Abbott (1997) puts it, "[The Chicago school] thought that no social fact makes any sense abstracted from its context in social (and often geographic) space and social time. . . . Every social fact is situated, surrounded by other contextual facts and brought into being by a process relating it to past contexts" (1152). Abbott suggests that the search for single causal factors, rather than accounting for social interactions that occur in context, came partly from the efforts to make social science more scientific in its determination of social outcomes. It came, as well, from the shift from community-based approaches, with attendant problems of ecological fallacies, to individual-based approaches that isolated individuals from the communities in which they lived. The efforts to use random sampling to generate survey respondents encouraged the search for individual-based variables that could be analyzed in terms of independent-dependent relationships, devoid of concerns about the social contexts in which these behaviors take place. Whereas mapmakers are encouraged to verify the facts in their maps through "ground truthing," social scientists rarely involve themselves in "context truthing."

Abbott advocates describing interactional fields. He says that we require, as well, ways of looking at spatial interdependence, which has a temporal character. According to Abbott, the revival of the Chicago perspective derives from a concern with this interdependence and the richness it brings to our understanding of social behavior. This is exactly the form of research that we advocate in the study of criminal events—research based on the assumption that behavior that can be understood only in its spatial and temporal context (Anselin et al., 2000).

The incidence of crime may also depend on interethnic and interracial relationships that develop in areas where groups with different backgrounds come together. The confusion and misunderstandings that arise from differences in family practice and cultural values can lead to tensions and conflicts, which in turn can develop into criminal behavior along the lines proposed by Sellin (1938). In addition, Suttles (1972) found that, particularly in ethnic communities, boundaries are set by public displays of territorial marking (for example, threatened gang fights); these boundaries indicate, through spatial mechanisms, with whom it is safe to associate. The marking of territory plays a role in reducing neighborhood conflict by excluding those who are considered to be different or undesirable. Conflict with people outside of the neighborhood takes on a symbolic character of protectiveness of the turf.

In disorganized areas, people are less likely to know their neighbors or to be interested in their welfare. The high level of cultural distance between different groups inhabiting the area and the rapid turnover of population mitigate against the development of a strong sense of community spirit. Monitoring the behavior of others in the neighborhood is more difficult when residents do not recognize their neighbors and thus do not know whether they have a "right" to be there (Stark, 1987). Under such circumstances, residents are not only less likely to fail to recognize neighbors but also less likely to recognize their property; thus, stolen property that is carried around the neighborhood by a stranger, or even by someone we know, is unlikely to be identified (Felson, 1998). In contrast, in small, tightly knit communities in which the residents know one another both culturally and personally, informal community control is expected to operate more effectively.

Many of the social institutions that might be expected to control the behavior of youthful offenders are also less effective in socially disorganized areas. Formal social controls such as churches and schools, for instance, may not enjoy a high level of community support, in which case their social control functions may be undermined (Stark, 1987). In well-integrated areas, community organizations might be expected to form in response to the problem of local crime or delinquency. However, when the level of social disorganization is high, voluntary groups formed to address community problems are less likely to develop.

In a recent restatement of the social disorganization perspective, Bursik and Grasmick (1993) distinguish three types of social controls that are rendered less effective in areas characterized by high levels of social disorganization. The first type of control functions at the private level and includes controls associated with the family, the friendship group, or other groups with which one has an intimate association. The second type is parochial control and represents the effects of broader patterns of interpersonal association. Such controls are exerted by local schools, stores, churches, or voluntary organizations. The third type is public or external control, the ability of the local community to mobilize sources of control that originate beyond its boundaries. Local communities will not be equally successful in their attempts to get the urban bureaucracy to allocate funds to neighborhood projects or to get the police to take neighborhood problems seriously. This discussion of private to public social control mirrors our approach to the discussion of social domains that we will elaborate in the chapters that follow.

Bursik and Grasmick argue that such controls, when operating, discourage crime by discouraging both criminal motivation and the opportunities for crime. The researchers also note that these controls do not emerge instantaneously. Instead, they emerge slowly, as residents associate with one another and establish relationships over time. Factors that contribute to residential instability undermine the processes that lead to effective community controls and therefore make higher rates of crime and delinquency more likely.

We see the logic of the social disorganization argument manifested in many forms of crime prevention that attempt to re-create a sense of community in high-crime neighborhoods. Neighborhood Watch and similar programs seek to increase the level of interaction among residents and at the same time encourage them to develop a sense of responsibility for their neighbors.

The connection between daily behavior and instability in neighborhoods has been translated through the filter of social cohesion and social control. This approach, however, had difficulty in articulating the mechanisms whereby criminal actions are facilitated in the structure of routine daily activities. An important shift in the ways in which we study crime origins relates to the observation that communities maintain crime patterns despite the characteristics of the people living in these areas. Although Shaw and McKay (1942) made this observation, they had difficulty explaining it. The recent focus on hot spots has helped refocus our attention on patterns of behavior rather than on patterns of social characteristics. But hot spot analysis still suffers from the limitation that we are studying the residue of misbehavior—police arrest data—and not the behavioral patterns that bring about these outcomes. This realization has demanded a shift from analysis of social disorganization or community cohesion to a focus on the component parts of behavior patterns in neighborhoods. The leading hypotheses on the ways in which individual behaviors combine to create crime comes from routine activities theory.

ROUTINE ACTIVITIES AND LIFESTYLE EXPOSURE THEORY

That offenders are ready and willing to engage in criminal conduct—because of their personalities, background, or views of the law—does not in and of itself explain the occurrence of criminal events. Potential offenders must encounter opportunities that allow their criminal inclinations to be given expression. This is no less true of crime than of anything else. An inclination to learn to play the saxophone, to go to graduate school, or to become a skydiver does not ensure that these things will happen. In such cases, as in the case of criminal events, it is useful to consider how opportunities spur individuals to act on their inclinations. Some theorists have argued that crime is a function of exposing oneself to crime by being in environments that attract offenders, because of one's lifestyle or patterns of movement through urban spaces (Brantingham and Brantingham, 1999; Felson, 1998). These lifestyle exposure and routine activities theories suggest that criminal event spaces become likely locations for crime because the opportunity is provided through low guardianship and enhanced risk.

Since the late 1970s, lifestyle exposure and routine activities theories have focused on how variations in levels of crime from place to place or over time are related to variations in the opportunities to commit crime rather than to variations in the numbers of people who are motivated to commit crimes and who feel that they will be rewarded by this action. The lifestyle exposure theory of criminal victimization was formally developed by Michael Hindelang, Michael Gottfredson, and James Garofalo in their 1978 book, *Victims of Personal Crime*. Their theory, which was grounded in victimization survey data, sought to explain what it is about being male, young, single, or poor that increases the chances of being victimized.

The linchpin of their argument is the concept of lifestyle. In general terms, *lifestyle* refers to the patterned ways in which people distribute their time and energies across a range of activities. We have no trouble recognizing that the lifestyle of a teenage male differs quite markedly from the lifestyle of an elderly female. Such differences relate to how and where time is spent, with whom one associates, and what type of leisure pursuits one enjoys. These lifestyle differences are not merely a matter of personal choice; they also reflect the social roles that one is required to play and the various types of social constraints to which one is subject.

Where and how people spend their time is related to their risk of victimization. Although the number of evening activities in which people engage outside the home increases their chances of becoming a crime victim, research suggests that crimes are more likely to occur in some places, at some times, and in the course of some activities than in others. Data from the 1998 National Crime Victimization Survey revealed that 1 in 5 violent crimes took place in the victim's home. Another 10 percent occurred near the home. Close to 20 percent transpired on the street away from the victim's home, and less than 1 in 10 happened in school or on school property. About 4 percent transpired inside a restaurant, bar, or club.

Hindelang, Gottfredson, and Garofalo (1978: 251–264) offer the following eight propositions about victimization that summarize the link between lifestyle and key demographic variables such as age, sex, marital status, family income, and race:

- The more time that individuals spend in public places (especially at night), the more likely they are to be victimized.
- Following certain lifestyles makes individuals more likely to frequent public places.

- The interactions that individuals maintain tend to be with persons who share their lifestyles.

- The probability that individuals will be victims increases according to the extent to which victims and offenders belong to the same demographic categories.

- The proportion of time individuals spend in places where there are a large number of nonfamily members varies according to lifestyle.

- The chances that individuals will be victims of crime (particularly theft) increase in conjunction with the amount of time they spend among non-family members.

- Differences in lifestyles relate to the ability of individuals to isolate themselves from those with offender characteristics.

- Variations in lifestyles influence the convenience, desirability, and ease of victimizing individuals.

Recent literature has discussed the importance of risk taking in influencing the degree to which certain individuals are likely to become crime victims. Those who live on the edge may seek out areas that enhance risk, because those areas are more exciting and less predictable. Individuals who live in the mainstream might also pursue risky behavior—for example, drug use or prostitution—as a way to get kicks and excitement. Through risky behavior, individuals come together with others who are living equally risky lives, and they encounter situations that raise the likelihood of crime victimization (Lyng, 1990).

Lifestyle in a sense structures victimization opportunities. Rates of personal victimization are relatively high for young minority males because these individuals tend to associate with people who are likely to offend (that is, other young minority males) and because they tend to frequent places (for example, bars) where offending often occurs. An elderly female, by contrast, is likely to associate with other elderly females (whose level of offending is very low) and to avoid high-risk settings. In explaining empirical variations in levels of personal crime, Hindelang and colleagues (1978) advance these opportunity structures, not offender motivation, as a central theoretical issue.

Cohen and Felson (1979) note that traditional motivational theories in criminology are unable to explain the dramatic increase in many forms of crime that occurred in Western nations in the post–World War II period. Many of the explanatory factors (for example, poverty, unemployment, size of inner-city population) indicated trends that suggested that crime rates should have been falling during this period rather than climbing. How, then, could the problem of rising crime rates be accurately reconceptualized?

According to Cohen and Felson, the presence of a motivated offender is only one component necessary to the completion of an assault, sexual assault, homicide, breaking and entering, or other direct-contact predatory violations. For such crimes to occur, two other conditions must be met. First, a "suitable target" must be present, against which the criminal motivation can be directed (for example, homes to break into, people to assault, and goods to steal). Second, there must be an "absence of capable guardianship," meaning that the motivated offender must meet the suitable target in the absence of anything (or anyone) that might prevent the crime from occurring.

Cohen and Felson suggest that variations in levels of crime are determined not only by the numbers of people willing to commit crimes but also by the numbers of suitable targets and by the levels of guardianship that are routinely exercised over these targets. Even if the numbers of suitable targets and the levels of guardianship remain unchanged, higher crime rates can be expected if the tempos and rhythms of social life affect the rate at which motivated offenders encounter suitable targets in the absence of capable guardianship. For Cohen and Felson, illegal activities must be understood as behaviors that depend on, and feed on, the "routine activities" of the population: "Although the fox finds each hare one by one, the fox population varies with the hare population upon which it feeds" (Felson, 1987: 914). As the structure of the routine activities changes, so does the frequency at which crimes occur. Felson (1998) gives the example of how theft and robbery rates have been affected by the implementation of ATMs (automatic teller machines), which provides both easy access to money and easy targets for offenders who know that people coming away from an ATM have money in their pockets.

How do these insights inform our theoretical understanding of why crime rates changed as they did after World War II? Cohen and Felson (1979) argue that changes in patterns of routine activities substantially altered levels of target suitability and guardianship, as well as the rates at which these elements and motivated offenders came together in time and space. This period witnessed a broad shift in the locus of routine activities. In increasingly large numbers, women whose lives had revolved around the household entered or returned to the paid labor force or school. In addition, vacation periods became longer and travel became cheaper, so that holidays were more likely to be spent away from home. Even the frequency with which people dined at restaurants increased and gave rise to a booming fast-food industry. At the same time, divorce rates increased, and people were waiting longer before getting married. These latter changes resulted in a significant rise in the number of smaller, single-person households and further contributed to the likelihood that leisure interests previously pursued at home would now be pursued elsewhere, among nonfamily members.

Not coincidentally, this period also witnessed a revolution in the design of small durable products. A general increase in the standard of living combined with technological advancement to produce a wide range of lightweight, durable consumer goods. Demand for tape recorders, television sets, and stereo equipment increased, as it later did for products like personal computers, CD players, and VCRs (Felson, 1998).

These changes, according to Felson, exerted a profound impact on the rates of direct-contact predatory crimes. Through their effects on target suitability and guardianship levels, they provided greater criminal opportunities and pushed crime rates upward. The shift in routine activities away from the home exposed increasingly large numbers of people to criminal dangers from which they previously had been insulated. Moreover, in greater numbers, people's homes were unoccupied for increasing periods of time and thus deprived of capable guardianship. At the same time that guardianship was being lowered, homes were being stocked with larger numbers of highly desirable durable consumer goods that were easy to steal, carry, and sell or use. As guardianship declined, target suitability increased. One need not agonize over the question of criminal motivation, Felson concludes, in order to understand an increase in crime through the 1970s and 1980s.

The routine activities theory emphasizes the role that opportunities play in the commission of crime. Social patterns that separate people from their property and from their family members increase the opportunities for crime. Liska and Warner (1991) agree that public reactions to predatory crimes (like robbery) keep people at home and away from strangers. Although this reduces their sense of community, it also allows them to exert greater guardianship over their persons and property. As this happens, opportunities for crime are decreased and greater control of crime is achieved. As a consequence, crime rates drop.

An important theoretical question in the study of criminal situations relates to the manner in which these events unfold over time. They are set in motion by offenders who are inclined to make use of available criminal opportunities. In order to explain why they follow a particular course of action, we must ask questions about the specific behavioral choices that offenders, victims, and others make in the situational contexts in which they find themselves. In particular, we must understand how the choices that each participant makes influence the choices made by others. Victims and offenders act and react, and in so doing, they exert mutual influence. Stated differently, crimes have an interactional character: what any one participant does depends on what others do. Although interactional dynamics have not attracted as much attention as issues like offender motivation, a general appreciation of how criminologists attempt to understand these interactions is necessary.

Also looking at opportunities for crime, rational choice theories focus on offenders' actions based on perceived benefits rather than on some precipitating social or psychological factors (Clarke and Felson, 1993). Moreover, as offenders seek benefits and attempt to avoid losses, they make decisions and choices that can be understood as reflecting rational thought. Therefore, the rational choice theorist argues that, rather than studying whatever broad social factors might influence offending behavior, it makes more sense to study how offenders make their decisions. Two broad types of offender decisions invite attention.

One type of offender decision relates to the commission of particular crimes. How do burglars choose the neighborhood where they will look for targets? How do they decide which house to break into? How do they decide what to do if they see a window sticker indicating that the home is protected by an alarm system? The answers to such questions allow rational choice theorists to develop an understanding of criminal events and the role that offenders play in such events (Tunnell, 1992). Obviously, when compared with many traditional theories of motivation, rational choice theory is more interested in the situational character of crime (Birkbeck and LaFree, 1993).

In attempting to answer questions about offenders' decisions, rational choice theories do not assume that offenders operate in purely rational fashion. Instead, offenders usually employ a "limited rationality." In other words, they may inaccurately perceive the benefits of committing a particular crime, lack the time to weigh the possible outcomes, or have only limited access to information with which to make a decision.

Rational choice theorists argue that because specific situational factors are so important and because offender decision making varies across situations, it makes little sense to try to develop a generic theory of crime. The choices that must be made when an offender is deciding whether to rob a convenience store will be very different from the choices that must be made if an offender is deciding whether to steal a car or defraud a bank (Clarke, 1992).

Criminologist Maurice Cusson (1993) addressed the specific character of the situations in which crimes occur. A typical research project might ask respondents to indicate how likely it is that they will be apprehended if they attempt to steal a car. Too often, however, the context of the automobile theft is not specified. Obviously, how risky one perceives car theft to be depends greatly on the specific circumstances under which the theft is attempted. Although study respondents may make certain assumptions in order to provide an answer to the researcher's question, the answers may have little to do with the actual assessment of risks that an individual makes in any specific situation.

In addition, Cusson notes, while researchers ask survey subjects to calmly assess the risks of apprehension, this research ignores the emotional character of the deterrence process. Deterrence, he argues, is not about the cold and rational calculation of risks but about fear. A burglar who breaks into a house may rationally believe that his chances of getting caught are low, but he may panic when he hears a noise. Fear can override rational calculation and make the deterrence process look quite different in reality from how it appears in theory. For these reasons, Cusson suggests the need to consider deterrence as a situational factor. Situational deterrence emphasizes the ways in which the offender's fear of apprehension is related to the specific circumstances of the criminal event.

According to Cusson, potential offenders face two types of danger in the precriminal situation. The first type is immediate. For instance, the robber worries that the victim may fight back or be armed, and the burglar worries that a barking dog might bite. The second type of danger refers to subsequent harm that is signaled by some element in the precriminal situation. Thus, the television monitor in the convenience store about to be robbed does not threaten the robber directly but may eventually if it leads to the robber's apprehension.

Cusson notes that the risks facing offenders prior to or during the commission of the offense do not guarantee that the offender will be deterred. Offenders differ in terms of the level of courage that they can muster in particular situations and also in terms of their ability to manage the fear they experience. In addition, some crimes (such as joyriding or vandalism) may be more attractive precisely because they involve an element of danger.

The value of Cusson's analysis is that it forces us to recognize that deterrence effects are embodied not solely in abstract legal threats but also in the risks that offenders understand themselves to be facing in the settings in which criminal events occur.

Victimization and Opportunity

In recent decades, a large body of research has grown up around the questions raised by opportunity theories of victimization (Cohen, Kluegel, and Land, 1981; Felson, 1998; Kennedy and Forde, 1990; Tremblay and Tremblay, 1998). As a result, the field has grown in a number of distinct ways.

Some writers, such as Terance Miethe and Robert Meier (1994), have attempted to refine and modify the theoretical approach to the study of victimization opportunity. Miethe and Meier have proposed what they call a structural-choice model of victimization. Building on the work of earlier writers (Cohen et al., 1981), they maintain that opportunity theories highlight the importance of four factors: the physical proximity of targets to a pool of motivated offenders, the target's exposure to high-risk environments, target attractiveness, and the absence of guardianship. In addition, they argue that current theories of victimization opportunity suggest two propositions. The first is that routine activities or lifestyles foster a structure of criminal opportunity by enhancing the contact between potential offenders and potential victims. The second proposition is that the subjective value of a person or of property, and the level of guardianship exerted over person or property, determines which targets are chosen for victimization. Thus, their model implies that although patterns of routine activities expose some people or property to greater risks, the selection of specific targets will depend on the rewards and risks associated with one target rather than another. For Miethe and Meier, then, proximity and exposure are considered "structural" factors because they predispose people to differing levels of risk. Target attractiveness and guardianship, on the other hand, are best viewed as "choice" components because they determine which targets are selected, in contexts characterized by particular levels of risk.

Some elaborations of opportunity theory focus on the ways in which arguments about criminal opportunity are compatible with arguments about the spatial distribution of crime. As pointed out earlier, research on hot spots in Minneapolis by Sherman and colleagues (1989) suggested that a relatively small number of urban locations (street addresses and intersections) host a relatively large amount of crime. Their explanation of this pattern emphasizes the need to focus on the routine activities of places. In other words, crime rates are high at specific locations because of the ways in which those locations are used by the people found there. Similarly, although most interpretations of social disorganization emphasize how neighborhood disorganization affects offending, it is equally reasonable to show how social disorganization might affect levels of criminal opportunity (Bursik and Grasmick, 1993; Smith, Frazee, and Davison, 2000).

Felson (1998) has written about the relationship between the character of community and levels of criminal opportunity. Of particular interest to Felson is the urban form he describes as the "metroreef." Such "communities" emerge when "metropolises themselves begin to fuse into a single organism, a seemingly endless suburban sprawl at moderate or low metropolitan density" (Felson 1998: 87). According to Felson, metroreefs promote crime because of the ways in which they "unpack" everyday activities. He has identified four related aspects of this unpacking process:

Dispersing by construction. As metroreefs develop, they spread homes and public building across metropolitan space. The buildup of such areas involves the construction of single-family homes, large numbers of buildings with few stories on large lots, wide roads, and huge parking areas. This kind of dispersion makes it difficult for neighbors to keep an eye on each other's property and for the police to patrol effectively.

Proliferating households. In the metroreef, young couples and the elderly generally maintain their own households (although in an earlier time, they might have lived with other family members). As well, boarders are rare, divorce rates are high, and college and university students tend to move away from home. All of this implies that, in the metroreef, people are spread out over more households, and thus within each household fewer people are available to discourage theft.

Spreading people over many vehicles. In the metroreef virtually everyone depends on cars for transportation. The huge parking lots, which the large number of cars requires, increase the number of criminal opportunities. Thousands of expensive cars and their contents, sitting unsupervised for hours at a time, attract thieves and vandals. Walking to and from cars in underground parking garages or in the massive parking lots that surround, for instance, the modern shopping mall, leaves people vulnerable to a variety of forms of criminal exploitation.

Dispersing activities away from the home. The reliance on the car in the metroreef has reduced the connection that people have to, and perhaps their interest in, their immediate environment. People are willing to travel farther to work, to shop, or to socialize. As an example of this pattern of dispersion away from the home, Felson comments on how the corner grocery store has been replaced by the megasupermarket. Whereas the former would have attracted local residents who most likely walk to get there, the latter attracts strangers from a much wider area who almost certainly drive to get there.

Thus Felson's analysis shows us how the social organization of everyday life in the metroreef makes large numbers of criminal opportunities available to those who are inclined—for whatever reason—to take advantage of them.

Some writers (Osgood et al., 1996; Riley, 1987) have argued that offending (like victimization) can itself be understood as a function of routine activities. Thus, the routine activities in which people engage increase or decrease the likelihood that they will find themselves in situations that encourage or allow offending behavior. Osgood and his colleagues argue that, for a range of criminal and deviant behavior, situations conducive to offending are particularly prevalent when routine activities frequently place young people in unstructured social activities with peers that occur in the absence of authority figures. The lack of structure leaves time available for deviance. In addition, when peers are present, various types of crime and deviance are not only more easy to accomplish but also more rewarding. Finally, the absence of an authority figure (such as a parent or a teacher) means that it is less likely that anyone will assume the responsibility for the social control of the offending behavior.

More specifically, Kennedy and Forde (1998) have attempted to develop what they refer to as routine conflict theory. This argument seeks to understand the social roots of violence by integrating routine activities theory with arguments about the ways in which violent responses to conflict situations are learned. For Kennedy and Forde, it is meaningful to speak of "routine conflict" in two respects. First, conflict situations (and in many cases, potentially criminally violent situations) in which individuals find themselves emerge out of the routine interactions in which people engage. These conflicts may involve a fight over money, sex, or drugs, or they may involve a trivial disagreement arising from a perceived slight. They may lead to threats or physical harm or to a parting of the combatants before real trouble begins. Conflicts may have long histories, suggesting that the combatants have been feuding for years, or they may spark between strangers who have never met each other before. Second, the ways in which each of us responds to conflict situations is a function of the "scripts" that are learned as part of the socialization process. In other words, when we find ourselves involved in conflict, we rarely understand what is happening as a "completely new situation" that requires a "completely novel solution." More typically, we draw on our experiences with conflict tactics in the past, and our actions are informed by our sense of what has worked in the past and therefore is likely to work again. Thus, Kennedy and Forde argue that violent routines are available to people based on what they have learned and what they expect to happen in particular situations.

The theory maintains that individuals come to situations with a predisposition to behave in particular ways. Moreover, individuals learn "repertoires" that they use to manage their daily lives, much as they learn other aspects of their lifestyles. In a sense, these repertoires include guidelines regarding the ways in which conflict situations that they routinely encounter should be managed. Kennedy and Forde note as well that individuals learn not only how to act when confronted by the actions of others but also that reactions to perceived threats are tempered by the situations in which they find themselves. Certain contexts (for example, bars or sporting events) may be more likely than others to encourage routine acts of violence.

Traditionally, researchers interested in the factors that place people at increased risk of victimization have focused on a relatively narrow range of lifestyle factors. These factors have included measures of alcohol consumption, the frequency of engaging in nighttime activities outside the home, and a range of demographic indicators (such as sex, age, or social class) that are thought to indicate differences in the kinds of roles people play in society. More recently, some researchers have begun to argue that the range of lifestyle risk factors that criminologists study should be extended. Two such variables are of particular interest: offending behavior and prior victimization experience.

With respect to the first of these variables, several studies have shown that an important, if imperfectly understood, relationship exists between offending and victimization (Jensen and Brownfield, 1986; Richie, 2000). In short, this research suggests that people who engage in offending behavior are at an elevated risk of criminal victimization. There are two very reasonable explanations for this relationship. First, as lifestyle models argue, people tend to associate with others who are socially and demographically like themselves. By implication, offenders tend to associate with other offenders. Moreover, because offenders often victimize those who are most accessible to them, it should come as no surprise to discover that those who tell researchers that they have offended are also likely to tell them that they have been victimized. A second explanation stresses the character of offending behavior itself rather than the social demographic characteristics of those who engage in such behavior. In short, those who engage in prohibited behavior often make perfect victims because they are unlikely to want the police to be involved in any investigation of their activities. In this sense, offending behavior can be seen as increasing one's vulnerability to predatory crime (Kennedy and Baron, 1993).

For many people, the recognition of a link between offending and victimization greatly complicates the understanding of crime. In the context of popular discourse, we are encouraged to think of criminals and victims as two separate categories of people who differ not only behaviorally but also morally. However, the empirical evidence suggests that the picture is not so straightforward. Not only do victims and offenders often share many characteristics in common (both, for instance are typically young and typically poor), and not only is offending a risk factor for victimization, but other research also shows that victimization is a risk factor for offending (Agnew, 1985; Fleisher, 1995; Widom, 1995). Thus, people who have been criminally exploited by others (for a wide variety of understandable reasons) may be more likely to engage in certain types of criminal behavior themselves. In short, the relationship between offending and victimization is extremely complex and may not neatly conform to our idealized moral visions of how the world should look.

What is the nature of the relationship between offending and victimization? Baron (1997) attempted to answer this question by investigating a group that is at high risk for both kinds of behavior—male homeless street youth. Baron conducted detailed interviews with 200 street youths with whom he was able to establish prior contact. The respondents were asked about a variety of issues— especially their involvement in criminal events as offenders and as victims. The results of the research were illuminating in several respects.

First, Baron found that almost all of the youth had suffered some kind of criminal victimization and that the majority had been repeatedly victimized.

Second, the results suggested a strong relationship between offending and chronic victimization. The greater the number of violent crimes the offender committed, the more likely he was to report having been victimized. It is quite likely, Baron reasoned, that the "capricious nature" of these crimes left the offender vulnerable to serious physical injury. As well, offenders who behave violently are often themselves at risk of violent retribution at the hands of those they have victimized. Third, and less expected, Baron found that violent offending can sometimes deter victimization. For example, those who are themselves not inclined to behave violently may be reluctant to try to steal from someone who is known to have no such inhibitions. Finally, Baron found that youths from abusive families were more likely to be victimized. Their experiences in abusive homes may have encouraged them to develop provocative and belligerent interactional styles that made them likely targets for victimization. Baron concludes that it is important to focus future analytical attention on the relationship between offending and victimization—especially because such issues affect those, like homeless youth, who are at high risk of both.

A second factor in which those who study victimization risk have become very interested is prior victimization (Farrell, 1995; Farrell, Phillips, and Pease, 1995; Hope, 1995; Johnson, Bowers, and Hirschfield, 1997). Analyses of victimization data suggest that much victimization is multiple victimization. Stated differently, these data indicate that people who have been victimized once have an increased risk of being victimized again. Of course, for some crimes—such as wife assault—we are not surprised to discover that this is the case. However, several studies suggest that the phenomenon may be somewhat more generalizable. In other words, an initial act of victimization appears to increase the risk of subsequent victimization in the case of property, as well as personal crime.

Pease and Laycock (1996) use the term *hot dot* to refer to a victim who is repeatedly victimized. In a sense, hot dots are the ultimate hot spots. In their review of the problem of repeat victimization, Pease and Laycock maintain that available research supports the following conclusions:

- Past criminal victimization of an individual is a useful predictor of his or her subsequent victimization.

- The greater the number of previous victimizations, the greater the likelihood that the individual will experience victimization in the future.

- High-crime areas differ from low-crime areas at least in part because in high-crime areas a small number of victims are victimized at higher rates.

- When victimization recurs, it tends to be soon after the prior occurrence.

- The same offenders seem to be responsible for the bulk of repeated offenses against a victim.

- Many factors, from policing styles to the nature of criminal justice information systems, inhibit a more detailed understanding how repeat victimization contributes to the crime problem.

Two general explanations can be offered for the patterns of repeat victimization. One argument suggests that perhaps the social or demographic characteristics that put people at risk for the first victimization continue to place them at risk after that first victimization. The second explanation maintains that something about the victimization experience itself may increase the risk of further victimization. Although we might assume that an offender who has burglarized a house once may not want to do so again, that may not be the case. Instead, the house that has recently been successfully burglarized once may be an even more desirable target the second time. After all, in the case of the already burglarized house (as opposed to some other random house), the offender probably has some prior knowledge about when the house is unoccupied and how easy it is to gain access. As well, the burglar might safely assume (given the empty cardboard boxes put out for trash collection) that the stolen television and VCR have been replaced by new equipment. Research evidence supports the conclusion that both prior risk and an increased vulnerability due to the victimization experience may be important sources of repeat victimization (Wittebrood and Nieuwbeerta, 2000).

Opportunity Reduction

Newman (1972) uses the ideas of opportunity theory in arguing that the most effective way to reduce crime is to redesign public and private spaces in such a way that opportunities for crime are removed—that is, removing criminal event places from urban environments. The "defensible space" concept proposes that one can "harden" targets by installing locks or by improving surveillance, such that criminals are deterred from committing the crime, either because they fear detection or simply because the target has been made inaccessible. The operators of 7-Eleven convenience stores redesigned their premises under the direction of Ray D. Johnson, who had served twenty-five years for robbery and burglary in the California state penitentiary system. The insights provided by a former perpetrator led to a design that removed the chance of concealment:

> To allow clear sightlines from the street into the store, they moved cash registers up front and removed all advertising from the front windows. They also put bright floodlights outside the entrance, forcing potential robbers to perform where any passerby could look in and see. They also installed special cash drawers that make it impossible to get at more than $10 every two minutes. This gives the would-be robber the choice of getting away with very little cash, waiting onstage to make the payoff worthwhile or simply going elsewhere. (Krupat and Kubzansky, 1987: 60)

The incidence of robberies in the redesigned 7-Eleven stores was 30 percent lower than that in the stores that had not been redesigned.

An outgrowth of this recent interest in spatial location of crime is an interest in environmental criminology that assumes a relationship between the physical character of cities and the potential for crime. Crime Prevention through Environmental Design (CPTED) suggests that we can reduce the likelihood of crime occurrence through the hardening of targets (Brantingham and Brantingham, 1984). If the physical design makes it difficult to steal or to attack someone (for example, fences or locked doors), the opportunity for crime is reduced. Further, problem-solving techniques that involve spatial analysis have begun to affect the way in which criminologists and police analyze crime patterns in social context.

Victimization research suggests that some types of housing structures are more susceptible to various forms of household crime than are others (Massey, Krohn, and Bonati, 1989). Most susceptible are dwellings that offer the thief or the burglar easy access or that provide cover during the commission of the crime. Thus, the risk of breaking and entering is higher when a housing structure offers multiple points of entry, when doors or windows are obscured by trees or shrubs, when the house is located on a corner or near a major route that allows easy escape, or when neighbors' houses do not directly overlook the target (Bennett and Wright, 1984; Evans, 1989).

Studies in which burglars themselves have served as informants have also provided information regarding what types of household settings are likely to be at high risk for this type of victimization. In a study with one hundred convicted burglars, for example, Reppetto (1974) found that the burglars were able to identify several characteristics that made a household a more (or less) attractive target: ease of access, appearance of affluence, inconspicuous setting, isolation of the neighborhood, absence of police patrols, and lack of surveillance by neighbors.

Burglary trends also seem to vary somewhat by time of day. Many studies have found that burglaries are quite likely to occur when houses are empty, often during daylight hours (Evans, 1989; Rengert and Wasilchick, 1985). Data from the 1998 National Crime Victimization Survey showed that among the burglaries for which the time of occurrence was known (60 percent of the total), about 60 percent occurred during daylight hours (U.S. Department of Justice, 2000).

The rhythms and tempos of family life affect the risk of household crime in other ways. A good deal of traffic in and out of the home is an expected characteristic of large families. Doors are more likely to be left open or unlocked, and property may not always be put away, which makes such homes an attractive target for thieves (Smith and Jarjoura, 1989). The summer months, which bring warm temperatures, open windows, and houses vacated by vacationers, may also increase the opportunities for household crime (Sacco and Johnson, 1990).

Sampson and Raudenbush (1999) conducted research using videotapes of a wide range of neighborhoods in Chicago to test the relative effects of social disorganization (what they refer to as community efficacy) and structural decay (for example, broken windows) on crime outcomes. They suggest that social control, which involves commitment on the part of community residents to oversee the behavior and physical order in their neighborhoods, is differentially applied across the city. The collective efficacy is the linkage of cohesion and mutual trust with shared expectations for intervening in support of neighborhood social control. The researchers believe that social control or efficacy should coexist with order in public spaces.

In proposing their research strategy, Sampson and Raudenbush suggest that their theory offers a different way to think about ecological "comorbity," that is, the association between public disorder and predatory crime, especially violent crime. As they characterize it, the "broken windows" literature (Kelling and Coles, 1998; Wilson and Kelling, 1982) sees disorder as a fundamental cause of crime. If this is true, Sampson and Rauderbush say, the association of structural characteristics of urban areas and collective efficacy with crime and violence ought to be largely mediated by social disorder. Their hypothesis (which their data analysis supports) suggests that disorder is a manifestation of crime-relevant mechanisms and that collective efficacy should reduce disorder and violence. Disorder, then, becomes unrelated to the etiology of crime events.

This characterization of disorder theories seems to extract them from the larger literature that relates disorder to the structure of crime opportunities that occur in urban areas. The broken windows analogy is not a static concept but should be seen as representing the temporal changes that occur in structural opportunities, both at any given time and in conjunction with what happened just previous to the time under question. Seen in dynamic terms, opportunity structures inevitably interconnect with elements of social control that appear in neighborhoods. Urban disorder is not simply a physical construct but rather a manifestation of complex social and physical interactions that involve decline, hazard, risk, and opportunity.

Jang and Johnson (2001) critique Sampson and Raudenbush's research, suggesting that they have misinterpreted what is intended in the broken windows metaphor proposed by Kelling and others. According to Jang and Johnson, although Sampson and Raudenbush state correctly that the broken windows theory proposes disorder as a fundamental cause of crime, their interpretation that disorder directly causes serious or predatory crime is incorrect. Jang and Johnson interpret the broken windows theory differently, saying that disorder indirectly causes crime through weakened informal social control. In fact, they suggest that the weakening of disorder effects by increases in collective efficacy provides positive support for this theory, rather than the negative support suggested by Sampson and Raudenbush.

Although the research of Sampson and Raudenbush is ambitious, they seem to be too literal in their view of social disorder and not open to the possibilities that we are discussing in this book—that crime places are created by the combination of social actions and physical structure. These places need to be studied as such, not in terms of individual variables that may have greater or less impact on social outcomes such as crime (see the discussion of Abbott's research, above).

COMMUNITY REACTIONS TO CRIME

We have examined the structural factors that determine crime opportunities in communities. Also important in the study of criminal events are the cognitive assessments that people apply when evaluating their environments. Do individuals' reactions to crime have implications for the communities in which they live? Theorists have provided two general answers to this question. The first, derived from the writings of the famous French sociologist Émile Durkheim (1933), suggests that public reactions to crime can make important contributions to the cohesion and stability of social life: "Crime brings together upright consciences and concentrates them. We have only to notice what happens, particularly in a small town, when some moral scandal has just been committed. [People] stop each other on the street, they visit each other, they seek to come together to talk of the event and to wax indignant in common" (102).

From this view, crime is thought to shock our sentiments and reaffirm our commitment to the common values that the crime violates. Our communal opposition to crime unites us. We might speak out against crime, be more vigilant in the exercise of informal social control, join a concerned citizens' group, or support the toughening of laws intended to control crime. The overall effect described by this view is one of social integration and a strengthening of social control whereby crime rates may decline or at least stabilize.

In sharp contrast, others have suggested that because crime generates fear, it is more likely to drive people apart than to bring them together. Conklin (1975) argues that when people are less afraid of crime, they are more likely to trust others and to think positively about their communities and less likely to restrict their activities and reduce their social interaction with other community members. In contrast, when levels of fear are high, people are more likely to stay home at night and less likely to get to know or to be interested in their neighbors. Some might even be tempted to flee the community for a safer haven. Overall, according to Conklin, crime does not build communities up, as the Durkheimian model contends, but rather undermines communities by weakening interpersonal ties.

This view implies that public reactions to crime weaken informal social controls. When the streets are empty and neighbors cease to care what happens to one another, potential offenders may feel freer to take advantage of criminal opportunities. Some researchers have argued that public reactions to rising crime rates can amplify subsequent crime rate increases. The central mechanism in this process is the breakdown of informal social control at the community level. Goodstein and Shotland (1982) have described the processes by which crime rates spiral upward as follows.

The cycle begins with actual increases in the crime rate or with the occurrence of one or several particularly noteworthy crimes. Such crimes might include an unsolved murder or a series of sexual assaults for which an offender has not been apprehended.

In the next stage, information about these crimes and the threats that they pose to other members of the community is disseminated widely. People learn via the mass media or rumor networks that crimes are increasing or that they might be at risk. As the information circulates, people begin to fear for their safety. This fear causes them to withdraw from community life. They stay home at night rather than go out, and they report that their enjoyment of the community has declined.

As people withdraw from the community, the delicate web of social relations begins to break down, as do the various informal social controls that regulate conduct. Thus, as the streets become less populated, they are subject to less control because citizen surveillance of them is reduced. As the levels of community control decline, the levels of crime may be expected to rise; and as the levels of crime continue to rise, the cycle begins to repeat itself.

Goodstein and Shotland's argument is consistent with the theoretical view that crime is made more likely by the absence of controls that check it. As the authors note, empirical evidence supports each of the individual linkages just described. What is less clear, however, is the validity of the overall model, which has not been rigorously tested in its entirety. In spatial terms, Harries (2000) has referred to these patterns as constituting "landscapes of fear."

Although the term *fear of crime* is widely used in the popular and social scientific literature, there is relatively little agreement regarding its meaning. Both *fear* and *crime* are complicated terms. Common usage of the term *fear* suggests an emotional or physiological reaction. We recognize that we are afraid when our mouths are dry, our hearts begin to pump, and the blood drains out of our faces. This, however, is not the meaning of the term as it is typically used by criminologists who do research in this area. After all, criminologists rarely have access to people at the moments when they are actually afraid.

Most research on the fear of crime comes from surveys (often victimization surveys) in which members of the public are asked about their beliefs or perceptions regarding crime. As a result, fear is usually treated as an attitude or a perception rather than as an emotion. In addition, we most often treat fear as a personal rather than an altruistic matter in that we ask people about their worries regarding their own safety or the safety of their property. Warr and Ellison (2000) argue, however, that people often are fearful not for their own safety but for the safety of other family members. Parents, for instance, may express less fear if asked about their own safety but more fear if asked about the safety of their children.

Skogan (1993) argues that the research literature indicates at least four distinct meanings of fear. The first meaning, concern, focuses on the extent to which people understand crime to be a serious problem in their communities. Concern is a judgment that people make about the frequency and seriousness of crime in the local environment. Using this definition, it is possible for a person to be concerned about crime without being personally fearful (Furstenberg, 1971).

A second definition of fear emphasizes risk. Research based on this type of definition asks respondents questions such as how likely they think it is that they will become victims of crime at some point in the future. Although this definition does not include an explicit emotional dimension, the assumption is that people who perceive their chances of being a victim of crime to be high will be more afraid.

Third, fear may be understood in terms of a threat. This definition stresses the potential for harm that people believe crime holds for them. Respondents to surveys are frequently asked, for instance, questions such as these: How safe do you, or would you, feel walking alone in your neighborhood at night? Would you say that you feel very safe, reasonably safe, somewhat unsafe, or very unsafe? Questions of this sort are designed to discover how likely people think it is that they would be harmed if they were to expose themselves to risk.

Finally, fear may be defined in terms of behavior. People may be asked not how they feel about their safety or how likely they think they are to be subject to harm, but about what they do (or say they do) in response to crime. Respondents may be asked, for example, whether they engage in "avoidance behavior" or about the other precautions they take to protect themselves from crime.

The term *public fear of crime* encourages the view that fear is a problem evenly shared by all members of society. As in the case of other social problems, however, the burden of fear falls more heavily on the shoulders of some than of others. We can identify two broad sets of factors that have been shown to be related to differences in the fear of crime. One set of factors suggests characteristics of individuals, and the other involves the characteristics of their social environments.

Both sets of factors are important to a comprehensive understanding of fear of crime. The individual-level factors of gender, age, and socioeconomic or minority status are often interpreted as measures of social and physical vulnerability. They explain why some people (women, the aged, the poor, minorities) might feel they are particularly susceptible to criminal victimization or less able to cope with the consequences of any victimization that does occur. In contrast, the environmental factors can be understood as describing dangers in the environment itself. When crime rates are higher, when public order is tenuous, and when people learn about local crime by talking to friends and neighbors, they define their environments as less safe.

In general, the fear of crime is a more significant problem in big cities than in small towns (Baumer, 1978; Moeller, 1989). The simple explanation for this is that big cities have higher crime rates, and the greater fear that urbanites have is a rational response to the reality of big-city crime.

Although this explanation is probably true, it is not necessarily the whole story. Urban sociologist Claude Fischer (1981) has suggested that fear is a more significant problem in cities because the "public world of city life" routinely presents residents with situations that increase their feelings of insecurity. As we travel through urban public places, we are likely to encounter people who are strangers not only in the personal sense but also in a cultural sense. Because cities are hotbeds of lifestyle innovation, Fischer argues, we always run the risk of finding ourselves on the street, in an elevator, or on a subway platform with people whose style of dress or public behavior strikes us as weird or threatening. Though many of the strangers we encounter are not criminals or delinquents, our unfamiliarity with groups whose lifestyles differ dramatically from our own may undermine our sense of security in cities.

Within communities, levels of fear vary from one neighborhood to another. Again, some of the difference is due to differences in crime rates (Miethe and Lee, 1990). Residents who live in neighborhoods where the levels of crime are higher are more likely to be concerned about their personal safety and the safety of their property than are people who live in neighborhoods with lower crime rates.

However, levels of neighborhood fear are also affected by what some writers have called social disorder or incivility (Baumer, 1978; Skogan, 1990a). These terms refer to those low-level breaches of the social order that, while not strictly criminal, in many cases seem to be related to a sense of unease. Incivilities are usually considered to be of two types. Physical incivilities include conditions such as abandoned buildings, unkempt residences, and strewn trash and litter. Social incivilities include public drinking or drug use, panhandlers, and groups of noisy youths. In a study of reactions to disorder in forty neighborhoods, Skogan (1990a) found that although disorder tends to be a problem where crime is also a problem, its effects on levels of fear supplement the effects exerted by the local crime rate (Kelling and Coles, 1996).

Why does social disorder promote fear of crime? A dominant interpretation stresses the role that disorder plays in signaling to people the breakdown of local social controls. People may read signs of incivility as indicating that in this neighborhood people don't care very much about themselves or their community. In effect, the message is that neighborhoods that can tolerate conditions like these can also tolerate more serious threats to person or property.

For instance, using data collected in six Atlanta neighborhoods, Gates and Rohe (1987) distinguished three types of reactions to crime—avoidance, protection, and collective action. They found that each type of reaction was related to a different combination of factors. Avoidance behavior (avoiding places or people in the neighborhood) was related to local crime rates and the fear of crime. Protective behavior (such as taking a self-defense course or obtaining a gun or watchdog) was more closely related to levels of interaction among neighbors and the amount of control that respondents felt they could exert in the local area. Finally, collective actions (such as involvement in local crime prevention efforts) were related to both sets of factors.

SUMMARY

Crimes occur in context at the household, neighborhood, and community levels. Two major approaches have been used to look at this context: social disorganization and routine activities. Exposure that comes from lifestyles that bring people into contact with motivated offenders can be seen as following certain set patterns or routines. These routines create opportunities for crime. Looking at the problem of exposure a little differently, social disorganization theory suggests that areas that lack strong community efficacy also lack the social controls that can be used to deter offenders and protect victims and property. This social disorganization can be signaled by social disorder, including abandoned buildings or unruly public behavior.

In recent research, efforts have been made to accommodate the strengths of both perspectives, suggesting that we need to know not only about the activities of individuals that may make them targets for crime but also the social and physical environments that facilitate or even promote offending. An important part of this analysis involves looking at the opportunities for crime that occur in social environments. If the routines of offenders, potential targets, or guardians create these opportunities, crime risk increases. A consequence of this exposure to crime is heightened levels of fear, which cause psychological damage and can create major behavioral changes in daily routines. Vibrant areas can quickly become wastelands, where disorder and low social control creep in.

Prevention strategies that look at these perspectives suggest that the strongest form of crime reduction medicine comes from the removal of opportunity, either through target hardening, greater surveillance, or changes in routine activities to reduce exposure to crime. Further, prevention needs to be considered in terms of changing the nature of urban places, where multiple strategies can be used in removing crime opportunities. The eradication of crime in urban neighborhoods, then, comes not only through increased policing but also through increased community involvement. This requires greater participation by the community in controlling deviant behavior, as well as a greater involvement of the police and social agencies in directing resources toward disorder.

4

Private Places:
The Family and the Household

The most intimate places, among family and close friends, have long been considered to be private, operating under different sets of social control than behavior conducted in public. The authority of parents, the ties of marriage, and the sanctity of private spaces have meant that deviance and crime that occurs in households is often undetected and, until recently, unsanctioned by authorities.

Routines that people follow in private may increase the chance of victimization at the hands of intimates but also may protect people from exposure to strangers. The public's view of these private spaces has changed over the last few years, particularly with the widespread concern that has developed regarding the dangers of family violence. Though still hidden away from public scrutiny, violence in homes that comes to the attention of authorities is now treated as crime. Because of difficulties that the police have had in dealing with private relations, new laws force police officers to respond to private violence without using discretion in arrest if they have probable cause that a violent act occurred.

Privacy also plays an important role in households in the protection from surveillance that it can provide offenders who steal from or burglarize homes. At the same time, the right to privacy allows homeowners to take steps to protect property and restrict access to outsiders, which reduces their exposure to crime. In this chapter we will examine both violence in families and victimization of households as the context for looking at how social actors in these places experience and respond to crime.

VIOLENCE IN THE HOUSEHOLD

Precursors

Not surprisingly, as both children and adults, females face greater risks of intimate violence than do males. According to data from the 1995–1996 National Violence against Women Survey, about 22 percent of surveyed women and 7.4 percent of surveyed men reported having been physically assaulted by an intimate partner at some time in their life. These percentages translate into approximately 1 out of every 5 women and 1 out of 14 men (Tjaden and Thoennes, 2000).

Some studies have reported findings suggesting that, in the context of the family, women are as violent as men. Such findings have led some observers to argue that we need to focus attention on the battered husband as well as the battered wife (Steinmetz, 1977–1978). However, recent findings from the National Violence against Women Survey do not support this symmetry of violence (Tjaden and Thoennes, 2000). Also, critics have argued that when we look at counts of violent acts, we need to clarify the context, motives, and consequences associated with the violence (DeKeseredy and Hinch, 1991). As Saunders (1989) notes, by most measures of victimization—who initiates the violence, who uses violence offensively rather than defensively, and who is injured most—there is little question that women are more frequently victimized.

In the case of children, patterns of violence also reflect patterns of inequality and dependency. Family assaults—by both parents and siblings—are alarmingly common among all children, and especially among the very young. The first National Family Violence Survey performed by Straus and Gelles in 1975, for example, found an estimated rate of severe violence perpetrated on children by their parents of 142 per 1,000 (a rate considerably greater than that for partner violence) and a rate of severe violence among siblings of 530 per 1,000 children (Straus and Gelles, 1990). In a report based on 1995 data, the FBI (2000) found that family murder disproportionately affects children under 11 (who account for more than 12 percent of family murders and only 5.5 percent of overall murders) and women (52 percent of family murders and 32 percent overall) to their victimization at the hands of nonfamily members. Likewise, children are much more likely to be abducted by family members (at a rate of 2.6 per 1,000 children) than by strangers or nonfamily members (at an estimated rate of 0.05 to 0.07 per 1,000 children) (Finkelhor, Hotaling, and Sedlak, 1990). Another form of abuse that reflects hierarchy and dependency relationships is elder abuse, the victims of which may be infirm and reliant on an adult or child caregiver or a spouse for the basic necessities of life (Pillemer and Finkelhor, 1988; Quinn and Tomita, 1986; but see Pillemer, 1985).

Violence can occur in dating relationships, as well, where intimate places serve as locations for abuse. Drawing on a large body of empirical data, the Centers for Disease Control and Prevention (2001) in Atlanta, Georgia, provides the following profile information about courtship violence:

- Young women aged 12–18 who are victims of violence are more likely than older women to report that their offenders were acquaintances, friends, or intimate partners.

- The likelihood of a female's becoming a victim of dating violence is associated with having female peers who have been sexually victimized, lower church attendance, greater number of past dating partners, acceptance of dating violence, and having personally experienced a previous sexual assault.

- Studies have found the following to be associated with sexual assault perpetration: the male having sexually aggressive peers; alcohol or drug use; the male's acceptance of dating violence; the male's assumption of key roles in dating such as initiating the date, being the driver, and paying dating expenses; miscommunication about sex; previous sexual intimacy with the victim; interpersonal violence; traditional sex roles; adversarial attitudes about relationships; and acceptance of rape myths.

- Men who have a family history of observing or experiencing abuse are more likely to inflict abuse, violence, and sexual aggression.

- As the consumption of alcohol by either the victim or perpetrator increases, the rate of serious injuries associated with dating violence also increases.

Conflict, privacy, ambivalent attitudes about violence, and inequality are not the only factors that serve as precursors to the occurrence of violence in the family. When families are isolated from the wider community of kin, friends, and neighbors, the negative effects of privacy may increase (Straus, 1990). Under such conditions, those who behave violently may become increasingly insensitive to prevailing community standards regarding appropriate conduct. Further, they and their victims may lose or find less accessible the social supports that could be crucial in ending or preventing violence or in mediating the conflicts that lead to violence.

Conditions of economic stress may also contribute to violent conduct (MacMillan and Gartner, 1999). A husband or father who is out of work may use violence to compensate for feelings of inadequacy that the perceived failure to play the breadwinner role may promote (Frieze and Browne, 1989). This interpretation is consistent with the widely reported finding that rates of family violence are generally higher among lower-income groups (Klaus and Rand, 1984; Schwartz, 1988; Steinmetz, 1986; Straus and Smith, 1990). Strain may also arise from non-economic sources such as illness or the death of a loved one. In the case of child abuse or elder abuse, stress may originate from the demands of the caregiving experience itself (Fattah and Sacco, 1989).

Transactions

Straus and Gelles (1990) report that, according to the 1975 and 1985 National Family Violence Surveys, more than 90 percent of parents said that they had hit their children. Further, the rates are quite high with respect to severe violence, which includes hitting the child with an object; 11 percent of parents reported hitting a child in a way that probably fits most people's definition of abuse.

Research on violent events involving elderly victims is represented by a study by Pillemer and Finkelhor (1988). They investigated the extent of elder abuse among a sample of 2,020 elderly residents of Boston. The study, which defined elder abuse as physical violence, verbal aggression, and neglect, found that the rate of overall mistreatment was 32 per 1,000 elderly persons. In all, 20 per 1,000 had experienced physical violence, 11 per 1,000 had experienced verbal aggression, and 7 per 1,000 had experienced neglect.

The location and timing of violent events in general reflect the importance of the precursors discussed previously. Most violent events involving family members occur in the home. About 86 percent of spousal homicides, for example, occur in the victim's home. Only about 20 percent of homicides involving nonfamily members occur in the victim's household (U.S. Department of Justice, 1994b). The reason for this pattern is fairly obvious: the home is the place where family members are most likely to confront each other and where privacy allows these events to develop.

Intrafamily violence is most likely to erupt in the evening or late at night. Arguments that begin in the early evening may turn violent if they are unresolved as the night wears on (Gelles and Straus, 1988). The late-night and early-morning hours bring with them a reduction in the options available to the parties in the conflict through which the matter could be resolved without violence. It is too late to call a family member or to leave the house in order to visit a friend. Stressful events that fuel tensions or challenge parental or patriarchal authority increase the likelihood of a violent episode involving children. Despite the attention paid to the physical mistreatment of very young children by parents, it appears that much violence is directed against teenage children whose various forms of adolescent rebellion may be viewed as requiring strict physical discipline (Pagelow, 1989).

On some occasions, the factors that contribute to the likelihood of a violent event come into sharp relief. Gelles and Straus (1988) note that violent events occur with higher-than-usual frequency during the Christmas and Easter holidays. At these times, the sources of both economic and non-economic stress may be especially pronounced. Family members spend more time than usual together and may entertain unrealistically positive expectations about how others will behave. In addition, family celebrations may involve drinking alcohol, which can facilitate the movement toward violence.

Perhaps the most distinctive characteristic of family violence events is their repetitive and cyclical character. In contrast to forms of victimization that result from a chance encounter between victim and offender, the intimate relationships in which family members are involved increase the probability that violent events will recur or escalate. Minor acts of violence may be self-reinforcing when those who engage in them come to see violence as an effective means of achieving compliance and when the use of violence carries few sanctions (Feld and Straus, 1990). Although most victims try to resist the physical violence, their resistance is more likely to be passive (reasoning with the offender, trying to get help) than active (Harlow, 1991; Klaus and Rand, 1984). Silverman and Kennedy (1993) note that most spousal homicides are not the result of a sudden blowup but rather represent the culmination of serial violence, which is fueled by drugs and alcohol, a lack of problem-solving skills, and the effects of longstanding quarrels and antagonisms. Many cases of family violence escalate into more serious forms of victimization. At a minimum, the physical violence that does occur is probably part of a much larger pattern that involves a variety of forms of emotional and psychological mistreatment.

The violent events in a household may take on the character of "routine conflict" that escalates to violence (Kennedy and Forde, 1998). The opportunities for this violence are facilitated by the privacy of the home, which protects the offenders from detection and provides them with objects with which to vent their anger. The violence is likely to be repeated (the opportunities for victimization rarely change), at least until the victim decides to flee or seek outside help.

Increasingly, researchers have begun to argue for the need to focus on the differing contexts within which various types of family violence occur. With respect to partner violence, for instance, Johnson and Ferraro (2000) argue that several distinct subtypes can be identified. "Common couple violence" is not part of a general pattern and arises primarily in the context of a specific argument in which one of the partners responds violently to the other. In contrast, "intimate terrorism" involves violence as just one tactic in a general pattern of control. "Violent resistance" refers to the use of violence as a form of self-defense. Finally, "mutual violent control" suggests a pattern in which both husband and wife are controlling and violent in a situation that "could be viewed as two intimate terrorists battling for control" (Johnson and Ferraro, 2000: 950).

Aftermath

Family violence may result in severe physical injuries and even death. In fact, some evidence suggests that violence in the home is more likely than other types of violent episodes to result in injury (Harlow, 1991; Klaus and Rand, 1984). This finding may be explained by the repetitive character of family violence and by the relatively limited ability of victims to escape such violent encounters.

Violence has emotional and psychological effects as well as physical effects. Victims of violence in the home, like other victims of violence, experience many forms of fear, trauma, and stress (Wirtz and Harrell, 1987). Indeed, violence in the home may be more likely than other forms of violence to produce these consequences (Gelles and Straus, 1988). Violence may be more threatening if it occurs in environments that individuals have defined as "safe" (Burgess, Holmstrom, and McCausland, 1977). In addition, being victimized by an intimate may produce greater stress because the victim has to cope with the fact that the violence has been at the hands of a trusted individual (Sales, Baum, and Shore, 1984).

Despite the seriousness of their injuries, victims may decline to seek medical aid, so as to avoid having to explain to others the sources of the injury. The stigma of being a victim may also keep many from seeking help. Even when they do seek help, they may encounter emergency room personnel who are less than sympathetic. According to Kurz (1987), some ER personnel describe abused wives as "AOBs" (alcohol on breath) and as troublesome people who deserve the predicament in which they find themselves.

Victims of family violence may, for similar reasons, decline to report the incident to the police (Klaus and Rand, 1984). For many female victims of spousal abuse, calling the police is a last resort, even when the violence is severe (Kantor and Straus, 1987). Victimization surveys suggest that the victim's fear that the offender will retaliate through violence against the victim (and possibly against dependent children) figures largely in the decision not to report. The victim may also have concerns about how an arrest may lead to a loss of financial support (Steinman, 1992).

In the past, police have been reluctant to intervene in family situations or, when they did intervene, to remove the offender (most often the husband) from the situation to cool off. Increasingly, however, the police are taking steps to invoke the law as it applies to family violence. Williams and Hawkins (1986) argue that applying sanctions to offenders may deter future offending, although more recent research on the impact of mandatory arrest procedures suggests a more complex picture. Sherman (1992) reports that although arrest will reduce repeat offending among most groups, for certain individuals (for example, those who are unemployed) arrest may actually increase the probability of reoffending.

Members of victim groups share a strong sentiment that more must be done to help victims of family violence. The number of safe houses is considered inadequate to meet the needs of women who feel at risk. At a more basic level, some assert, it is unfair that women have to flee their homes for safety's sake. Browne and Williams (1989) attribute the 25 percent reduction in female-perpetrated spousal homicide in the United States since 1980 to the public's greater awareness of the difficulties women face when dealing with violent spouses. Accompanying this awareness has been an increase in the resources available to women victims—resources that have enabled them to escape their partner's violence rather than to suffer alone or respond with violence themselves, although such resources may be not be easily accessible to some groups, particularly the poor and minorities (Johnson and Ferraro, 2000).

Providing resources such as shelters is helpful in managing the more serious forms of violence, but the day-to-day problems that people most often encounter do not come to the attention of the authorities. Many of these problems are, however, known to neighbors, friends, and others. We are becoming increasingly aware of situations of serial violence, eventually resulting in homicide, in which outsiders knew of the conflict over a long period but were either reluctant to intervene or were not taken seriously by authorities when they attempted to do so.

One important issue being considered by researchers interested in the aftermath of family violence is the way in which violent behavior by one family member promotes violent behavior on the part of others. The fact that courts are becoming increasingly willing to accept the psychological consequences of violence as a defense for killing indicates that we cannot always rely on the notion of rational behavior when judging why people act as they do. Arguments about acts performed in the "heat of passion" have always been recognized when one partner kills another in a jealous rage. However, the idea that violence begets violence is only now being viewed as contributing to a condition that may constitute a justifiable defense.

How does physical violence against children increase the risks of their delinquency? Several types of effects may derive from such violence. First, social control theorists have argued that the bonds between juveniles and their parents (and other conformist models) provide a certain insulation against involvement in delinquency. A high degree of parental attachment means that the parent is better able to teach the positive social skills that facilitate an individual's success in the workplace or at school (Currie, 1985; Patterson and Dishion, 1985). Obviously, parental abuse may weaken this bond and lessen the degree of juvenile sensitivity to parental expectations of appropriate behavior (Rankin and Wells, 1990).

Second, if a parent is abusive, the child or adolescent may seek to avoid contact. To the extent that delinquency is prevented by the ability of parents to monitor and supervise the behavior of children, delinquency in such situations may be expected to increase, as predicted by control theory (Gottfredson and Hirschi, 1990; Thornberry, 1987).

Third, violent delinquency may be a form of acting out on the part of the child (Agnew, 1985). Children may run away from home or engage in other "escape crimes." Their resulting homelessness, combined with a lack of labor market skills, may increase the likelihood that, in order to support themselves, they will make use of whatever delinquent or criminal opportunities they encounter (McCarthy and Hagan, 1991). In addition, they may behave violently toward classmates or other acquaintances as a way of expressing their frustration about the abusive home situation.

Fourth, growing up in a violent home may provide children with lessons in the use of violence as a means of achieving goals and controlling others (Peek, Fischer, and Kidwell, 1985). A child who witnesses spousal violence may come to see it as a legitimate way of resolving conflict (Fagan and Wexler, 1987; McCord, 1991). According to Hotaling and Straus (1990), homes in which child assault or spousal assault occurs have higher rates of sibling violence and higher rates of violence by the dependent children against children outside of the home.

The privacy of the home makes the interactions that take place there less open to scrutiny. Opportunities for violence occur and are hard to deter without the victims coming forward to report abuse or others in the family being willing to involve authorities in stopping the conflict. The household place is an environment where violence can be learned from others, and the modeling that children bring away from violent encounters in their homes may result in intergenerational violence. In the aftermath of these events, the police must charge offenders if they witness injury. Victims, then, must find help to deal with the psychological consequences of the assaults as well as the economic and social consequences of the arrest of their partners. The resulting fear and the need to find safe places away from the home have put great pressure on social agencies to provide resources to families in need of shelter and protection from violent family members. Thinking of family violence as an event helps us view these violent interactions as situated in private locations operating over sustained periods of time. It is important to remember that the event doesn't end with the arrest of an offender but has long-term consequences for the family and the intimate relationships that have been disrupted by these actions.

THE HOUSEHOLD AS TARGET: PROPERTY CRIME

Precursors

Although we may think about opportunities for property crime directed against households as an objective feature of the social environment (for example, an open door invites theft), the situation is more complicated. Criminal opportunities also have a subjective quality. For a criminal event to occur, a potential offender must define the open door as an opportunity for theft. Whereas one person might see the large shrubs blocking a residential window as nothing more than interesting landscaping, another might see this shrubbery as providing cover during a robbery attempt.

Crimes against the household are common in the United States. In 1998, data from the National Crime Victimization Survey showed that about 18 percent of the nearly 7.5 million crimes of violence occurred at or in the respondent's home (U.S. Department of Justice, 2000). At the same time, a little more than 10 percent of the nearly 18 million thefts were reported at or in the respondent's home, and 30 percent occurred near the home.

What are the characteristics of the property offender? Like many other types of predatory offenders, these individuals tend disproportionately to be young males, many of whom come from socially disadvantaged backgrounds (Maguire, 1982). Data from the 1999 Uniform Crime Reports, for example, indicate that 70 percent of those arrested for all index property offenses (burglary, larceny, motor vehicle theft, and arson) were males, and 58 percent of those arrested were under age 25 (FBI, 2000). Larceny theft was the offense for which females were most likely to be arrested, constituting 14 percent of all female arrests and 71 percent of female arrests for index offenses. Furthermore, 56 percent of all female larceny-theft arrestees were age 25 or younger (FBI, 2000).

Transactions

Household theft is a crime that easily resists detection because the routines of household members may leave houses empty for long periods of time (Maguire, 1982). Offenders learn from their own and others' experiences that the chances of getting caught in the commission of any particular crime are slim (Bennett and Wright, 1984). They also recognize, however, that if they become known to the police as thieves and they fail to vary their method of crime commission, their chances of getting caught become greater over time, thus reducing the attractiveness of this form of crime (Cromwell, Olson, and Avary, 1991). Whereas professional thieves may be said to have lengthy records, supporting the theories that these types of offenders follow a criminal career, a substantial number of juvenile offenders commit crimes only rarely, and with even less frequency as they get older (Shover, 1983). The number of repeat offenders, as measured by the recidivism rate for burglary, is higher than that for many other crimes, but many juvenile offenders do not repeat the crime at all (Maguire, 1982).

As events, crimes against the household can be relatively uncomplicated affairs. An opportunistic thief may pass a house and notice some item of value lying unguarded on the front lawn or in the driveway (Lynch and Cantor, 1992). Seeing no one about, the thief will grab the item and continue on his or her way. Similarly, under cover of darkness in the early hours of the morning, the thief may happen upon an unlocked car and steal either its contents or the car itself.

The crime of breaking and entering varies in terms of how much planning it requires. In a large number of these events, young offenders target a house not far from their own residence (Brantingham and Brantingham, 1984). The proximity of the target may reflect two distinct considerations: offenders' relatively limited mobility (they may be too young to drive) and offenders' direct knowledge of both the contents and routine activities of the households they encounter in the course of their own routine activities. In such cases, entry may be "child's play" (Maguire, 1982). The offender tests the door and, if it is open, enters the house. (According to the National Crime Victimization Survey, almost half—46 percent—of the household burglaries reported by victims in 1992 did not involve forcible entry [U.S. Department of Justice, 1994a]). The thief moves through the house quickly, more interested in getting in and out with something of value than with the wanton destruction of property (Maguire, 1982; Waller and Okihiro, 1978). The items stolen may include money, alcohol, and light electronic goods such as portable TV sets or VCRs.

The more professional burglar may select a target more carefully. The selection process may include several stages as the offender makes decisions about which neighborhood, which block in the neighborhood, and which house on the block will be victimized (Taylor and Gottfredson, 1986). Relationships may be cultivated with "tipsters" who can provide information about vacant homes and potentially large "scores" (Shover, 1973). Some tipsters may be "fences" who are attempting to boost their inventory, whereas others may be thieves who for some reason are unable to undertake the crime themselves. Additionally, thieves may, in the course of their regular travels through the neighborhood, be attentive to homes that appear empty or that promise easy entry. Waiting at a traffic light may provide potential burglars with the opportunity to view potential targets without attracting attention (Cromwell et al., 1991).

Irrespective of the level of professionalism, burglars who are intent on breaking and entering must consider three questions: Can they get away with the crime (degree of risk)? Can they commit the crime without great difficulty (ease of entry)? Can they get anything out of it (potential reward)? Of these three factors, the first (degree of risk) is probably the most important (Bennett, 1989; Bennett and Wright, 1984). Homes that provide cover from surveillance by other homes present the offender with fewer risks. The mere presence of passersby may not influence the decision to offend, because thieves are concerned not about being seen but about being seen *and* reported (Cromwell et al., 1991).

The occupancy of the household may be the most important aspect of risk. The presence of a car in the driveway or signs of movement or activity in the house may encourage the potential offender to look elsewhere (Bennett, 1989). Some offenders may engage in more sophisticated occupancy probes in order to establish whether the household is vacant.

An occupied home is to be avoided not only because of the risk of detection but also because of an offender's concern that, if someone is home, the crime of breaking and entering could escalate into a more serious offense. Some researchers (Kennedy and Silverman, 1990; Maxfield, 1990) have observed that, although a rare occurrence, a higher-than-expected number of homicides involve elderly victims in their homes. The reason for this anomaly may be that the elderly occupy households that appear uninhabited during the day. The burglar who is surprised by an unexpected encounter may strike out against the elderly person, with fatal consequences. The occurrence of such unpremeditated homicides, coupled with uncompleted burglaries due to the presence of the householder, suggests that offenders may not be quite as adept at assessing occupancy as is sometimes thought (Hough, 1987).

The second factor (ease of entry) concerns the relative difficulty burglars encounter in attempting to enter the residence. In general, this factor cannot be assessed until the offense is under way (Bennett and Wright, 1984). In many cases, breaking a door or a window is a simple matter; even the presence of special locks and security hardware may not serve as a strong deterrent (Lynch and Cantor, 1992; Maguire, 1982). Although many professional burglars report that they can, if required, deal effectively with alarms or watchdogs, they also report that the large number of households that are unprotected by such measures makes attempted burglary of protected homes unnecessary (Maguire, 1982).

In their interviews with burglars, Cromwell and colleagues (1991) discovered that these offenders use several imaginative methods to determine whether anyone is home:

- If working as part of a team, the most "presentable" burglar knocks on the door or rings the doorbell. If someone answers, the burglar asks for directions or for a nonexistent person.
- The burglar rings the doorbell and, if someone answers, claims that his or her car broke down and that he or she needs to use the phone. If the resident refuses, the burglar may leave without attracting suspicion. If the resident consents, the burglar may have an opportunity to check out the merchandise in the home as well as whatever security measures may exist.

- The burglar telephones the residence to be broken into from a nearby phone. The burglar then returns to the residence. If he or she can hear the telephone ringing, it is unlikely that anyone is at home.

- The burglar targets a house next to a residence that has a "for sale" sign on the front lawn. Posing as a buyer, the burglar can examine the target household from the vantage point of the sale property.

One informant in the study by Cromwell and colleagues would dress in a tracksuit, jog to the front door of the target household, remove a piece of mail from the potential victim's mailbox, and ring the doorbell. If anyone answered, he would say that he found the letter and was returning it. The tracksuit explained why a stranger might be ringing a doorbell in the neighborhood, while the apparently neighborly gesture suggested that the burglar was a good citizen and therefore above suspicion.

The final factor (the potential reward) is probably the least important consideration. Offenders who engage in breaking and entering may be unable to determine before the commission of the crime whether anything of value is to be gained (Lynch and Cantor, 1992; Miethe and Meier, 1990). As noted previously, information from a tipster may decrease uncertainty, and higher-status households may hold the promise of greater rewards. However, in most situations, the thief can be relatively certain that something of value will be collected in the course of the crime (Cromwell et al., 1991).

Aftermath

Data from the 1998 National Crime Victimization Survey (U.S. Department of Justice, 2000) indicate that almost 95.4 percent of the property crimes reported resulted in some economic or monetary loss; about 19 percent of all household crimes resulted in loss of money or property valued in excess of $500. Perhaps not surprisingly, completed motor vehicle theft was the crime most likely to result in a loss greater than $500 (88.4 percent), and theft was least likely to involve monetary loss that great (about 10 percent). Some of the net loss for property crimes may be mitigated by either recovery or insurance. Members of lower-income groups, who are less likely to have insurance, generally experience the greatest net loss for household crimes.

Such figures provide only a partial picture of the impact of household crime. Incidents of illegal entry that escalate into assaults, robberies, sexual assaults, or homicides have direct and immediate physical consequences (Warr, 1988). Because incidents of this type are relatively rare, and because household crimes generally involve rather small net losses, these crimes are sometimes assumed to have little psychological impact on victims. But such is not the case, especially with respect to breaking and entering. Many victims—particularly women—may be badly shaken by the event (Maguire, 1982). Victims may experience feelings of vulnerability, concern that the offender will return, and fear of being alone, even in situations that are not directly related to household crime. They may also experience long-term sleeping disorders or require tranquilizers for an extended period. Maguire (1982) found that, in a sample of

British burglary victims, negative effects were reported by 65 percent of the victims four to six weeks after the crime.

Like other criminal events, many crimes against the household are not reported to the police. Data from the National Crime Victimization Survey indicate that in 1999 about 26 percent of all household crimes were reported: 49 percent of burglaries, 27 percent of thefts, and 84 percent of motor vehicle thefts (Rennison, 2000). These figures represent a big drop from early NCVS reports (in 1992 the reporting of property crime was more than 40 percent). Respondents who said that they had reported their victimizations were most likely to cite "a desire to recover property" as the reason (26 percent of respondents gave this reason). The single most common reason for not reporting household crimes was because the stolen property was recovered or the offender was unsuccessful in his or her attempts (30 percent) (U.S. Department of Justice, 1994a).

Crimes against the household also indicate that it is what happens to the victim rather than who the victim is that determines whether an event will be reported (Evans, 1989). In other words, the likelihood of reporting is not strongly related to the social and demographic characteristics of victims. Instead, the crime is more likely to be reported when it has characteristics that might be interpreted as indicators of greater seriousness, such as when there is evidence of forced entry or malicious destruction and when the loss is relatively high (Waller and Okihiro, 1978). Thus, unreported crimes against the household, at least in the legal context, are generally less serious than those that come to the attention of the police (Maguire, 1982).

Victims who report household crime do so with the hope that the police will be able to apprehend the offender and recover the stolen property. At a minimum, victims expect that the police will undertake an investigation and treat them with some sympathy (Maguire, 1982). In the aftermath of household crime, victims may seek the assistance of a friend, neighbor, or landlord in addition to, or instead of, the police. When losses are substantial, victims may seek compensation through private insurance.

Reported household crimes carry with them a low certainty of arrest. A major factor in the low clearance rates for such crimes is that, by the time they are reported to the police, the perpetrator is long gone. In addition, unlike in the typical crime of violence, there is no immediate suspect (Maguire, 1982).

In the aftermath of the crime, offenders are probably less concerned with arrest than with the uses to which the stolen merchandise might be put. Cash or alcohol may be used for "partying." Although some stolen merchandise may be kept and used by the offender, the amount of loot one can put to personal use has a limit. Retaining too many stolen goods may also increase the risk of arrest.

Much of what is stolen may be converted into cash through the sale of merchandise. Although a substantial market exists for stolen goods, particularly lightweight electronic goods, offenders recoup a relatively small amount from each item. Some stolen goods are sold directly to private buyers for their own use. Such people may see this exchange not as a criminal activity but as "good business." Their reasoning may be, "It was already stolen, and if I don't buy it, someone else will" (Cromwell et al., 1991). Merchandise is also sold to "fences," who purchase the items for the purpose of resale. Some fences are businesspersons who do not have a criminal record, and others are former thieves (Maguire, 1982).

SUMMARY

Violent events within families can be partially attributed to the values that our society places on family privacy. There is increased interest in dealing with crimes that both occur in and are directed toward the household. Intrafamily violence is attracting a great deal of public concern, and demands are being made that more action (in the form of education and changes in the law) be taken to reduce the likelihood that such violence will occur. Attempts have been made to give victims of family violence greater protection under the law and to provide them with safe havens, as well as to provide treatment for offenders. As our review of family violence has shown, it is important to consider different theoretical approaches to the problem. New perspectives that draw attention to such things as power differentials in the family have become increasingly effective in providing explanations of family violence and in suggesting ways in which it should be addressed.

For a more complete understanding of family violence, we must also consider the stress placed on families, the reluctance of victims to report the violence, the modeling of parental behavior in managing conflict and anger, the breakdown of social control mechanisms that restrain interpersonal violence, and the paucity of deterrence strategies. The discovery in recent years of the extent of family violence, coupled with changes in societal values, has been influential in defining violent events within families as criminal events. Changes in relevant laws and in the police enforcement of those laws increasingly reinforce such a definition.

Property crime is a booming business. The target of most of this crime is the household, which is filled with portable appliances that can be easily transported and resold. Much property crime is opportunistic in nature, involving the presence of a thief at a place and time in which property is unguarded and easy to steal. A good deal of the property crime committed by youthful offenders falls into this category. The more complicated crime of breaking and entering, which often requires considerable planning and technical expertise, tends to be committed by professional burglars, who not only take the time to plan the event but also ensure that the merchandise can be disposed of after the fact. Sometimes, because of a miscalculation by the offender, residents may be unexpectedly encountered in the course of a household burglary; the consequences—especially for elderly victims—may be fatal.

Many property crimes are not reported to the police. People who do not report them may feel either that the police can do little to solve the crime or that the crime is not serious enough to warrant such action. Increasingly, homeowners are engaging in target-hardening activities intended to discourage both opportunistic and professional burglars.

5

Semiprivate Places: Workplaces

In this chapter, we consider crime in the social domain of the workplace. This social domain, perhaps more so than those discussed in previous chapters, has been largely neglected by criminologists until recent years (Gill, 1994). Although people enter into and out of this domain through economic enterprise or purchase of goods, the organization of work largely restricts access. Rules pertain to workers that keep records private and transactions under restricted public view. This level of privacy protects both workers who target crime opportunities within the workplace and offenders who come from outside. Work can also be viewed as criminal enterprise where transactions take place to buy and sell illicit goods.

Our discussion is organized around two broad topics. The first broad topic is the relationship between participation in the legitimate labor force and the occurrence of criminal events. Included within that topic are two major issues of concern to our studies. First, in what ways are patterns of victimization associated with patterns of employment? In other words, how do the jobs we have affect the victimization risks we face? Second, in what ways does seemingly honest work make available opportunities for criminal behavior, involving employers, employees, or members of the general public?

The second broad topic to be explored in this chapter is crime as a type of occupational activity. Here, we examine "enterprise crime," which involves the exploitation of opportunities for the development of criminal business.

CRIME, EMPLOYMENT,
AND UNEMPLOYMENT

Precursors

Theories that emphasize the role of social inequality in the generation of crime quite naturally suggest that not having a job may encourage the development of criminal motivations. Moreover, this view is perfectly consistent with common sense. We would expect measures of unemployment to be related, in empirical studies, to measures of criminal offending for many reasons. First, some property crimes may be committed out a sense of need or desire for things that people cannot afford to buy. If people lack a stable income, they may experience greater temptations to take what is not theirs. Second, occupational status arguably is an important mechanism for integrating people into conventional society; that is, jobs provide a "stake in conformity" (Toby, 1974). Not having a job may weaken the hold that conformist institutions have over people. Third, being unemployed may contribute to the adoption of behaviors, such as drug use, that are themselves associated with criminal offending (Hartnagel and Krahn, 1989). Fourth, unemployment may be related to family instability and thus to the inability of parents to monitor the criminal behavior of dependent children (Sampson, 1987). Fifth, because rates of unemployment are high among young people, who seem to be the most crime prone, we might expect the criminogenic effects of unemployment to be particularly strongly related to offending among this segment of the population.

Despite these theoretical and commonsense connections between unemployment and offending, several criminologists question the validity of this relationship (Chiricos, 1987; Gottfredson and Hirschi, 1990). Although many criminologists would argue that unemployment is causally related to crime, they are unsure of the size and significance of the effect. Others dispute whether being unemployed has any independent causal influence on the propensity to behave criminally.

Sorting out the relationship between unemployment and offending is no simple task. First, just as efforts to measure crime are fraught with difficulties, measuring unemployment in a valid way is also quite difficult (Gramling, Forsyth, and Fewell, 1988). Unemployment is usually measured in terms of the number of people who are not employed but who are actively looking for work. Such measures thus exclude those who have "dropped out" of the labor pool. This bias in our measures of unemployment may have the effect of including those who are most highly motivated to gain entry to the conventional world and excluding those who are least motivated to do so. The overall effect may be to weaken the measured relationship between crime and unemployment.

A second difficulty, some researchers have argued, is that not only unemployment per se but also the quality of labor force experiences is related to criminal offending (Allan and Steffensmeier, 1989; Currie, 1985; Hartnagel and Krahn, 1989). Precarious, low-paying jobs that offer few of the advantages generally associated with employment are counted as employment in labor force surveys, even though such jobs might not provide a strong cushion against the various criminogenic influences to which the jobholder may be exposed.

Yet another difficulty lies in the attempts of many researchers to study the relationship between unemployment and crime at the state or national level— for example, by asking if the national unemployment rate is related to the national crime rate (Chiricos, 1987). This may be too broad a level for the investigation of this issue, in that it may obscure relationships that exist at the community or neighborhood level.

Despite the popular view of the relationship between unemployment and crime, studies support alternative interpretations. Some researchers have suggested, for instance, that delinquent involvement is greater among employed teenagers than among unemployed ones (Tanner and Krahn, 1991). The former group, it is argued, may be less susceptible to parental controls and more susceptible to delinquent peer influences. Other researchers have suggested that crime causes unemployment (not the other way around), in that people who are criminally inclined are less interested in conforming to the routines demanded by legitimate labor force participation (Wilson, 1983). Still others maintain that the relationship between crime and unemployment is spurious in the sense that no real relationship exists between them; the appearance of a relationship is created by the fact that being unemployed and behaving criminally are both related to a "common cause," such as a low degree of self-control (Gottfredson and Hirschi, 1990; Wilson and Herrnstein, 1985).

Ultimately, making generalizations about the relationship between unemployment and crime may be impossible. The nature of the relationship may depend on the type of crime, the social characteristics of the labor force group, and the social policies in place to assist those who are not employed (Allan and Steffensmeier, 1989; Currie, 1985). Cantor and Land (1985) have argued, moreover, that the rate of unemployment may have more than one type of effect on the overall rate of crime. They suggest that unemployment may encourage the development of criminal motivation among some people. This suggestion implies that unemployment will be positively related to the crime rate, such that the crime rate increases as the unemployment rate increases. However, Cantor and Land also argue that the unemployment rate may have a negative effect on the crime rate. This effect is related not to criminal motivation but to criminal opportunity. According to Cantor and Land, the unemployed are much less likely to engage in routine activities that take them away from the home for predictable and extended periods. In other words, unemployment may be related to increases in the level of guardianship exercised over persons and property. In addition, because the unemployment rate can be understood, at least in part, as a general indicator of the overall well-being of the economy, we can assume that when the unemployment rate is high, fewer goods will be in circulation for thieves to steal. Cantor and Land's analysis of UCR data for the period 1946 to 1982 supports the argument that both types of effects may be possible.

Labor force participation may also make crime possible. Two issues interest us here. The first is the relationship between the jobs people have and the victimization risks they face. The second is the ways in which the jobs that people have give them opportunities to behave criminally. Public awareness of workplace stress has been increasing in recent years. Studies have estimated that approximately 15 percent of the U.S workforce will experience health problems because of stress ("Helping to Eliminate Stress," 1994). Workers' compensation claims for stress-related problems tripled in the 1980s (Karasek and Theorell, 1990). Stress-related losses are estimated to cost the U.S. economy as much as $150 billion per year (Freudenheim, 1987). Work-related stressors include job demands and hours of work, the threat of layoff, poor interpersonal relations, the risk of accident or injury, harassment, and discrimination—and even fear for one's life.

Although it is not generally recognized as such, the threat of criminal victimization may be an important source of job stress for many people. Victimization surveys tell us that the chances of being a victim of crime are not randomly distributed across occupational groups. Although work roles may have much in common, irrespective of the unique characteristics of particular jobs, there are dramatic differences in what types of work people do, where they do it, and with whom it brings them into contact. As we will see, the characteristics of some jobs increase risk, whereas the characteristics of other jobs decrease risk. Such differences may be obscured when the victimization experiences of the employed are compared with those of the unemployed.

Yet, even when we compare the victimization risks associated with different occupations, it may be difficult to determine whether it is the job itself or the characteristics of the people who hold such jobs that affect the risk of victimization. For instance, if we were to discover that part-time employees of fast-food restaurants faced particularly high risks of victimization, we would not necessarily be justified in concluding that something about cooking or serving hamburgers makes one more vulnerable to criminal danger. Fast-food employees tend to be teenagers and, in view of the relationship between age and victimization, the higher risks may involve age-related rather than work-related factors. In fact, we might not even be surprised to discover that, though these employees report higher rates of crime, the experiences that they tell us about typically occur outside of work rather than on the job. Thus, a cursory review of victimization risks and occupation may be misleading.

Information about how victimization risks vary across occupations is hard to come by. This is because the statistical rarity of victimization incidents does not, in many cases, allow survey researchers to compute separate victimization rates for a detailed inventory of occupations. Some research indicates that risks are higher for members of the military (Harlow, 1991), probation officers (Lindner and Koehler, 1992), police officers, welfare workers, and those who work in bars (Mayhew, Elliott, and Dowds, 1989) and other occupations that involve regular and frequent contact with high-risk populations.

Perhaps the most comprehensive study of this type was undertaken by Block, Felson, and Block (1984), who calculated victimization rates for 426 different occupations, using data on 108,000 crime incidents reported to National

Crime Victimization Survey interviewers between 1973 and 1981. For the five offenses these researchers examined (robbery, assault, burglary, larceny, and automobile theft), victimization risk was inversely related to "occupational status," which they defined as the average income for each occupation. In other words, as the average income of an occupation increased, the risks of being victimized decreased. More specifically, the study revealed marked differences in levels of victimization risk. For instance, amusement and recreation workers and restaurant workers such as busboys, dishwashers, and servers were among the five highest-risk occupations for all offenses. Sheriffs and police officers had the highest assault rates, and taxi drivers and newspaper vendors were among the most frequently robbed. The lowest rates of victimization were found among certain farm workers, as well as telephone and electrical workers, opticians, stenographers, and radio operators.

Block and colleagues (1984) readily acknowledge that data of this sort are difficult to interpret.

> On the one hand, better jobs tend to provide more good things in life, presumably including safety and security from crime. More income and credit allow people to purchase security devices, safer locations to live in, better parking spots and the like. Better jobs may also help people avoid public transit and unfavorable hours for trips to work and elsewhere. Better credit allows avoidance of cash. In general, more resources, including money, credit and control over time, should help people to obtain security from crime.

> On the other hand, better jobs may bring with them more luxury goods to attract offenders. Higher strata individuals may also go out more at night, enjoying sport and cultural events or visiting restaurants or other night spots. Good jobs are often found within a metropolis rather than in rural areas with lower risk. One suspects that modern offenders have little trouble finding the higher occupational strata in order to victimize them, security efforts notwithstanding. (442)

Transactions

Thus, although analyses of the victimization rates of different occupational groups are interesting and informative, they do not necessarily tell us much about crimes that occur in the workplace. That requires a more focused investigation of the crimes that happen while people are at work.

A more recent analysis of the NCVS data from 1992 to 1996 provides a helpful discussion of the relationship between work and victimization risk (Warchol, 1998). The analysis revealed that the most common violent crime experienced by victims working or "on duty" at the time of their victimization was simple assault. However, the rate per 1,000 workers of violent workplace victimization varied quite dramatically across occupations. These data suggest that of the occupational categories listed, the highest rates of violent workplace victimization were experienced by those involved in law enforcement and the lowest rates were experienced by teachers.

In general terms, workplace settings have characteristics that both encourage and inhibit victimization. On the one hand, full-time employees spend many hours "at risk" to whatever threats the workplace presents. On the other hand, workplace settings tend to be much more highly structured than, for instance, leisure settings and thus more subject to a variety of social controls that discourage victimization. Some degree of order and control is usually deemed necessary if the organizational goals of the workplace are to be achieved in an efficient fashion.

How much crime occurs in the workplace? Data from the 1998 NCVS provide a broad answer to this question (U.S. Department of Justice, 2000). According to this survey, about 16 percent of violent crimes occurred while the respondents were "working or on duty," including 34 percent of assaults, 6 percent of robberies, and 9 percent of rapes. An additional 4.5 percent of violent crimes occurred while respondents were on their way to or from work. With respect to crimes of theft, about 16 percent occurred while the respondents were at work. However, these data underestimate the relative proportion of workplace crime, in that they represent proportions of the total number of incidents—that is, incidents involving those who are and who are not members of the paid labor force.

One type of worksite for which detailed information regarding the nature of victimization risk is readily available is the school. In recent years, much attention has been focused on schools as settings that pose serious criminal dangers to both students and teachers. Following tragic shootings at a number of high schools, President Bill Clinton commissioned in 1997 a report on school safety in the United States. Overall, the authors concluded that schools are safe. In fact, they showed statistics that indicate a decline in school crime over the decade and a reduction in children carrying weapons to school. Despite this drop, the fear of crime in schools was higher than a decade before. Important to note about the crime that did occur in schools is that violence was a small proportion of all crime, and homicide was a rare occurrence (U.S. Department of Justice, 1998). In explaining the reasons for the drops in crime rate, the report suggested that schools responded with many situational crime prevention strategies that were implemented with zero-tolerance policies. A zero-tolerance policy was defined as a school or district policy that mandates predetermined consequences or punishments for specific offenses. The report listed the following findings about zero-tolerance policies in schools.

- At least 9 out of 10 schools reported zero-tolerance policies for firearms (94 percent) and weapons other than firearms (91 percent).
- Eighty-seven and 88 percent of schools had policies of zero-tolerance for alcohol and drugs, respectively.
- Seventy-nine percent of schools had zero-tolerance policies for violence and for tobacco.

The commissioned report also included information on a number of measures that public schools used to increase security in 1996–1997.

- Ninety-six percent required visitors to sign in before entering the school building.
- Eighty percent had a closed-campus policy that prohibited most students from leaving the campus for lunch.
- Fifty-three percent controlled access to their school buildings.
- Twenty-four percent controlled access to their school grounds.
- Nineteen percent conducted drug sweeps.

In the case of schools, the structure of the school population might lead us to expect more crime than we observe. Schools, after all, are settings that concentrate on a daily basis the age groups at greatest risk of offending and victimization. Toby (1983) argues that the risks associated with school populations are compounded by the requirement of compulsory attendance. Disruptive or troublesome students who do not wish to attend school are required to do so. For this reason, he suggests, junior high schools have more serious rates of victimization than do senior high schools.

In addition, until recently, schools have been relatively open settings, easily accessible to potential offenders who do not attend them. These "intruders," as they are usually referred to by school officials, might include not only the stereotypical predator but also the angry parent or the student who is disgruntled at having been expelled. Although schools are capable of exercising some degree of guardianship against victimization, a school of above-average size that allows students considerable freedom of movement may provide many settings that facilitate criminal activity. Within school buildings, more victimizations typically take place in less supervised areas, such as hallways and rest rooms, than in more controlled places, such as classrooms and libraries (Garofalo, Siegel, and Laub, 1987).

Violent school crimes, except perhaps those involving intruders, are probably more likely than other workplace crimes to include as participants offenders and victims who are known to each other (Whitaker and Bastian, 1991). According to Garofalo and colleagues (1987), many of these events result from frictions among peers that arise from normal daily activities: "School grounds and trips to and from school provide ample opportunities for interactions that can escalate into relatively minor victimizations. 'Weapons' often consist of available items grabbed on the spur of the moment. Items stolen from victims often seem to be the targets of malicious, even mischievous motivations" (333).

Several high-profile incidents in Canada and the United States in the late 1990s and early 2000s led to a widespread concern about the threat of mass murder in schools. Although such incidents might be statistically rare, the horrific violence associated with such cases has had profound consequences for the ways in which politicians, security experts, and parents think about school safety.

Criminologists John Alan Fox and Jack Levin (2001) stated that, for the public, "lethal violence inside the school struck a nerve" (94). To some degree, such incidents were made all the more shocking by their contexts. Because they did not occur in primarily minority communities in urban centers, where drugs and street violence might be seen as pervasive problems, they shocked the consciousness of those who had thought that they were safe from violence.

Fox and Levin note that the search for explanations of these incidents quickly settled on the family. Popular wisdom suggested that bad kids come from bad homes. Though parenting is an important factor, these researchers also direct our attention to the social dynamics of the school. They argue, for instance, that with respect to perhaps the most notorious incident of school violence—the mass murder at Columbine High School in April 1999—the schoolyard snipers were seen by others as "geeks" or "nerds." Largely excluded from student cliques and from the mainstream of school life, they banded together with fellow outcasts in what they called the Trench Coat Mafia. The image of themselves that they attempted to construct was one that emphasized power, invincibility, and incivility.

Fox and Levin conclude,

> Birds of a feather may kill together. Harris, the leader, would likely have enjoyed the respect and admiration from Klebold, who in turn would have felt uplifted by the praise he received from his revered buddy. In their relationship, the two boys got from one another what was otherwise missing from their lives—they felt special, they gained a sense of belonging, they were united against the world. As Harris remarked, as he and his friend made last-minute preparations to commit mass murder: "This is just a two-man war against everything else." (94)

How do workplace characteristics relate to variations in the levels of workplace danger? Do these risks, for instance, have something to do with the nature of the work or with the location of the workplace? Answers to such questions are still fragmentary. Respondents in the 1988 British Crime Survey blamed the nature of their jobs for nearly one quarter of the violent and theft incidents they experienced (Mayhew et al., 1989). The "public" rather than fellow employees were blamed for nearly three quarters of the violent incidents and one half of the thefts.

Data from victimization surveys have been used to describe the types of workplace conditions that seem to facilitate employee victimization (Collins, Cox, and Langan, 1987; Lynch, 1987). These studies suggest that the risks of becoming a crime victim on the job are greater when the job involves:

- face-to-face contact with large numbers of people on a routine basis (if the workplace restricts access to authorized persons, the risks of crime are lower)
- handling money
- overnight travel or travel between worksites
- the delivery of passengers and goods

The importance of these factors becomes apparent when they are assessed in reference to routine activities theory and associated concepts such as exposure and guardianship. People who work in settings that leave them unprotected and at the same time exposed to large numbers of people (some of whom may be "motivated offenders") are more likely to be victimized in the workplace. Desroches (1995) argues that although department stores and supermarkets are known to carry large amounts of cash, they are generally not viewed as desirable targets by robbers. Not only are supermarkets likely to have security equipment, but also many people are often in the store at any one time. The high shelves in most grocery stores do not allow the potential thief an unobstructed view of the setting, and because there are usually two exits, it is difficult to control movement in and out of the store. The separation of the cash registers by relatively wide aisles makes the collection of the stolen money a time-consuming activity. In short, such targets offer too many risks for too little money.

Much of the violent victimization that occurs in the workplace results from conflicts between employees and customers or clients. These situations include the bartender who tells the inebriated customer that he is "cut off," the teacher who tries to enforce classroom discipline, the sales clerk who refuses to accept returned merchandise, and the police officer who tries to intervene in an argument.

This pattern of employee-customer conflict is reflected in British Crime Survey data that describe "verbal abuse" at work. In a survey by Mayhew and colleagues (1989), 14 percent of respondents said that they had been verbally abused by someone other than a coworker during the 14-month period preceding the survey. Although not strictly criminal, verbal abuse can contain threatening statements and may precipitate a conflict that escalates to violence. Although male and female workers were about equally likely to be abused in this way, younger women appeared to be particularly susceptible. Whereas incidents involving abuse by an adult were more likely to involve a single offender, incidents involving adolescents were about as likely to involve a group as a single offender. Intoxication was a factor in almost a tenth of the incidents. In 80 percent of the incidents, workers were sworn at, and insulting comments about job performance were made in 40 percent of the cases.

The nature of the situational context of much workplace victimization is revealed in a study by Salinger and colleagues (1993) of assaults of flight attendants. This study found that flight attendants have rates of assault as much as 10 times higher than the average person. Most assaults involved a conflict between the passenger and the attendant over some mandatory aspect of the flight, such as baggage arrangements or food or drink service. The researchers discovered that first-class passengers, who comprise only 10 percent of the traveling public, accounted for 20 percent of the assaults, a finding that may be explained by the higher expectations of service, passengers' perception of their status relative to that of the attendant, and the amount of alcohol that is typically consumed. The study also found that assaults are most likely to occur during takeoff or landing, the most distressing time for passengers who are afraid of flying. In addition, at takeoff, the authority role of the attendant may not yet be clearly understood.

Victimizations that occur in the workplace do not seem to differ appreciably from other categories of crime in terms of their levels of property loss and injury (Garofalo et al., 1987; Mayhew et al., 1989; Whitaker and Bastian, 1991). One important factor that probably reduces the potential severity of much workplace crime is the presence of other coworkers, who can provide or summon assistance.

Aftermath

As in the case of other social domains, much of the crime that occurs in the workplace is not reported to the police (Warchol, 1998). At least two specific characteristics of the work domain may discourage such reporting. First, many work environments may have alternative means for dealing with crime. The handling of an incident might proceed no further than bringing it to the attention of a supervisor or private security officer. Businesses, restaurants, and even schools may choose to avoid the publicity associated with the visit of a police patrol car by using informal processing or nonprocessing to deal with the majority of less serious incidents.

Second, employees who are victimized as a result of their dealings with the public may be persuaded by their employers that such incidents occur only when they are not doing their job properly. In other words, they may come to believe that among their job responsibilities is to "cool off" belligerent customers or clients. Even in more severe cases, the victim may fear being blamed for having started the incident by behaving rudely toward the customer (Salinger et al., 1993).

As crime in the workplace has become a public issue, many people feel less secure in their work environments than they once did. However, we know relatively little about the character of workplace fear of crime. Sociologist Esther Madriz (1996) has used data from the American National Crime Survey to investigate the factors that affect fear at work. She found the people were more likely to judge the workplace as unsafe when they

- lived in bigger cities
- had contact with potential offenders
- handled money in their jobs
- worked in places that employed fewer security measures
- worked during the evenings
- used public transportation
- had been victims of crime

As Madriz notes, many of these factors are related not only to fear of crime but also to the risks of actual victimization.

Jobs can become hazardous when they expose employees to clients and situations that may provide an opportunity for crime. One step that can be taken to deter these crimes is to provide employees with the resources they need to deal with client-related problems. Employers must further resolve to react strongly to crimes that occur on their premises, thereby ensuring that their employees can do their job with a greater sense of security.

We have seen that the relationship between crime and unemployment is less straightforward than is commonly supposed. Being employed is no guarantee of immunity from crime or victimization. In the next section, we explore some of the ways in which work makes offending possible. Put simply, how do particular types of work routines and particular forms of the social organization of work relate to particular styles of offending?

CRIME AND LEGITIMATE WORK

Many people (including many criminologists) tend to think about criminal offending and legitimate work as mutually exclusive. As Fagan and Freeman (1999) note, however, the relationship between crime and legitimate work should not be understood in quite so deterministic a manner. Many individuals are simultaneously involved in the legitimate labor force and in the world of crime. Crime, after all, need not take all that much time and energy, and often the legitimate jobs that people have (especially low-paying jobs) do not necessarily remove criminal motivation. Even more important is that the legitimate jobs that people hold provide them with criminal opportunities to which they would otherwise not have access. In this section, we explore some of the ways in which work makes offending possible.

Precursors

The scope of work-related crime is potentially as broad as the types of jobs that exist within an economic system (Croall, 1987). Employees who have unsupervised access to the stock of their employers may find that their work role allows them a unique opportunity for theft. Physicians and lawyers may charge for services that are not performed (Arnold and Hagan, 1992). Stores may use illegal sales practices to defraud the public. Large corporations may engage in the sale and manufacture of dangerous products, pollute the environment, and maintain unsafe working conditions. Work-related crime ranges from pilfering by a disgruntled employee to the gargantuan thefts associated with the American savings and loans scandal.

Modern interest in the concept of work-related crime is usually traced back to the writings of the famous American criminologist Edwin Sutherland. Sutherland (1940) used the term white-collar crime to refer to "a crime committed by a person of respectability and high status in the course of his occupation." Sutherland saw a need to correct the imbalance in criminological thinking that associated crime almost exclusively with the actions of the poor and the powerless. Through a study of major American corporations, he sought to prove that individuals who were fully and gainfully employed, and whose jobs accorded them considerable power and economic security, were frequently responsible for serious breaches of the law.

Since Sutherland's time, the concept of white-collar crime has undergone adjustments that reflect changes in the meaning of white-collar work. For Sutherland, the term *white-collar crime* denoted the criminal conspiracies of major corporations. Today, many forms of white-collar work (for example, sales or computer programming) do not involve manual labor, but they cannot be considered positions in some sort of economic or corporate elite. Criminologists have attempted to capture important distinctions in the study of crime and legitimate work by introducing such terms as *professional crime, elite deviance, corporate crime, organizational crime, respectable crime,* and *business crime.* Our interest in social domains as the context of criminal events requires us to focus attention not only on the crimes of powerful jobholders but also on the crimes of those whose jobs denote lower-ranked positions. Encompassing both types of crime is the term *occupational crime,* which Akers (1985: 228) defines as the "violation of legal norms governing lawful occupational endeavors."

Occupational crimes may be distinguished in two important ways. First, they differ with respect to the nature of the offender–victim relationship. Some kinds of crimes are intended to provide only the jobholder with direct benefits. The person who pilfers from an employer does so for personal benefit, as does the bank teller who embezzles or the systems analyst who steals computer time. In such cases, the agency or organization is the victim, and the employee is the offender.

In other cases, the organization may be understood not as the victim but as a weapon that is used against those outside of the organization or at the bottom of the organizational hierarchy. In the context of such criminal events, the crime may profit the jobholder indirectly, in that direct benefits accrue to the organization itself. Included among the victims might be other business organizations (a corporation hires industrial saboteurs to steal competitors' secrets), clients or customers (a corporation engages in deceptive advertising or sells untested pharmaceutical or food products), or low-level organizational members (employers maintain unsafe working conditions or violate laws relating to labor relations). Finally, we can recognize more general patterns of victimization with respect to offenders who inflict harm on very broad segments of society. Such crimes include political bribery, which undermines the political system; tax frauds, through which people indirectly distribute their losses to members of the taxpaying public; and industrial pollution, which threatens the air, land, and water.

A second way in which occupational crimes differ concerns the nature of the organizational settings in which they occur. Some types of occupational crime involve an offender who acts alone or only a small number of offenders. Medical fraud or dishonest household repair schemes might each involve the actions of a single offender who deals directly with victims and whose activities are not dependent on institutional support from coworkers. At the other extreme, corporate crime might involve "large vertical slices" of complex organizations (Snider, 1993). In such cases, it may be difficult to say who did and who did not behave criminally, because each individual's actions contribute in small ways to the criminal event.

The relationship between work routines and criminal offending may be understood with reference to the concepts of opportunity and motivation

(Coleman, 1987, 1991). In other words, the social organization of work may give people the means with which to violate the law, and their feelings about their jobs or employers may supply them with the reasons for doing so.

Although a majority of adolescents spend some part of their youth in the workforce, criminologists have spent little time investigating their work-related delinquency. Wright and Cullen (2000) investigated this issue through the use of survey data collected from more than 300 employed juveniles enrolled in 8 high schools. The research revealed the following:

- Two-thirds of the students reported committing at least one work-related delinquent act in the previous year. The most common acts were calling in sick (when the individual was not), giving away goods or services for nothing and without permission, and drinking alcohol or using drugs while on the job.

- The overall quality of the workplace had no effect on the likelihood of engaging in delinquency.

- The likelihood of delinquency was related to the presence of delinquent peers in the workplace.

- Youths who were delinquent outside of the workplace were more likely to be delinquent on the job.

- Individuals with delinquent propensities were selected (by themselves or by others) into work environments in which delinquency is more likely.

In terms of opportunity, some work routines give employers or employees access to people and things to victimize. Doctors have access to patients, lawyers have access to clients, corporations have access to markets, and bank tellers have access to "other people's money" (Calavita and Pontell, 1991). Though such access does not necessarily result in criminal action, it does make such action possible.

According to Coleman (1987, 1991), at least four factors influence the evaluation of opportunities to commit white-collar crime. The first factor is the perception of how large a gain can be expected from using the opportunity. The second is the perception of potential risks associated with the opportunity. The exploration of criminal opportunities is more likely when effective control is lacking. Many professional groups, for example, claim to be self-regulating and discourage the efforts of government agencies to assume an investigative function, except in the most extreme cases. Many crimes that are associated with large corporations are so complex that they are policed only with great difficulty. Some observers have argued that the power of professional groups and large corporations discourages effective enforcement by state agencies (Hagan, 1992). The third factor is the degree of compatibility between the use of the opportunity and the potential offender's beliefs, attitudes, and ethical view of the situation. Finally, the evaluation of the opportunity is based on the potential offender's perception of the benefits of one opportunity relative to other opportunities to which the person has access.

The motivations for occupational crime are a matter of considerable debate. Some observers assert that these motivations reside in the nature of work itself or in the wider socioeconomic setting of the workplace. Insofar as capitalism promotes a "culture of competition" that encourages the pursuit of economic profit, the profit motive may be said to be the criminal motive (Calavita and Pontell, 1991). However, the ways in which particular businesses and industries are organized may also serve as important motivating factors. Industries that experience severe competition, that operate in an uncertain economic environment, or that are engaged in the sale or distribution of potentially dangerous goods and are therefore highly regulated may feel pressure to operate unlawfully as a means of achieving organizational goals (Coleman, 1991; Keane, 1991; Snider, 1993).

In very large corporations or businesses, the pressures to behave criminally may be accentuated by the pressure placed on underlings to achieve organizational goals. Creating what Simon and Eitzen (1993) describe as "corporate Frankensteins," senior management may establish goals or quotas that everyone knows cannot be achieved within the limits imposed by current regulations. At the same time, management may be able to insulate itself from any covert criminal action that results from establishing such corporate objectives (Hagan, 1992). Those who follow rules that lead to criminal wrongdoing may be actively or passively discouraged from reporting their activities to senior management (Coleman, 1987; Hagan, 1985). If the acts are discovered by enforcement agencies or the public, management can disavow any knowledge of wrongdoing. If the acts are not discovered, management can claim credit for the high profit yields (Snider, 1993).

By way of illustration, Farberman (1975) argues that the North American automobile industry is characterized by a criminogenic market structure. He maintains that the economic organization of the automobile industry almost necessitates criminal behavior on the part of car dealers. The large automobile manufacturers require dealership franchises to sell cars in large numbers but at comparatively low prices. A small profit markup per unit on a large number of units benefits the car manufacturer but not the dealer, who, as a result, may feel compelled to compensate for financial losses by resorting to dishonest repair schemes and other forms of fraud.

The role of market forces in shaping criminal events in the automobile industry is even more clearly illustrated in the case of the Ford Pinto. This car was placed on the market in 1970, largely in response to feared competition from Japanese car manufacturers. Lee Iacocca, who was president of Ford at the time, told his engineers that they had to produce a car that weighed less than 2,000 pounds and cost less than $2,000. Although the Pinto met these specifications, it also contained serious design flaws. Most critical was the placement of the gas tank, which increased the likelihood that the car would explode in a rear-end collision. It was subsequently discovered that the corporate officers had known about this design flaw and about the actions that could be taken to correct it. Rather than act on this knowledge, however, they calculated the cost of these modifications and compared them to the costs likely to be incurred in lawsuits resulting from injuries to or deaths of Pinto drivers. Because the costs of the improvements in the car were estimated to be greater than the costs associated with deaths and injuries, Ford decided not to repair the defect.

Despite organizational and market pressures and a culture that seems to extol success at any cost, not everyone uses his or her occupational role to achieve criminal ends. Criminologists have stressed the significant role played by "definitions of the situation" that favor criminal offending (Benson, 1985). Coleman (1987) offers six examples:

- acts of theft are "borrowing"
- white-collar crimes do not result in any real harm
- laws that prohibit the criminal behavior are unfair or unjust
- certain types of criminal behavior are necessary if organizational goals are to be achieved
- the behavior is normal and "everybody does it"
- employee theft is not really stealing, because the money was "owed" (for example, uncharged overtime)

Thus, acts that others may see as criminal may be seen as excusable behaviors by the embezzler who defines theft as "borrowing" and by the corporate executive who defines the violation of fair labor laws as "just good business."

Much of the debate about the motivations to commit occupational crime has centered on the distinctiveness of occupational offenders. Many criminologists have long argued that white-collar offenders differ from street criminals in important ways that influence the likelihood of law violation. Many white-collar offenders are neither poor nor powerless. Their crimes are not impulsive, irrational, or the product of inadequate planning. Thus, numerous factors that are usually associated with crime and criminals would seem to have little to do with the behavior of white-collar offenders, particularly those at the top of corporate hierarchies. Therefore, the causes of these types of crime must lie elsewhere.

By contrast, Gottfredson and Hirschi (1990) believe that the similarities between street criminals and occupational criminals are more important than the differences. For Gottfredson and Hirschi, the key explanatory mechanism for both groups is self-control. Special theories are no more necessary to explain the criminal in a legitimate business than they are to explain the criminal in the university, the military, or the church. People who have low self-control are likely to engage in a variety of types of crime and deviance, as the opportunities to do so present themselves.

Because occupations that present significant criminal opportunities tend to be occupations that require a considerable degree of self-control, Gottfredson and Hirschi argue that the rates of occupational crime are lower than is popularly believed. Moreover, they suggest that when differences in opportunity are taken into account, demographic correlates of street crime and occupational crime are similar. They conclude that there is no need to presume special motivational circumstances in the case of the occupational offender, such as "the culture of competition" or other types of factors described here. Instead, Gottfredson and Hirschi assert that "the distinction between crime in the street and crime in the suite is an *offense* rather than an *offender* distinction [and] that offenders in both cases are likely to share similar characteristics" (200).

Benson and Moore (1992) used data on the sentencing patterns for a large number of white-collar crimes (bank embezzlement, bribery, income tax evasion, false claims, and mail fraud) and common crimes (narcotics offenses, postal forgery, and bank robbery) to test some of the implications of Gottfredson and Hirschi's theory. Specifically, Benson and Moore attempted to determine whether white-collar offenders were as "criminally versatile" as common offenders and whether they were as prone to as wide a range of deviant activities. They found that although a minority of white-collar offenders behaved as the theory predicted, the majority did not.

According to Benson and Moore, low self-control is not the only path to occupational crime. Offenders with high self-control may employ it to pursue ego gratification in an aggressive and calculating manner. The culture of competition rewards such individuals by giving them positions of trust and opportunities for committing serious but frequently undetected crimes. In between those with high self-control and those with low self-control are individuals who may take advantage of occupational opportunities, depending on their personal situations. For these individuals, fear of economic or occupational failure may create a circumstance in which a previously adequate level of self-control may become inadequate. As a result, the individual's ability to resist occupational opportunities for crime may be weakened.

Transactions

Determining the amount of crime that is committed in the course of legitimate work is quite difficult, for many reasons. Above all, the nature of much of this crime ensures that it will never be discovered. Corporate crimes that victimize consumers, clients, or members of the general public are often "invisible" (Coleman, 1987). For example, people do not necessarily know that some of the illnesses they experience are the result of inadequately tested drugs. Workers who are injured by hazardous working conditions may be inclined to blame themselves rather than their employers for their injuries (Croall, 1987). Our terminology encourages this tendency—we routinely call such occurrences accidents rather than assaults.

Unlike more garden-variety forms of offending, occupational crimes are largely hidden from public view. The employee who has access to opportunities for offending may escape public scrutiny. The offender who uses the computer to embezzle may do so in such a way that the crime goes undetected by the employer, coworkers, or enforcement agencies. Corporate conspiracies are even less visible. Evidence about corporate decisions regarding offending are not accessible to those outside the corporation. Moreover, because a corporate crime may involve actions by members at all levels of the organization, many of those who participate in the event may not even be aware of the true character of their actions.

As is the case with other categories of crime, occupational crimes do not come to the attention of policing or regulatory agencies as a result of vigorous enforcement practices. At the same time, victims may be poorly positioned to know about—and respond to—the occupational crimes that victimize them. The regulatory agencies that are supposed to police and scrutinize corporate behavior face many obstacles. According to Snider (1992), these obstacles include the following:

- lack of staff and funds
- frequent lack of support from the governments that appoint the regulatory agency
- the high cost of investigating each complaint
- support only from weak consumer or labor groups
- minimal accountability to public or media scrutiny
- the massive economic and political power of corporations

A consequence of these obstacles is that many kinds of occupational crimes that are discovered are not reported. A business that learns that its employees have been embezzling funds may not wish the matter to be widely known because it would in all likelihood reduce public trust in the company. Thus, the long-range negative consequences of reporting may be seen to outweigh the immediate benefits of doing so.

Police data on occupational offenses are of only limited use. Not only are such offenses underreported, but in many cases (for example, cases of fraud) it is not possible to determine whether the crimes occurred in the context of work roles. This ambiguity exists partly because occupational crime is a conceptual rather than a legal category. Although victimization surveys may supplement official record-keeping systems, the surveys, too, are limited, given the absence in many cases of a "direct victim" as well as the inability of the victim to recognize occupational and corporate offending.

Aftermath

Our best estimates suggest that the crimes that people commit in the course of legitimate occupational activities result in considerable levels of financial and physical harm and loss of life. Snider (1993) states that "corporate crime is a major killer, causing more deaths in a month than all the mass murderers combined do in a decade." According to one estimate, Americans are twice as likely to die as a result of unsafe or unhealthy workplace conditions as they are to be murdered (Reiman, 1990). The economic costs of corporate crime also exceed the costs of street crimes like burglary or larceny. It is estimated that the savings and loan scandal alone will cost American taxpayers as much as $500 billion by the year 2022 (Calavita and Pontell, 1991). In 1993 the FBI estimated the total dollar losses due to index property crimes to be $14.8 billion (U.S. Department of Justice, 1994a).

Controlling crimes that occur in the context of legitimate work roles is no easy task. Members of the public are sometimes assumed to be less concerned about occupational crimes than about more direct forms of predatory crime; however, this does not appear to be the case (Hans and Erman, 1989). Nonetheless, the fact remains that the low level of visibility associated with occupational crimes makes effective deterrence difficult (Coleman, 1987). Some studies suggest that the threat of legal sanction has less impact on corporate crime than does the market environment in which companies operate (Keane, 1991; Simpson and Koper, 1992).

ENTERPRISE CRIME
VERSUS ORGANIZED CRIME

In some cases, crime can itself be thought of as an occupation or business. We can define *enterprise crimes* as the "sale of illegal goods and services to customers who know that the goods or services are illegal" (Haller, 1990: 207). The nature of such goods or services may be highly varied and may ultimately depend on what the law disallows. The sale of illegal drugs or pornography, the operation of illegal gambling houses, loan sharking, and "contract killing" are all examples of enterprise crime.

What we call enterprise crime is usually referred to by criminologists and noncriminologists alike as organized crime. This concept conjures up a number of familiar images gleaned from movies like *The Godfather,* television shows like *The Sopranos,* and newspaper coverage of "mob trials" like the trial of John Gotti. However, for reasons that will become clear, the concept of organized crime obscures rather than enhances our understanding of the types of events in which we are interested.

Precursors

In popular usage, the study of enterprise crime has been compromised by what some writers have referred to as the "official myth of organized crime" (Kappeler, Blumberg, and Potter, 2000). In this context, the term *organized crime* has been most often used to refer to long-term, highly organized criminal syndicates that are involved in a number of criminal businesses. These syndicates are said to be organized along ethnic lines and to function in much the same way as legitimate business corporations (Cressey, 1969) and thus to have well-established patterns of recruitment and authority. In this view, organized crime functions largely as what Smith (1975) has called an "alien parasitic conspiracy."

The most widely discussed group of organized criminals in the criminological and popular literature on the subject is the Mafia, also known as La Cosa Nostra. This particular form of criminal conspiracy is said to have dominated organized crime in North America for most of the twentieth century, although its significance is generally thought to have declined in recent years (Jacobs, 1999; Reuter, 1995).

How useful is it to think of organized crime as the exclusive domain of alien ethnic conspirators (irrespective of whether the conspirators' ethnicity is Italian, Russian, Aboriginal, or Vietnamese)? Critics contend that the tendency to equate organized crime with particular types of criminal organizations discourages our understanding of the wide variety of other parties who are involved in organized crime. In other words, there is more to organized crime than organized criminals. There are victims, customers, regulators, suppliers, competitors, and innocent bystanders. The criminal association is only one part of a much larger web of social relationships.

Even more basically, the concept of organized crime is confusing and misleading (Friedrichs, 1996). Logically, we might think that it refers to any type of activity that involves more than one offender acting in coordinated fashion. From this point of view, two juveniles who break into a house could be said to have engaged in organized crime. However, the term is almost never used this way. Instead, it is used to refer to large-scale criminal efforts that are diverse in nature and that seem to have little in common beyond our associating them with particular stereotypical notions of who organized criminals are. Adding to the confusion, the term *organized crime* is sometimes used to refer to a particular type of activity (as in the statement, "Gambling is a form of organized crime") and other times to particular groups of criminals (as in the statement, "We must prosecute members of organized crime"). Such usage results in circular reasoning. If we say, for example, "Organized crime is involved in the drug trade," we have not really said anything, because, by definition, the drug trade is an organized crime and any group involved in this activity must necessarily be involved in organized crime.

Transactions

Beare (1996) has argued that the most useful way to think of organized crime is to view it as a process rather than as a structure or a group. Organized crime is thus viewed as a way of committing crimes rather than as a type of crime. One way to circumvent some of these definitional difficulties is to shift our focus away from the alien parasitic conspiracies and so-called organized crime and toward the study of enterprise crime.

As previously defined, enterprise crime involves the sale and distribution of illegal goods and services. What kinds of social conditions make enterprise crime likely? The first such condition, of course, is the existence of laws prohibiting the goods and services in question. In other words, enterprise crime is made possible when the reach of law creates market opportunities. Prohibition of alcohol, which was in force in the United States between 1920 and 1933, created an opportunity for financial gain that was exploited by criminal entrepreneurs (Packer, 1969; Schelling, 1967). In a similar way, attempts to use laws to control the availability of illicit drugs—such as marijuana and cocaine—or to use high rates of taxation to control the availability of legal drugs such as tobacco make enterprise crime possible. The gap between what people want and what the law allows them to legitimately have is a major way in which our society provides the sources of enterprise crime. This point is obscured when we think of such crime as merely the product of an alien parasitic conspiracy.

The second condition that makes enterprise crime likely is systematic corruption. To the degree that enterprise criminals have access to police or political officials who are interested in developing cooperative ventures with them, the effects of agencies of legal control may be neutralized. Bribery and corruption may afford some enterprise criminals protection from the law, while others may discover that they are the objects of much more aggressive enforcement. Just as occurs in the more legitimate sectors of the economy, the establishment of cozy relationships between those who do the policing and those who are supposed to be policed may facilitate the conditions by which greater market control is assured. In the absence of such mutually advantageous relationships, criminal enterprise markets are more unstable.

A third precondition for the establishment of stable enterprise crime is the existence of partnership arrangements. Such arrangements have the same role in illegal businesses that they have in legal business ventures. They allow entrepreneurs to share risks (especially the risk of business failure), and they allow people to pool different types of resources. Thus, individuals who have political influence, capital, or managerial skills can combine their talents in a way that increases the potential for profit.

This emphasis on partnerships suggests that, rather than being hierarchically or bureaucratically organized, enterprise crime is much more likely to involve informal styles of association (Haller, 1992; Ianni and Reuss-Ianni, 1972). Partnerships may arise when they are deemed necessary or desirable for business purposes, and they may be dissolved when they have served their purpose or when they cease to be profitable. Moreover, Haller (1990) notes, not everyone need be thought of as equal in these partnerships. Some entrepreneurs exercise much more power than others because they have the political or economic resources that allow them to participate in several enterprises simultaneously.

Haller (1990, 1992) suggests that, like the chamber of commerce or the Rotary Club, La Cosa Nostra should be viewed, not as an organization that operates illegal (or legal) businesses but as an association that businesspeople join partly to further their business careers.

Finally, Haller notes, many types of economic factors shape the structure of illegal enterprises—factors that serve both to enhance and to reduce cooperation. Enterprises that involve the importation of drugs like cocaine or heroin may involve a high degree of cooperation among many groups located in both the exporting and the receiving countries. Drug networks also exist at the local level. In addition, substantial drug transactions may require a large initial capital investment. Factors such as these may encourage the development of monopolistic tendencies, because relatively few groups are able to marshal the economic resources or possess the contacts needed to facilitate large-scale arrangements. By contrast, the illegal market for marijuana may be structured quite differently. This illicit commodity does not have to be imported and can be distributed on a small scale by independent entrepreneurs who cater to the needs of a small, local clientele. Markets of this type are much more resistant to monopolization.

If we think about enterprise crime as a type of business, then the questions to which we seek answers are not unlike the questions we might ask about more legitimate businesses. What is the nature of the market? How are goods and services produced and distributed? What are the sources of capital that underwrite the costs of doing business? How do the various groups involved in these businesses cope with changing markets? What types of people are attracted to this particular line of work, and why?

Criminologists are particularly concerned, however, that the business is illegal (Haller, 1990). As economist Thomas Schelling (1967) notes, when a business is made illegal, entry into the marketplace is restricted to those who are willing and able to behave criminally. In other words, the illegal nature of the business is perhaps most attractive to those who have no strong reservations about involvement in behaviors that are prohibited by law.

As we pointed out previously, much has been made of the ethnic character of organized crime. Apart from La Cosa Nostra, commonly cited groups include the Chinese Triad, the Jamaican Posse, and associations loosely referred to in the popular press as the Colombian, Irish, and Vietnamese "mafias." This emphasis on ethnicity frequently reinforces the popular view that criminal enterprise is an "alien" problem because it is associated with ethnic groups.

Rejecting this view, sociologist Daniel Bell (1953) observed half a century ago that organized crime functions as a "queer ladder of social mobility" in societies that emphasize material success but fail to provide all racial and economic groups with equal opportunities for achieving it. Like Merton (1938), Bell maintained that, as a result of the pressure to achieve social goals, groups that find the legitimate channels of upward mobility blocked may turn to illegal alternatives. A key implication of this argument is that enterprise crime, seen as a form of economic activity, is most attractive to those located at or near the bottom of the social hierarchy.

O'Kane (1992), like Bell, has argued that involvement in enterprise crime is characterized by an ethnic succession rather than by an enduring criminal conspiracy. Particular ethnic groups may dominate organized crime until legitimate channels of upward mobility become generally accessible. At this point, the influence of any particular group may decline as other groups move in to fill the void created by the outward movement. Thus, the Italian presence in organized crime, which peaked in the period immediately before Prohibition, was preceded by an Irish and Jewish presence and succeeded by a Cuban and African American presence. The emergence in Canada of Vietnamese, Chinese, and Aboriginal gangs may illustrate a similar process of ethnic succession.

This is not to say that the domination of enterprise crime by any particular group is irrelevant to the ways in which markets are structured or exploited (Light, 1977). Members of ethnic groups may be able to draw on their cultural capital in ways that enable them to be especially effective in particular types of enterprise crime. They may also share in particular forms of cultural traditions that facilitate criminal organization. According to Ianni (1971), the significance of the family as a central organizing theme in Italian culture has contributed to the creation of criminal enterprises—structured along kinship lines—that are remarkably durable.

A second important implication that flows from the illegal nature of criminal enterprises relates to the role of regulation. Obviously, when a market is declared illegal, it cannot be controlled by the government agencies responsible for the mediation of disputes or the resolution of conflicts (Reuter, 1984). Criminal entrepreneurs are unable to seek recourse for harm done against them by going to the police or initiating lawsuits. One mobster cannot sue another because a promised shipment of heroin was not delivered or because a promise to influence the vote of a labor union was not kept. It is for such reasons that violence, or the threat of violence, looms so large in the business affairs of criminal entrepreneurs. Violence represents one of the few means by which contracts can be enforced and compliance with agreements can be assured (Black, 1983).

The types of criminal events that are central to enterprise crime—the acquisition and distribution of illegal goods and services—are complicated affairs, but much popular thinking on the subject glosses over these complexities. We are used to thinking about enterprise crime as nothing more than the acts of vicious gangsters whose ways of thinking and acting are foreign to the societies in which we find them. Though this makes for good pulp fiction, it is not very illuminating. Organized crime events are shaped by the societal context and are in no fundamental way alien to it. The gap between popular demand and efforts to legally control supply makes illegal markets possible in the first place. By declaring these markets off-limits to legal regulation, society helps create circumstances in which the potential for violence is considerable. The stratified nature of society and the restrictions that society imposes on upward mobility cause some who are adversely affected to see enterprise crime as a viable means of achieving the goals to which their societies encourage them to aspire.

Aftermath

Public reactions to enterprise crime often fail to take account of the wider context, which, we have argued, is necessary if we hope to achieve an appropriate understanding of this type of crime. When we read about a gangland killing in an urban ethnic restaurant or a police seizure of drug assets, we rarely consider the social character of these crimes. We are encouraged to think about organized crime as a force at war with "decent society," as it preys on citizens and threatens to corrupt our public officials and undermine our basic social institutions. Rarely are we encouraged to think about criminal enterprise as a logical product of prevalent social conditions. As McIntosh (1975) argues, criminal entrepreneurs are part of a larger configuration that includes not only the criminal but also victims, the police, politicians, customers, and others. The activities of the criminal entrepreneur cannot be understood by focusing on the entrepreneur alone. As these larger configurations change, so do the types of events in which criminal entrepreneurs are likely to be involved. In the absence of this more complex and detailed understanding, enterprise crime will be seen as alien and parasitic.

One important implication of traditional views of enterprise crime relates to the means by which such crime is to be controlled. The image of enterprise crime as an alien parasitic conspiracy, rather than as a social product, supports the position that this type of crime is a law enforcement problem. From this perspective, enterprise crime is best controlled through the aggressive prosecution of criminal entrepreneurs. And yet, when we conceptualize the problem in terms of criminal enterprise rather than in terms of organized crime, we recognize that this "gangbuster" mentality has serious limitations. If enterprise crime really does function like other economic markets, then the removal of criminal entrepreneurs (through arrest and imprisonment) will not significantly affect market operation, because such actions have no effect on the demand for illegal goods. We recognize this fact quite explicitly in the case of legal markets. When an entrepreneur who sells legal goods—for instance, shoes—is removed from the market as a result of death, illness, or retirement, shoes remain available (Van den Haag, 1975). The demand for shoes will prompt others to enter the market to fill the void. In fact, it might even be argued that, because an aggressive policy of prosecution increases the risks of doing business, the going rate for goods and services will increase and the profits to be gained may increase accordingly.

SUMMARY

We have seen in this chapter that the roles we play in the domain of the workplace will structure the kinds of involvement we are likely to have in various types of criminal events. Some jobs increase employees' risks of criminal victimization, whereas other jobs provide them with opportunities to victimize others, be they subordinates, coworkers, clients, customers, or society at large. Alternatively, illegal though they may be, various types of enterprise crime nevertheless constitute a form of work.

Throughout much of its history, criminology has focused attention on how exclusion from the world of legitimate work motivates criminality. Although this remains an important (if unresolved) issue, it is equally important to understand how the organization of the domain of work facilitates or hinders the development of criminal events within this domain. Theories that emphasize the role of social inequality in the generation of crime quite naturally suggest that not having a job may encourage the development of criminal motivations. Victimization risks differ between those who are employed and those who are not. More importantly, particular forms of workforce participation make crime possible. Relevant here are two factors: the relationship between the jobs people have and the victimization risks they face; and the ways in which jobs provide people with opportunities to behave criminally.

Victimization risk at work is inversely correlated to occupational status, measured by income, with those in lower-income occupations being more vulnerable. However, occupation alone is not enough to define victimization risk. Workplace settings can be very important in influencing the opportunity for crime. Risk can be heightened by the availability of money that can be stolen. Sometimes, the nature of the job has a provoking effect on customers, who may vent their anger and frustration at the employee. Crimes that occur in these circumstances are not easy to deter and are underreported. In the aftermath of violent encounters, employees may accept the blame or assume that the employer will blame them for handling the situation poorly. Alternatively, these incidents may be handled informally to avoid the problems associated with police involvement.

Work-related crime may range all the way from pilfering by a disgruntled employee to the gargantuan thefts associated with the savings and loans scandal in the United States. Sutherland (1940) used the term *white-collar crime* to refer to crimes committed by a person of respectability and high status in the course of one's occupation. He saw a need to correct the imbalance in criminological thinking that associated crime almost exclusively with the actions of the poor and the powerless.

Occupational crimes may be distinguished in two important ways. First, they differ with respect to the nature of the offender–victim relationship. Some kinds of crimes are intended to provide direct benefits only for the jobholder, as in the case of the employee who steals. In such instances, the agency or organization is the victim, and the employee is the offender. In other cases, the organization may be used to attack those outside of the business or at the bottom of the organizational hierarchy. With respect to these criminal events, the crime may profit the jobholder indirectly in that more direct benefits accrue to the organization itself. Finally, more general patterns of victimization result from crimes that inflict harm on broad segments of society. Such crimes include political bribery, tax fraud, and industrial pollution.

Occupational crimes differ according to the nature of the organizational settings in which they occur. Some types of occupational crime involve either a lone offender or a small number of offenders, as is exemplified by medical frauds and dishonest household repair services. At the other extreme, corporate crime might involve large vertical slices of complex organizations. In such cases, it may be difficult to say who did and did not behave criminally, because each individual's actions constitute only a small portion of the criminal event.

Gottfredson and Hirschi (1990) argue that the mechanism of self-control is equally applicable to understanding the behavior of the occupational criminal as it is to understanding the behavior of the street criminal. What distinguishes occupational crime from street crime is, in Gottfredson and Hirschi's view, not the offender but rather the offense. People who have low self-control are likely to engage in a variety of types of crime and deviance, as the opportunities to do so present themselves. Despite the significant financial and physical harm caused by occupational crimes, their low visibility makes them difficult to detect and deter.

We can also view crime as operating in a marketplace in which illicit substances and services are sold to customers who know that they are illegal. Rather than view such activity in terms of ethnically based organized crime, we instead use the term *enterprise crime* to refer to this type of criminal activity. Enterprise crime occurs as a result of laws that prohibit certain goods and services. In other words, enterprise crime is made possible when the reach of law creates market opportunities. More than requiring a definition of illegality, however, enterprise crime needs the presence of systematic corruption, partnership arrangements between illegal and legal businesses, and favorable market conditions, such as a monopoly on the illegal goods.

When we conceptualize the problem of "organized crime" in terms of criminal enterprise, the serious limitations of law enforcement responses to crime become apparent. If enterprise crime functions like other economic markets, removing criminal entrepreneurs (through arrest and imprisonment) will not significantly affect market operation or reduce the demand for illegal goods.

6

Public Places: Leisure

In this chapter, we discuss the leisure domain. As we will see, the relationship between leisure and crime has several interesting dimensions. People who are "at leisure" seem to be particularly susceptible to the risk of many types of criminal victimization. Moreover, many types of offending—particularly juvenile offending—are themselves forms of leisure. Our language reflects this fact when, for instance, we describe illegal drug use as "recreational drug use" or when we describe stealing a car to use for fun as "joyriding." The leisure preferences of young people may also be seen as a cause of crime. This is evident in periodic scares in our society about the criminogenic effects of violent television, popular music, fantasy role-playing games, and video games.

We will also see that certain leisure settings, such as bars and sports complexes, are frequently scenes of crime and victimization. The street is also a likely location for crime victimization, as we begin to adopt lifestyles that take us away from our homes and into public areas in search of leisure pursuits.

What does leisure have to do with the timing, location, and relative involvement of particular types of people in particular types of criminal events? There are two answers to this question. One stresses the ways in which specific types of leisure activities motivate offenders toward, or free them from constraints against, offending. The other suggests that leisure activities and settings facilitate encounters between offenders and potential victims. These perspectives are not contradictory, but they do differ in their fundamental emphases. The former is offender centered, whereas the latter is opportunity centered.

LEISURE AS A CORRUPTER

Precursors

Arguments about the corrupting influences of leisure have typically been made with respect to the youthful offender. Throughout this century, every major form of youth leisure preference has been characterized by interest groups as a corrupter of young people. Feature films, rock and roll, rap and heavy metal music, video games, comic books, and Saturday morning cartoons and television commercials have all, at one time or another, been accused of weakening youthful inhibitions, providing negative role models, destroying childhood, and disrupting the bonds between adolescents and adult authority figures (Maguire, Sandage, and Weatherby, 2000; Tanner, 2001).

Hundreds of studies have investigated the potentially negative effects of television violence, and the issue has been the focus of attention from the general public as well as royal commissions in Canada and presidential panels in the United States (Tate, 1998). The argument that television violence has some causal relationship with real-life violence would seem to be supported by much anecdotal evidence (in the form of so-called copycat crimes, for example) and by common sense. We know that television is a powerful persuader; otherwise, advertisers would not spend so much money buying commercial time in order to persuade consumers to purchase their products. We also know that television is a violent medium and that young people (who are most likely to behave violently) have high levels of exposure to such content.

However, despite anecdotal evidence and commonsense notions, the nature and significance of the effects of televised violence are unclear. The effects of television violence on criminal motivation are likely limited by several factors. First, Uniform Crime Reporting data indicate that violent crimes make up a small proportion of total crime. Therefore, unless we want to argue that violent portrayals affect nonviolent crime in some as yet undetermined fashion, the amount of crime that could be causally linked to violent content is limited, even if the effects on violence are substantial. In fact, some researchers have suggested that the real effects of television may be on property crimes rather than violent crimes (Hennigen et al., 1982). The basis for this argument is that the media emphasis on consumerism raises expectations about the amounts of material goods to which people think they are entitled (Surette, 1992). The link between television and property crime has not, however, received sufficient research attention to warrant firm conclusions.

A second limiting factor regarding television violence is that criminal motivation is a complex issue, so whatever effects media exposure produces must be understood in the context of many other factors that encourage or restrain offending. The amount of variation attributable to media exposure is likely to be smaller than many observers would argue. Some researchers assert that 5 to 10 percent of the violent and nonviolent behavior may be attributed to exposure to media violence (Surette, 1992). Whether this means that television violence is a relatively important or unimportant factor in real-life violence remains unresolved.

Third, although many research experiments have been able to show that exposure to violent content in the laboratory setting triggers violent arousal, the same effects are not necessarily produced by media exposure in the real world (Howitt, 1998). In laboratory experiments, subjects may be encouraged to behave violently (or at least not discouraged from doing so); by contrast, violent behavior in most social contexts is discouraged. Also, the ways in which violence is measured in the lab (for example, the willingness of children to play with violent toys or of subjects to administer a harmless electrical shock to another person) may not have much to do with the willingness of people to beat, assault, rob, or kill others. Studies that attempt to link television violence to aggressive behavior in real-life settings have frequently been less successful than those that try to find these effects in the laboratory.

As the preceding discussion suggests, the relationship between television violence and criminal violence is more complicated, and perhaps less substantial, than we sometimes think. Much of the research supports the view that television violence may influence the behavior of a pool of at-risk individuals who may be particularly susceptible to its effects. In other words, television violence may be most likely to affect the behavior of individuals already predisposed to behave aggressively. Unfortunately, we lack detailed knowledge of the size of this at-risk pool and of the factors that put them at risk. The effect of media violence may be not to cause interpersonal aggression in any direct way but rather to reinforce preexisting tendencies or to shape them in particular ways. In the case of copycat crimes, for instance, media violence may not motivate someone to commit a crime, but it may affect how that person commits a crime.

In many cases, the effects of television (or movie) violence may be short-term. Anyone who has ever left a movie theater feeling excited or energized may intuitively understand the nature of this temporary arousal. We also know that such effects tend to dissipate rather quickly as we return to the family, work, or school responsibilities that structure our lives. Thus, whether people behave violently subsequent to such arousal may have as much to do with the situations and circumstances in which they find themselves as with their level of arousal. It is also important to note, though, that we know relatively less about the long-term effects of high levels of violent content in media on cultural beliefs and social practices.

The work of sociologist David Phillips (1983) illustrates how some of the effects might work. In a number of studies, Phillips has shown that media portrayals of homicide or suicide may exert temporary effects on the rates of such behavior. In the case of homicide, for instance, Phillips studied what happened to homicide rates after highly publicized prizefights. These media events are particularly interesting because they involve violence that is both widely publicized and generally condoned rather than condemned. In a careful assessment of homicide trends, Phillips was able to show that in the few days immediately following a highly publicized fight, homicide rates increased by about 12 percent and that such effects could not be attributed to seasonal, monthly, or other temporal patterns.

Critics contend, however, that the findings of such studies are not convincing. As Howitt (1998) argues, homicides do not occur randomly over time but vary according to the day of the week and month of the year. In a similar way, prizefights are not random events; rather, the date of a title boxing match is carefully selected to maximize the investment of the promoters. Given the non-randomness of both the cause (the boxing matches) and the effect (the homicides), it is possible that the statistical relationship between the two suggests a spurious outcome rather than a real causal process.

Much of the rancorous public debate about television violence has found a parallel expression in debates about video games. Not only is the content of these games typically violent, but they are also interactive, and thus it is argued that they may be more likely than television viewing to produce delinquency. Although we have not yet amassed a significant body of research on the subject of the criminogenic influences of video games, thus far the concerns about the effects of these games on serious criminal offending seem to be overstated (Provenzo, 1991).

Debates about the corrupting influence of popular culture are not restricted to juveniles. Public alarm about the effects of pornography on sex crimes reflects concerns similar to those voiced by the critics of television violence. Yet, in a similar way, attempting to draw direct causal links between violent pornography (for example, "slasher" movies that combine sexual scenes with violent ones) and sex crimes ignores the complexity of the issue. A large body of experimental literature suggests that exposure to such pornography promotes negative attitudes toward women, a greater acceptance of rape myths (for example, that rape victims are to blame for what happens to them), and a decreased sensitivity toward female victims of violence (Malamuth, 1983; Malamuth and Donnerstein, 1984).

Transactions

Public Places In the case of juveniles, it is sometimes argued that their patterns of leisure activity increase the likelihood that crimes will occur, by freeing youth from the social controls that might be expected to check or restrain delinquent conduct. Juvenile leisure is most frequently pursued out of the sight of parents or teachers and in the presence of peers (Agnew and Peterson, 1989; Osgood et al., 1996). The modern video arcade, like the pool hall of an earlier era, is off-limits to adults. "Hanging out" at the video arcade or mall or on the street corner may provide the behavioral freedom that makes group delinquency possible. A study by Riley (1987) of juvenile crime in England and Wales found that offenders and nonoffenders engaged in different types of leisure activities. Nonoffenders generally spent more time with parents and around the home, whereas offenders were more likely to spend their time in peer activities away from home. In addition, offenders were more often out in the evening, were expected home later, and were more likely to spend their money on youth-oriented amusements. Such leisure activities remove some of the obstacles to delinquency by lessening the chances of apprehension and by providing exposure to behavioral contexts that facilitate delinquent action.

By contrast, leisure activities organized by adults or leisure time spent with parents may be expected to decrease the possibilities of delinquency by strengthening social bonds and thereby rendering delinquency less attractive (Agnew, 1985; Messner and Blau, 1987). One study found that although "hanging out" and social activities such as dating and partying were associated with higher levels of delinquent involvement, organized leisure was associated with lower levels of delinquent involvement (Agnew and Peterson, 1989). The researchers also reported, however, that youths' engagement in "positive" leisure is not sufficient for a decrease in delinquency to occur—they also must enjoy the activity. In other words, coercive leisure activities cannot be expected to bring about a decrease in offending behavior.

Leisure activities provide important occasions for criminal events of various types, as evidenced by the times and places at which crimes occur. A large number of personal victimizations occur during the evenings and on weekends when most people are "at rest," when they have dropped their more serious work roles, and when the formal social controls of the school and the workplace are not operative (Luckenbill, 1977). Personal victimizations also occur disproportionately in leisure settings—informal contexts that host a wide range of activities such as drinking or gambling, dancing, and playing games. In a study of high school youth in Tucson, Arizona, Jensen and Brownfield (1986) found partying, cruising, and visiting bars—in general, the social pursuit of fun—to be significantly related to victimization risk.

Generally, activities that bring people out of their homes in the evening increase the likelihood of personal and household crime (Kennedy and Forde, 1990). Messner and Blau (1987) found that the volume of leisure activity in the home (indexed by levels of reported television viewing) is related to lower rates of victimization, whereas the volume of leisure activity outside of the home (indexed by the number of sports and theatrical facilities) is related to higher rates of victimization.

A similar pattern has repeatedly been revealed by victimization surveys. Violent and household victimization increase as evening activities outside the home increase, and this relationship is independent of marital status, employment status, and age (Gottfredson, 1984). Going out on weekends increases these risks more than going out during the week, and engaging in leisure pursuits increases risk more than does going to work or to school (Gottfredson, 1984; Lasley and Rosenbaum, 1988; Smith, 1982). The 1998 National Crime Victimization Survey data indicate that about 22 percent of violent or theft victimizations occur while people are taking part in a leisure activity away from home, whereas about 16 percent occur when people are at work and about 3 percent while they are asleep (U.S. Department of Justice, 2000).

In general, leisure can be part of a risky lifestyle that has dangerous consequences (Kennedy and Forde, 1990). Some types of leisure are clearly riskier than others. Young single males are more likely than others to go to bars where, as we have seen, the risks are higher. By contrast, elderly people are less likely to leave their homes for leisure in the evening; when they do, they are less likely to come into contact with potential offenders.

Several studies suggest that forms of leisure that are themselves criminal may pose particularly high victimization risks (Gottfredson, 1984; Jensen and Brownfield, 1986; Lauritsen, Sampson, and Laub, 1991; Sampson and Lauritsen, 1990). This is partially because offenders make good victims—they may be unlikely to call the police and, if they do, may be likely to have difficulty establishing their credibility.

As stated previously, the groups most vulnerable to assaults in public places are young, unmarried males who frequent bars, go to movies, go out to work, and spend time out of the house walking or driving around. This lifestyle creates exposure to risk. Though violent crime may be spontaneous, its targets tend to be people who are in places that are conducive to violent conflict. This observation does not account for the motivation behind violent crime, but it does explain the high levels of victimization among particular groups, based on their exposure to certain settings and activities. Kennedy and Forde (1990) report a similar pattern for robberies: young, unmarried males who frequent bars and who are out walking or driving around are more likely to be victims of this crime.

According to Tanner (2001), it is important to note that in addition to parental controls, the behavior of boys exerts a significant effect on the routine leisure activities of female adolescents. Girls are often missing from deviant youth cultures because males exclude them. Male delinquents do not always relish female participation except as ancillaries or as objects of sexual goals. As Tanner points out, there is no reason to think that delinquent males are any less sexist than nondelinquent males.

The behavior of young males who just hang around on the street is often seen as criminogenic. According to Skogan and Maxfield (1981), urban residents are most afraid of run-down urban areas where teenagers are hanging around on street corners. Even if the loitering is harmless and the individuals who engage in it never become involved in crime, the street is seen as a dangerous place.

If these youths are loosely attached to one another, those whom they encounter in street situations are likely to be acquaintances and the chances of violence tend to be low. When individuals are more closely affiliated, as in a gang, the chance of violence increases, although, as Kennedy and Baron (1993) report, violence may not be a routine outcome of activity by gangs on the street. Much of the crime in which gangs engage actually occurs when they come into contact with other gangs. Minor theft and robbery certainly occur, but not to the extent that the public believes.

The same individuals on the street who represent potential offenders can also be victims. Young men in risky areas can easily become targets of assaults and robberies (Baron and Kennedy, 1998). When alcohol or drugs are involved, spontaneous conflicts may arise between individuals who are complete strangers to one another. Motivation in the violence that occurs between young males, whether in gangs or not, may simply be based on tests of character (Luckenbill, 1977).

The importance of social context for offenders has been identified in research on street youth. In looking at "punks," Kennedy and Baron (1993) examine how the lifestyle of individuals promotes conflict with others and often leads to crime. The authors suggest that punks have been forced to adopt certain strategies of conflict management. In order to survive the rigors of the street with no jobs, the punks rob people and thus can be seen as motivated offenders. This robbery often involves multiple offenders. Victims are chosen who can be robbed with minimal resistance and conflict. Sometimes, third parties get involved, however, and they frequently instigate conflict and engage in physical attacks on the punks. Because the street culture includes acceptance that individuals will face violence routinely, attempts to seek resolution of conflicts are more difficult. However, certain characteristics of the dispute may include elements that prevent individuals from pulling back from violence.

These situations are often influenced by whether or not the participants are seen as insiders or outsiders. Often individuals are guardians for individuals under attack. Their affiliation may establish norms of protection whereby members of the punk gang are expected to intervene on each other's behalf during conflict situations. Conflict, then, provides an integrative function for the group, with punks victimizing those that are outside their social network. With individuals involved in highly violent lifestyles, it may seem surprising that they do not victimize each other. Likely, the context of the gang provides a mild form of conformity based on this affiliation and inhibits members from preying on one another. At the same time, gangs are formed to defend against conflict. By restricting their relationships to those of the same approximate age, the members can avoid some of the most obvious sources of conflict.

Although women may be present in street environments, they are less likely to become involved in conflicts directly, even though they may act as third parties in escalating or defusing the conflict. Women alone tend to avoid areas that they perceive as risky (particularly the street) or situations that may lead to violence or loss of property. Of course, women can be targets of theft just as easily as men—purse snatching is all too common. Nonetheless, street crime appears to be predominantly the domain of young men, both as offenders and victims.

Assaults or robberies may depend on conflict styles that vary according to the individual personality and the social situation that individuals confront (Hocker and Wilmot, 1985). Hocker and Wilmot assume that people develop patterned responses to conflict. Decisions about response style are based on past experience and learning—by observing others' behavior and by trying out different responses.

Third parties also play an important role in the conflict escalation or de-escalation. Young boys often jokingly exhort their friends to physically restrain them when they are confronting a foe. The opponent is advised, "You're lucky he's holding me back, or you'd be sorry!" While this type of posturing, which is facilitated by third parties, may work to dissipate conflict, it may also have the opposite effect. The joking may become serious, and third parties may promote the conflict instead of acting to reduce its outbreak. However, even when one participant lands a blow that, in legal terms, might be considered criminal assault, the parties involved probably do not view it as such. There is likely too much confusion over the identities of the instigator and the victim. Only when physical harm that requires medical assistance is inflicted do these situations lead to the involvement of a formal third party (that is, the police).

Kennedy and Baron (1993) found that members of punk gangs would absorb a great deal of verbal abuse but become involved in a fight only when they felt they needed to protect themselves, not when they felt that backing down would make them look foolish. This finding suggests not that the members of punk gangs were unprepared for the violence or that they would just walk away if attacked, but rather that the crime in which they engaged was more likely to be characterized by spontaneous outbursts of violence (Gottfredson and Hirschi, 1990).

Vandalism As discussed in Chapter 3, people's attitudes toward city streets may be affected not only by the presence of gangs but also by graffiti and other signs of vandalism and decay. When people see these signs, in addition to the patterns of movement around them, their fears tend be awakened. Although vandalism is not a criminal event in conventional terms (that is, an event in which at least two parties are involved in a criminal action), we can still view it in event terms. Vandalism differs from other criminal events in that there is a time delay between the offense and the victimization.

Criminologists have focused greater attention on the consequences rather than the causes of vandalism. Some criminologists (Kelling and Coles, 1996; Skogan, 1990a; Wilson and Kelling, 1982) identify vandalism as a major contributor to the public's declining sense of security in their neighborhoods. Wilson and Kelling (1982) argue that disorder and crime are inextricably linked in a kind of developmental sequence. Wilson (1983) notes that social psychologists and police officers tend to agree that if a building window is broken and left unrepaired, the remaining windows will soon be damaged. Vandalism occurs more frequently in areas in which surveillance is low. In generating what Wilson calls "untended" behavior, vandalism leads to a breakdown of community controls and the degeneration of the neighborhood into one that may become criminogenic. The fear that accompanies this degradation may discourage people from routinely using the streets or providing informal surveillance as a way of constraining disorderly behavior. As vandalism increases and the neighborhood continues its decline, residents may move to safer, more congenial environments.

Although abandoned buildings appear to be the most frequent targets of vandalism, we are witnessing the growth of public vandalism, which involves tagging (writing graffiti) on walls, public vehicles, or whatever else is available. Graffiti-filled trains and stations had long been the scourge of New York public transit and have created the impression of a dangerous system, even though fewer incidents of crime take place on the subway than on the streets of New York (Felson, 1998). The New York City Department of Transportation has taken extreme steps to ban all graffiti on its subway trains. Similar strategies have been used in other cities as well.

While most tagging takes place at night, when the possibility of detection is low, graffiti writers are becoming bolder and are sometimes recognized for their skills at leaving their mark in daylight hours. This bravado may be the natural response of taggers who have come to see themselves as artists. To most people, however, graffiti is nothing more than simple vandalism.

What motivates most vandalism? Thrill seeking and the fact that it doesn't appear to harm anyone are probably significant causative factors. And, notwithstanding the efforts made to curtail it in many cities, vandalism is almost impossible to detect and deter.

Bars Bars are good examples of permissive environs. Not only are bars themselves the site of large numbers of criminal events, but so are the blocks on which they are located (Roncek and Maier, 1991; Roncek and Pravatiner, 1989). There are many reasons for this. Bars do most of their business in the evenings when people are freed from many of the social controls that structure their working days. Bars also deal in cash and liquor, which are easily stolen and easily used by the offender. Further, bars tend to place no real restrictions on who can enter, and they are particularly popular among young people. Finally, for many people, the consumption of alcohol increases the probability of interpersonal conflicts and impairs judgments about the scale of these conflicts.

Bars (taverns, lounges, and so on) are places people go to relax, meet friends, listen to music, and drink. Although most bars escape the frenzied aggressiveness that may lead to crime, some attract it. In these locations, where alcohol and drugs mix with loud music and bravado, violence often erupts. Bar owners are increasingly concerned about this violence but often are confused about how to reduce it. They hire private guardians (bouncers) to remove the most raucous of their clients, but sometimes the actions of bouncers incite more violence. When college or university criminology students are asked where they would go to find a fight on any given night, they can easily list two or three notorious bars in town in which violence occurs with regularity.

Criminal events that occur in bars generally consist of minor assaults, particularly between young males. These events may also involve vandalism (breaking windows, chairs, and tables). Events that involve interpersonal conflict may conclude without violence, with the protagonists walking away or being pulled away from one another. When there is escalation, violence may erupt. As a member of a band that has played for student gatherings told the authors, a crowd that is docile throughout an entire gig may suddenly become violent when the band finishes its last set. It is, he said, almost as if they can now hear one another speak and don't like what is being said. The jostling and shoving that may occur in these situations may be seen by all parties as harmless, but violence may ensue if the aggressiveness accelerates. While this description suggests that the event is spontaneous, the idea that certain bars attract this type of problem implies that some individuals go there in search of trouble. The characterization by Luckenbill (1977) of character contests would seem to apply to such situations. The jostling and shoving that precedes a fight might be combined with insults and threats. When the fight breaks out, those around the combatants may fuel it by offering encouragement or by joining in.

Aftermath

Victimizations that occur in leisure settings frequently go unreported. If the loss or the injury is not great, the victim may decide that reporting the incident to the police may not be worth it. Victimizations may also go unreported when the leisure activity is itself regarded as a form of disreputable behavior. Victims who have been drinking or who encounter offenders in a known "deviant context" may be reluctant to bring the incident to the attention of the police. Given the generally negative attitude toward many forms of youthful leisure activities, it is not surprising that crimes that occur in these settings remain undiscovered or unrecorded by police.

Victims may respond to crimes committed against them in leisure settings in other ways. One response may be to avoid the types of encounters or circumstances in which the victimization occurred. Because leisure activity is, by definition, discretionary activity, it is easier to avoid than home- or work-related activities. Thus, the victim of courtship violence may refrain from dating, and the jogger who is mugged may stop jogging and take up "mall walking," which may be perceived as safer than running on city streets or park paths.

In other instances, a participant in a street fight or barroom brawl may prefer to seek revenge rather than report the crime to police. Of course, the status of such individuals as "victims" may itself be questionable, as they themselves may have struck the initial blow or instigated the fight. In addition, many criminal events involving young males may be of little interest to police. In recent times, police have been encouraged to manage their excessive workloads by assigning a higher priority to the victimization of women and children than to young males.

Although the long-term consequences of leisure-related victimizations are not yet evident, it may be that, with the exception of the sexual assaults, the effects are short-lived. For example, the punks that Baron (1989) talked with simply shrugged off their own victimization, regarding it as just a routine hazard of life on the streets. The degree to which individuals are deterred from becoming involved in leisure-related crimes may have more to do with the risk of being hurt than with the risk of being arrested. This is not to suggest that the police do not deter; their presence on the street and in bars plays an important role in keeping such potentially dangerous behavior under control. The evidence would seem to indicate that the behavior of young males on the street and in other settings can change from violent to passive fairly easily, particularly given that victims and offenders are often hard to distinguish and that public guardians (police officers and citizens) are not always available to stop a brewing conflict from becoming serious.

The need for guardianship has long driven the policy whereby police attempt to maintain a high profile on the street. This has been achieved through the use of random patrol—that is, cars cruising neighborhoods looking for problems. As a result, police departments are now experimenting with neighborhood mini-stations and increasing foot patrols and neighborhood consultations—tactics they believe can prevent and deter crime more effectively than can a highly visible police presence in the form of random patrol. Still, the most effective guardians against crime are not the police but rather other people who frequent leisure settings and who call the police when needed.

Attempts have been made to influence the use of leisure as a crime control mechanism. Particularly conspicuous have been efforts to develop positive leisure alternatives for young people who are actually or potentially delinquent (Agnew and Peterson, 1989). This approach reflects the maxim, made explicit in social control theory, that "idle hands are the devil's workshop." Youths get themselves into trouble, through various forms of "hanging out," because they lack positive options. The reasoning behind the positive-leisure approach is that summer camps, organized clubs, and other so-called forms of healthy recreation will expose youths to an environment that discourages involvement in crime and delinquency.

A parallel approach focuses on the need to control what are widely viewed in some quarters as negative and corrupting forms of youth leisure. This approach seems to reflect the view that if youths are left to make their own leisure choices, they will almost always make the wrong ones. The past several decades have witnessed numerous crusades intended to impose legal and social restrictions on the ability of young people to make these choices. These campaigns were directed against feature films in the 1930s; comic books and rock and roll in the 1950s; the presumed drug-influenced protest music of the 1960s; and rap and heavy metal music, fantasy role-playing games (for example, Dungeons and Dragons), and video games in the 1980s and 1990s. Television violence has been the subject of recurrent crusades every five to ten years since the 1960s (Best, 1990; Gray, 1989).

However, such crusades have an ironic character. According to Tanner (2001), they reflect a perennial tendency on the part of adults to rediscover, to stigmatize, and to attempt to control the culture and behavior of the generations that follow them. Thus, the Elvis Presley and the Beatles fans, the hippies, and the student radicals of earlier eras express bewilderment and concern about the corruptive nature of the cultural worlds in which they believe their own children to be immersed. Contemporary charges that modern heavy metal music inspires teen suicide and sexual promiscuity, or that it promotes mysticism and devil worship, tell us more about the ways in which anxieties about youth are reproduced across generations than about the uniquely deviant characteristics of contemporary youth.

TOURISM

Precursors

The growing importance of tourism in our society is impossible to ignore. Large amounts of money are spent on tourist attractions, and people are allocating increased amounts of their disposable income to travel. Despite the growing awareness that tourists are not immune to crime, however, hotels and travel agencies have been slow to warn tourists about potentially dangerous areas. Tourists tend to be easy targets for the pickpocket or the robber. Nor is it just the property that tourists take with them that is at risk. One scam involves thieves who read the identification tags of departing travelers and then go burglarize their now unoccupied homes.

Victimization of travelers is hardly a recent phenomenon. In the Middle Ages, castles were built in the south of France to protect pilgrims who traveled through areas inhabited by thieves and robbers. And although modern tourism has left the impression that tourists are not likely to be victims, they *are*, and they need to take precautions to protect themselves. As tourists become increasingly aware of their vulnerability, many once-popular tourist destinations are finding that visitors are staying away.

Major outbreaks of violence against tourists receive widespread media attention, which may also include advice about special precautions that tourists can take to protect themselves. Attacks on foreign tourists in parts of East Africa and Egypt, for example, led to a worldwide alert to avoid these areas. Also, travel agencies and tour groups steer clients away from areas they consider dangerous. The governments of many countries issue warnings to their citizens to avoid certain areas, particularly those characterized by political instability or violence against tourists. In such circumstances, travelers may become a target of local anger and frustration. Some countries are responding to crime against tourists by developing programs that enhance security in resort areas and that educate travelers about the hazards they may encounter in certain areas. Crime directed at tourists would seem to be best explained by opportunity theories, which would characterize tourists as vulnerable targets in areas where surveillance may be low and precautions more difficult to take.

Transactions

A tourist is more likely to be a victim of theft or robbery than of personal attack. Most commonly, luggage is stolen or pockets are picked. As thieves develop sophisticated techniques for picking or jimmying locks, they increasingly are preying on autos as well. In one scam, the car thief drives along a beach road that is not too crowded and checks out the parked cars. If they see signs of an attractive target (for example, a foreign license plate or a rental car), and if the owner is nowhere to be seen (and thus presumably down at the beach), the thief parks behind the car, approaches the car, and breaks the lock (with special tools, this can be accomplished fairly easily). Then the thief quickly searches the car and exits with whatever loot is found. Slashing a tire prevents the victim from attempting pursuit.

Tourists may also run into problems simply because they do not understand the local customs or language. In one case, a 16-year-old Japanese exchange student was shot and killed in a Louisiana neighborhood because he did not understand the warning "Freeze!" The youth had been looking for a Halloween party and did not stop when he was accosted by Rodney Peairs, who said that he had felt that his life had been threatened by the costumed youth. Peairs was acquitted under a Louisiana law that allows citizens to use deadly weapons to protect themselves. In response to the student's tragic death, the Japanese government published a guide of helpful phrases for U.S.-bound tourists. The guide included about thirty phrases that few Japanese learn in their language classes, among them, "Get lost," "Watch out," and "I mean it" (Sanger, 1993). Not only the translations but also the different cultural meanings of the thirty phrases will be imparted as a way of letting the visitors know that the person issuing the warning is serious.

Victimization data can be used to help us understand the ways in which tourism and other forms of traveling affect our chances of becoming crime victims. Using survey data, Wellford (1997) has been able to estimate the rates of victimization of domestic travelers in the United States. The results of his analysis are not what we might expect. He found that the rate of victimization for all crime types for domestic travelers was substantially lower than the rate of victimization for the general population. As well, he found that the gender differences that exist with respect to victimization in the general population also exist for travelers.

Aftermath

How do we reconcile these results with our assumptions about the dangers of travel? Wellford (1997) suggests that routine activities theory offers one way of understanding the survey results. Perhaps, crime rates are lower for travelers in large part because travelers tend to take more concrete steps to control target suitability and guardianship. Tourists, for instance, are generally more likely to go out in groups and to spend their time in well-traveled "tourist areas." This interpretation is consistent with the observation that the notorious cases of tourist victimization that we read or hear about typically involve people who wandered off the beaten path into high-crime areas or who took the wrong exit ramp off the highway. Clearly, the topic of tourism and victimization is one that deserves more focused attention.

SUMMARY

When people are "at leisure," they are also at risk of involvement in criminal events, as offenders or victims. The relationships that link leisure activity and criminal activity are highly varied. Some forms of leisure might be seen as causes of crime. The content of youth-oriented media, for instance, may seem to provide the motives for crime. Alternatively, engagement in peer activities may suggest freedom from the social controls that might be expected to inhibit offending.

Much leisure activity takes place in public spaces. Street crime involves people who are passing through areas in transit from one place to another or who are simply "hanging out." In these contexts, crime might itself constitute leisure, as appears to be the case with vandalism and graffiti writing. In leisure settings such as streets and bars, it is often difficult to distinguish the offenders from the victims when a conflict escalates into assault or other forms of violence. This form of opportunity crime tends to be based on the risky lifestyles of the individuals involved and is more likely to be deterred by retribution than by reporting the crime to the police.

Some types of leisure pursuits place people at particular risk of victimization. The risky lifestyles in which people engage may make the search for a "good time" result in a "bad time." It must be emphasized that, in the leisure domain, as in other domains, the processes that we are describing are not deterministic. In other words, exposure to criminogenic influences or to threats of victimization does not guarantee the development of a criminal event but rather only increases its probability by bringing together opportunities for crime and motivations to offend.

7

Applying Criminal
Event Analysis

Some important recent innovations have shifted focus to the criminal event as a unit of analysis in criminology. Opportunity reduction focuses on how social and environmental factors might be brought to bear on the reduction of targets of crime. Community-based policing (or problem-oriented policing) considers ways in which the policing role may be expanded beyond the narrow reactive role that brings the police into criminal events only after such events are under way or finished. Finally, social development approaches attempt to create social conditions that discourage long-term serious offending and empower potential victims while at the same time contributing to the rebuilding of communities.

CRIME PREVENTION
THROUGH OPPORTUNITY REDUCTION

Borrowing from the language of public health, we can think of crime prevention as having primary, secondary, and tertiary dimensions (Brantingham and Faust, 1976; Lab, 1992; van Dijk and de Waard, 1991). Primary prevention includes programs aimed at either the entire community or the population at risk. Exemplifying primary prevention are crime prevention programs that teach risk-reducing skills to large audiences (Sacco and Silverman, 1982). Pamphlets, brochures, and posters providing information on family violence are examples of primary prevention via the mass media. Secondary prevention involves programs aimed at segments of the population that are at particularly high risk, or, in public health language, that show early symptoms of the problem. Examples of secondary prevention include targeting high-crime areas for special treatment (such as neighborhood redevelopment or Neighborhood Watch programs) and installing security equipment in schools that have experienced problems with intruders. Finally, tertiary prevention consists of strategies for preventing the recurrence of crime. Examples include victim-offender mediation, training courses for drunk drivers, treatment programs for wife assaulters, and various forms of diversion and community service.

As crime prevention specialists have become more skilled at implementing principles of situational prevention, the broad applicability of the approach has become evident. Although common uses of the approach might suggest that it is best suited for controlling minor nuisance crimes (such as trespassing and vandalism), it has also been used successfully to control much more serious kinds of offenses.

For instance, the Los Angeles Police Department employed situational prevention principles in an attempt to reduce levels of assault and homicide. Known as Operation Cul de Sac (OCDS), the program involved efforts to control and reroute traffic so as to "design out" crime by reducing the opportunities to commit it. Thus, traffic barriers were placed in neighborhoods where gangs and gang violence had become especially serious problems. The analysis of police data indicated that the majority of drive-by shootings and violent gang encounters occurred in clusters on the periphery of neighborhoods linked to major thoroughfares. To control the problem, the police closed all of the major roads leading to and from these identified hot spots by placing cement barriers at the ends of the streets that led to these roads. This redesign in effect created cul-de-sacs.

The situational prevention approach assumed that although gang violence may have a deep-seated structural cause, it also has significant opportunity dimensions. Thus rather than focus on the root causes of gang violence in this case, it focused on "proximate causes." A subsequent evaluation showed that the number of homicides and assaults in the OCDS area fell significantly during the two-year program period and rose after it ceased operation (in a comparison area it remained constant). The evaluation also showed another important result—that crime was not displaced to other areas (Lasley, 1998).

In recent years, a great deal of attention has been focused on proposals that encourage secondary prevention as a major form of opportunity reduction. Among the most popular measures intended to activate natural surveillance at the local level are Block Watch or Neighborhood Watch programs that are sponsored by the local police. These programs are intended to encourage neighborhood residents to "share information about local crime problems, exchange crime prevention tips, and make plans for engaging in surveillance (watching) of the neighborhood and crime-reporting activities" (Rosenbaum, 1987: 104). Surveillance programs increase interaction among neighbors at the same time as they remove opportunities for crime. The U.S. Bureau of Justice Statistics reported in 1986 that about 1 in 5 families lives in a neighborhood with a surveillance program and that, in those areas, 38 percent of residents participate (Garofalo and McLeod, 1988). Although opportunity for crime can be thwarted by the self-help actions of potential victims, individuals who take the law into their own hands may do so in a manner that constitutes vigilantism (Black 1983; Rosenbaum and Sederberg, 1976).

Finally, crime may be made less attractive by reducing the rewards associated with the offense. For example, requiring bus riders to have exact change decreases the amount of money that must be handled by any particular bus driver and makes the robbery of drivers a less attractive proposition. Similarly, markings that identify individual ownership of property may discourage the conspicuous use of stolen merchandise and seriously hurt the chances for resale.

The most sophisticated forms of situational prevention attempt to employ knowledge about all elements of the criminal event. Paul and Patricia Brantingham (2001), the foremost authorities regarding this approach, identify several such elements:

The offender. Of course, all crimes require offenders. Although traditional approaches to crime prevention have focused on changing the offender's motivation, the situational approach directs our attention to the routine activities of offenders and to their patterns of decision making.

Target. All predatory crimes have targets or victims. Situational approaches are sensitive to the role played by victim precipitation and carelessness in crime causation.

Site. Every criminal event has a site—a discrete location in space and time— at which the criminal action by the offender against the target takes place. Such sites are positional and can be analyzed to reveal patterns that help prevention planners understand the spatial (and temporal) regularities in crime occurrence.

Situations. Crimes require specific behavioral settings and situations. Thus, merely because a potential offender and victim find themselves in each other's presence does not mean that a crime will happen. It is also essential that the offender define the situation as appropriate. This determination could involve, for instance, the absence of official protectors—guardians or property managers, such as landlords or security guards.

Mechanics of the crime. The criminal event model of crime prevention also directs our attention to the sequence of actions the offender must take to accomplish the crime once the offender, target, site, and situation have combined to create a criminal opportunity. Criminal action sequences are normally short and technically simple, but they are sometimes quite complex. Knowledge of the mechanics of this process makes possible the development of strategies intended to disrupt this sequence.

The Brantinghams argue that situational prevention strategies must not only account for each of these factors but also be informed by an awareness of their various combinations. The numerous ways in which each combines and intersects with the others suggest to careful planners a wide range of prevention opportunities. Brantingham and Brantingham (1990) provide the following examples to illustrate the logic and the value of their approach.

Example 1. In a large suburban municipality, a brewer's warehouse had experienced repeated problems with people breaking into delivery vans at night. The vans were empty but were backed up to the loading bay doors and locked up overnight. Offenders, apparently in search of beer, repeatedly cut through a fence on the perimeter of the warehouse lot and broke into the vans. No beer was stolen, because the vans were empty, but the brewer incurred repeated repair costs to fix the damaged fence and delivery vans.

A crime prevention officer persuaded the warehouse manager to park the delivery vans away from the loading bay doors (which were themselves secure) and leave them unlocked overnight. The vans were opened on a few subsequent occasions, but they were not damaged as before.

Example 2. A church experienced a less serious but more common problem than that of example 1. A high school was located opposite the church, and a convenience store was located on the street behind the church. As might be expected, students from the high school walked through the church parking lot to get to and from the convenience store. Unfortunately, the students dumped lots of litter in the church parking lot. Church members were upset by the mess but unable to stop either the trespassing teenagers or their littering.

A crime prevention officer found an effective, low-cost solution. He persuaded the church to dig a ditch across the front of its property (except for an entranceway) and to build a direct pathway from the school to the convenience store along one edge of the church property. The new pathway had a tall cedar fence on one side to separate it from adjacent houses and a chain-link fence on the other side. The littering on the church grounds stopped, and, perhaps surprisingly, the student pathway stayed litter- and graffiti-free. General research on littering and graffiti finds that keeping an area "clean" is a deterrent to further problems.

Example 3. To combat shoplifting, video stores are changing how they display the videos they have for rental. Previously, they tended to place the actual cassettes out on the shelves. Customers would select a cassette and carry it to a central desk for rental. This system had the benefit of reducing staff time spent on telling customers whether particular videos were available for rental. If they were on the shelves, they were available; if they were not on the shelves, they were not available.

Many small video stores display the small empty boxes that the videos originally came in or else small plastic display cards with advertising material. The customer must exchange the box or card for the actual video at a central station. Although this system requires more staff time, it reduces shoplifting dramatically.

Unquestionably, opportunity reduction has proven effective in a variety of specific settings. According to Merry (1981), a neighborhood may be architecturally designed to discourage crime but still not be adequately defended, because it has little or no social cohesion. Krupat and Kubzansky (1987) note that even when buildings are low and the entrances and public spaces focus around a small set of families, people will not react to crime when they believe that they are on someone else's turf, when they do not consider the police effective, or when they fear retribution.

Critics have suggested that removing opportunity is more likely to displace crime than to prevent it (Gabor, 1990). In other words, if we make it difficult for a motivated offender to offend in one situation, he or she might simply find another situation more conducive to offending. If one store takes precautions to prevent theft, can we really be sure that the would-be thief will not simply seek out targets where such precautions are not taken? The evidence suggests that displacement may be a problem with particular types of crime and particular types of offenders. However, many forms of opportunity reduction do in fact prevent crimes rather than just displace them (Brantingham and Brantingham, 1990; Felson and Clarke, 1998).

More specific forms of opportunity reduction invite more specific criticisms. Various target-hardening methods, such as installing locks on doors and bars on windows, may be faulted for encouraging a "fortress mentality" that enhances the fear of crime in society (Graham, 1990). Some critics see the use of electronic surveillance as part of a gradual shift toward a "surveillance society" (Clarke, 1992). Critics of Neighborhood Watch programs assert that despite the highly favorable publicity such programs receive and the high regard in which they are held by police and politicians, little evidence suggests that they accomplish what they are supposed to accomplish. According to Rosenbaum (1987),

> There is some evidence to suggest (a) if given the opportunity to participate, residents in the majority of high-crime neighborhoods would not participate, and (b) when citizens do participate, the social interaction that occurs at meetings may lead to increases (rather than decreases) in fear of crime, racial prejudice and other crime-related perceptions or feelings. More important, there is little evidence that these block/neighborhood meetings cause local residents to engage in neighborhood surveillance, social interaction, and bystander intervention behaviors that are posited as the central mechanism for strengthening informal social controls and reducing opportunities for crime. (127)

Notwithstanding these critiques, opportunity reduction rather than offender targeting has had a major impact on crime decline. Recent analysis of crime data drops indicate that incarceration, size of offender cohorts, and police force size appear to account for only a small percentage of decreases in crime (Blumstein and Wallman, 2000).

If we think of crime opportunities in terms of crime potential, we can begin to model the prospective crime events that are likely to occur. In analyzing crime potential, we can see that certain areas are more likely to be hazardous (hot spots), certain people are more likely to be dangerous (high risks), and certain individuals experience greater risk (risky lifestyles) and can experience more harm over time (multiple victims). Certain locations spread risk (broken windows). Crime potential can also be curtailed, might move to other areas (displacement), or might remain in an area over time (momentum). This potential can relate to the precursors of the event or can influence the aftermath of the event, setting the stage for a repeat. Prevention strategies may curtail crime occurrence.

Evident in these propositions is the interrelationship between individual and community factors, as well as an emphasis on spatial and temporal processes. Of particular importance in these propositions is the view that crime potential is not a static factor but rather a dynamic factor, such that previous victimization may influence future experiences or risky lifestyles may lead to criminal careers. The multidimensionality of this approach is illustrated in the discussion (below) of what makes up a hot spot. We can list a number of factors, including the following:

- concentration of behavior that is risky
- congregation of offenders
- reduced guardianship or more intense policing
- social decline
- containment
- expectations that support risky behavior
- ambiguity and uncertainty
- lowered trust
- heightened exposure
- greater opportunity, more targets
- multiple victimization
- spatial concentration of similar activities

The concentration effects increase the crime potential. It is this aggregation of crime that interests us and will form the basis of the rest of our discussion of opportunity reduction.

Criminal event analysis can be performed using new technological applications that allow us to track the occurrence of behavior with the social characteristics of locations, or crime places. For example, geographic information systems (GIS) have become major tools for incorporating temporal and spatial dynamics in the study of crime. It could be argued that with current processing speed and high capacity for handling large data sets, GIS applications are providing analytical tools that go beyond the standard cross-sectional analytical packages that we have come to rely on in criminology. In analysis with GIS, dynamic change and patterning can become the focal point. Central to this method is the view that crime analysis can be constructed on the building blocks of criminal events.

The innovations in crime analysis procedure are mirrored in the development of new information technologies that are transforming the nature of social life and providing new possibilities for crime prevention. Cellular telephones allow people to intervene anonymously in a variety of situations that would not have been possible before. Computer terminals in patrol cars allow police to tap databases that provide instant information about known offenders and unsafe locations.

Other trends that bring with them increases in the levels of guardianship and decreases in levels of victimization risk include the growth of remote worksites, which can reduce commuting time; the spread of computer technologies, which allow many people to spend part of the working day at home; the expansion of part-time work in the service economy; and the increasing popularity of video and other home entertainment technologies (Felson, 1987). All of these changes suggest that the shift in routine activities away from the home may be undergoing a reversal. Though the long-term impact of such changes on the community remains to be seen, they may eventually permit some forms of community prevention that were not viable in the past.

Felson (1987) provides an interesting example of how our prevention planning must be informed by careful social forecasting. He believes that metropolitan areas in North America are undergoing profound changes that involve the emergence of a new dominant urban form, the "metroquilt"—"a patchwork of coterminous facilities intervening between homes, business and the larger society." He adds, "The metroquilt would divide urban space among a large set of corporations, whose facilities managers would be responsible for organizing everyday movements, including security" (Felson, 1987: 920). This patchwork is apparent in the landscape of any major city. Stores are replaced by malls, single-family dwellings by condominiums and apartment complexes, and businesses and factories by industrial parks. In the metroquilt, Felson maintains, we have decreasing need to walk from one place to another and increasing need to drive from the parking lot of one facility to the parking lot of another facility.

In Felson's view, the growth of the metroquilt has far-reaching implications for crime prevention. As facilities develop, the distinction between public urban space and private space becomes increasingly blurred. As people spend increasing amounts of their time shopping in malls, working in office complexes, and visiting friends and relatives in apartments, private businesses rather than the government assume greater responsibility for their safety. As a result, the facility could become the major organizational tool for crime prevention. Felson is optimistic about these developments because they suggest the possibility that prevention can be rationalized and that security can be planned. He maintains that safety will become part of the marketing strategy because, as facilities compete for customers and tenants, private developers will have a strong incentive to make environments more crime-free (see also Shearing and Stenning, 1983; Walsh and Donovan, 1989).

However, there is a disturbing side to all of this. If the production of safety is increasingly the domain of the private developer, then safety becomes a commodity accessible only to those who can afford it. The patron of the upscale shopping center, the resident of the luxurious condo, and the employee in a gleaming office tower may find safety more accessible than those who spend most of their time in facilities where profit motives or government cost-cutting militate against extensive crime prevention planning. The risk that safety may become a commodity to be bought and sold, rather than a public good, suggests that issues other than technical effectiveness must inform prevention efforts. The prevention of crime must involve not only logistical matters but also matters of justice and equality. This concern is one that police agencies are now facing as they attempt to adopt crime prevention as a primary focus of their activities.

COMMUNITY-BASED POLICING

Gottfredson and Hirschi (1990) argue that the natural limits of law enforcement are set by the spontaneous nature of crime: the offender sees that he or she can get something for nothing and seizes the opportunity. No increases in law enforcement, they suggest, can truly deter this type of behavior. Research has provided strong evidence that no relationship exists between the level of crime in a society and the number of police available to control crime (Bayley, 1985; Jackson, 1989). Gottfredson and Hirschi (1990) maintain that, in the overwhelming majority of robberies, burglaries, assaults, homicides, thefts, and drug deals, the offender does not know or care about the probability of being observed by the police. The primary role of the police, they suggest, is to respond to criminal activity and to maintain social control; there is no evidence that increasing police tactical resources has the effect of reducing crime rates.

When police resources have become scarcer, police officers primarily respond to complaints (not crime), maintain visibility in neighborhoods, and control traffic. In a study of police activity, Lawson (1982) discovered that the police spend only 10–15 percent of their time engaged in actual law enforcement; the rest of their time is taken up with order maintenance.

More recently, the pressures of order maintenance and restricted resources have forced police agencies to begin to rethink their strategy of law enforcement. The role of the police has expanded partly because they belong to the only twenty-four-hour social agency that is easy to reach and that will make house calls. The emergency telephone line, 911, overwhelms the police with calls that require them to serve not a law enforcement function but rather a regulatory or order maintenance function. In addition, the police are being called upon to become more actively involved in crime prevention, partly as a response to the high levels of unease that people feel in urban areas.

Given the assumption of routine activities theory that crime is made possible not only by the availability of offenders and victims but also by the absence of visible guardians (such as the police), it is hard to believe that the police have *no* effect on deterring crime. However, as the research consistently indicates, a direct correlation between policing levels and crime does not exist. Hiring more police officers does not necessarily lower crime, for many reasons. In previous chapters, we examined the police role in defining criminal events. The criteria that the police use in determining whether to arrest a person are shaped by a number of factors. Such factors include the nature of the police organization and its strategies of policing, differing interpretations of criminal events and differing assessments of the characteristics and motivations of participants in these events, and variations in the interpretations of the law and the cooperation of the public. We will examine how each of these factors can influence the new problem-oriented strategies that are intended to assist the police in dealing with crime. But first we will consider the changes that have taken place in the ways in which the police have functioned over the years.

The original mandate of the police in the nineteenth century was order maintenance (Wilson, 1983). The order maintenance, or compliance, role of the police was coterminous with "community relations." The police were to protect the community from disorderly behavior and to control conflict where they found it (Monkkonen, 1983). This role required them to act as "watchmen," keeping track of the comings and goings in the community and looking out for behavior that might constitute a threat to public order. As Klockars (1985) has stated, the police are not law enforcement agencies but rather regulatory institutions—their job is not to enforce the laws but to regulate relationships between people.

The principal objective of compliance law enforcement is to secure conformity with the law by resorting to means that induce that conformity (Reiss, 1984). Compliance systems return to the original mandate of the police whereby they seek to create law-abidingness through preventive or remedial actions. Under these systems, the primary focus of policing shifts from detecting and penalizing violators to providing incentives to individuals to comply with the law. Compliance-based policing also recognizes the need to include the public in controlling social disorder, beyond merely reporting crime to the police. The public is encouraged to include the police as intermediaries in situations of community conflict (Lawson, 1982).

The public has demanded more social order since at least the 1850s (Monkkonen, 1983). In fact, in comparison to crime control, order control as practiced by the police has had a long and successful record. As Monkkonen puts it, Victorian morality has triumphed in most of America's city streets. We expect, and get, quiet and predictable behavior from almost everyone. Vice is no longer highly visible. Yet the dramatic rise in crime rates in the 1980s and the apparent ineffectiveness of the police in dealing with crime and its consequences, again raised concerns about social order. Monkkonen attributes the increases in crime rates in the late twentieth century to a number of factors, including urbanization and changes in the demographic composition of the population. The effect of these increases was to narrow the focus of police agencies to crime control alone, leaving the problems of general order maintenance to other agencies.

The principal objective of crime control, or deterrence law enforcement, is to detect violations of the law, identify offenders responsible for violations, and penalize perpetrators. These actions are taken to diminish the chance of future offenses both by the offender (specific deterrence) and by others who may contemplate the same criminal act (general deterrence) (Reiss, 1984). Until recently, contemporary policing has had as a stated objective the apprehension of offenders through arrest, which has led to the form of reactive policing that dominates the way that police agencies operate (Reiss, 1984).

Police have now begun to realize that crime control, by necessity, requires broadening their mandate once again to include order maintenance or compliance law enforcement. In the last decade, community-based policing has replaced professional crime control policing as the dominant ideological and organizational model of progressive policing. Bayley (1988) identifies four major features of community-based policing: community-based crime prevention; proactive servicing, as opposed to emergency response; public participation in the planning and supervision of police operations; and the shifting of command responsibility to lower-level ranks. Accompanying these organizational and procedural changes is an emphasis on identifying and solving problems, which are defined in terms of breaches of both law and social order. Further, the solutions to these problems do not merely reside in the rules and regulations of the police service; they must also acknowledge the concerns and desires of the community in which the problems occur.

According to Goldstein (1990), community-based policing requires at least five major adjustments in thinking. First, to do their job well, police officers must be encouraged to search for alternatives to law enforcement. This encouragement must be reflected in a consistent, agencywide commitment to improving the quality of police service. Second, the police must not restrict their attention to those actions that have a potential for reducing crime. In some cases, crime is only the final consequence of unresolved non-crime-related problems. Third, consistent with the view that policing encompasses all of a community's problems, problems that do not fit strict law enforcement criteria must also be addressed. Fourth, some effort must be made to understand the nature of the problems that are encountered in any given area prior to setting out alternatives. Too often, alternatives are prescribed that do not work because they are not suited to the area being policed. Like any other large organization, the police have difficulty resisting internal pressures to follow established but rigid objectives and procedures. Fifth, the police must be open to the idea of allowing other agencies to fulfill the job in conjunction with (or in place of) the police. According to Goldstein (1990), this strategy "is intended to dissuade the police from applying a generic response to a generic problem, or to applying a single response haphazardly to a wide range of different types of problems" (104).

Bayley (1988) suggests that community-based policing constitutes the most fundamental change in policing since the rise in police professionalism early in this century. In fact, community-based policing has had differing levels of success (Rosenbaum, 1994). At the heart of the concept is neighborhood team policing, which involves the long-term assignment of officers to a particular area. This strategy allows officers to make a commitment to an area and to assume a broader level of authority in providing policing that is more sensitive to community needs. Neighborhood team programs have not been embraced by many police managers, however, who see the decentralization that is associated with them as limiting their control over their officers (Scheingold, 1984). In addition, aggressive patrol tactics used in crime control may diminish police rapport with the public, thereby undermining the effectiveness of community-based policing, as witnessed in the debates about the impact that these strategies had on the police community relations in New York City (Reppetto and Lardner, 2000). Finally, their fear of being seen as indecisive may cause many officers to play the role of order restorer rather than that of peacemaker (Palenski, 1984).

The police must look to community members to support them in their efforts to bring about order in the community. This support can take the form of self-help, as discussed earlier, or it can involve a kind of coproduction, whereby the police use community members as supporters of police activity (Krahn and Kennedy, 1985). Coproduction can range from passive responses, such as locking doors, to more active responses, such as participating in crime prevention programs or acting as informants (Skolnick, 1966). As Black (1980) points out, because the typical criminal act occurs at an unpredictable time and place, the police must rely on citizens (most often the victims of a crime) to involve them.

How should police do "problem-oriented policing"? One answer to this question suggests that the police need to collect better crime data and need to think imaginatively about how to put those data to use. A good example of problem-solving logic is provided by Eck (2001), who argues that, traditionally, police managers have not been attentive enough to the way in which crimes are clustered. Eck repeats the observation that we made earlier that the 10 percent of the places with the most crime account for about 60 percent of crime, that the 10 percent of the offenders committing the most crimes are involved in about 50 percent of the offenses, and that the 10 percent of the most victimized people are involved in about 40 percent of the crimes.

The implications of these empirical generalizations are quite profound. A community might have a high crime rate because a small number of offenders commit a lot of crime (career criminals), a small number of victims are repeatedly victimized (hot dots), or a small number of places host a large number of events (hot spots). Eck nicknames these problems "ravenous wolves," "sitting ducks," and "dens of iniquity" respectively. Clearly, these represent quite different types of crime problems. Merely knowing that the crime rate is high or that it has increased doesn't tell us whether we have a wolf problem, a duck problem, or a den problem—or some combination. If, for instance, a housing project has a high rate of breaking and entering, we need to know whether this rate reflects a small number of offenders victimizing a lot of residences; a small number of victims being repeatedly victimized; or a certain group of residences that get victimized repeatedly, no matter who lives there. Maybe it is even more complicated. Perhaps the problem is 80 percent wolf, 10 percent duck, and 10 percent den—or some other combination. These differences matter because wolf, duck, and den problems require different types of police interventions.

Wolves. The primary response to a pure wolf problem is, of course, to remove the wolves through incapacitation or rehabilitation. This is the traditional approach of the criminal justice system. Because many offenders use tools, another wolf solution is to make such tools less effective. Metal detectors in schools, for instance, can be used to systematically disarm potential wolves.

Ducks. Pure duck problems require solutions different from those for wolf problems. Because victims and offenders must persistently come together at the same place for a crime problem to occur, one approach to preventing repeat victimization is to keep victims away from offenders or away from places with offenders. It is possible to improve tool use by potential victims. This can include locks, lighting, and other things that help them detect and avoid offenders. Police crime prevention programs can be important sources of relevant information and hardware.

Dens. Addressing pure den problems requires other types of tactics. Places can be made less accessible to victims or offenders, or places can be removed permanently. For example, the open hours of ATMs can be limited. The best-known den solution involves changing the physical environment. Again, the police can be expected to play an active consultative and facilitative role with respect to the implementation of crime prevention through environmental design.

Eck's analysis demonstrates that a careful and judicious use of crime data by policing agencies can facilitate a range of interventions that do not appear as obvious options in the context of traditional models of policing. As people withdraw from the community, the delicate web of social relations begins to break down, as do the various informal social controls that regulate conduct. Thus, as the streets become less populated, they are subject to less control because citizen surveillance of them is reduced.

Providing resources for community-based policing (outside of community support) has proven to be problematic. Police budgets still depend on caseloads of calls for service and on crime rates. Community-based policing activity, which is directed at problem solving and referral to outside programs, may create an impression of reduced activity, which in turn would suggest a need for lower budgets. The use of alternative programs also brings the police into conflict with other agencies, which makes it more difficult for them to define their role in the community and obtain the resources they need to realize their objectives.

Further, it is difficult for some police agencies to remain apolitical when fighting for budget allocations and arguing for certain policing strategies. The lobbying by communities and by volunteers in community-based policing programs may make the police appear more politically active than local politicians would want them to be, thereby making their requests for more funds even more tenuous. Police chiefs are thus confronted with a plethora of community constraints. These constraints need to be overcome before the chiefs can show that they are fulfilling the objectives of compliance-based policing. In a discussion of policing programs in Britain, Shaffer (1980) argues that improving police-community relations is a crucial first step. The members of a community must get to know the police as concerned and sympathetic individuals, as well as controlling and disciplining law officers. Without communication and co-operation between the police and the public, she concludes, "policing in a democratic society is impossible" (38).

Of particular interest to criminologists are the new techniques that allow interactive problem solving by encouraging community members to visualize crime problems, using geographic information systems (GIS) that map where these crimes occur. GIS applications have been particularly popular in police agencies that have access to computer-assisted dispatch (CAD) systems, which provide not only a tracking program for the allocation of police officers but also electronic data records that can be analyzed in spatial and temporal terms. Police agencies have moved as far as using this analytical tool in tactical planning sessions or Compstat. Developed in New York City, Compstat sessions, which include the computerized display of crime maps, are used by police leaders to identify daily changes in crime patterns in different police districts.

Although based on map technology, Compstat sessions also include a great deal of information about other factors in the environment, including police action, deployment, community agencies available, command structure, demographics, and so on. This accountability device has had a major impact in the ways in which police operate, particularly in urban areas. The Map, a comprehensive multilayered geo-referenced database for New York City, is the first integrated system for coding the many different data layers used by the multitude of agencies in New York into one standardized grid. This multilayered data source will be invaluable in police analysis, allowing crime statistics to be constantly compared with changes in land use, transportation flows, social service delivery, and whatever else seems related.

With the increased interest by the police in GIS applications, the presentation of crime patterns in Compstat sessions is often based on point maps that compare incidents from one time period to another in patrol areas or police districts. Although helpful to the police in examining the immediate impact of their efforts, this type of analysis tends to limit the overall analysis of hot spots. In the more sophisticated applications that are available, the police are either querying their databases themselves or, with the help of criminologists, identifying patterns that would help them be more effective in problem solving. In an exercise performed in 2000 in Newark, New Jersey, members of the School of Criminal Justice (SCJ) at Rutgers University worked with police command staff to identify problems related to specific types of crimes (in particular, theft of and theft from cars) and to suggest ways in which these crimes could be abated.*

In Newark, auto theft is widespread, and the police understand that they face a difficult task in trying to solve this problem. As an initial approach to problem solving, the police were briefed on the elements of environmental criminology, with suggestions for hardening targets and removing opportunities from offenders. The police were then apprised of the basic principles for applying

---

*Members of SCJ involved in the project were Les Kennedy, Ron Clarke, Marcus Felson, and Erika Poulsen.

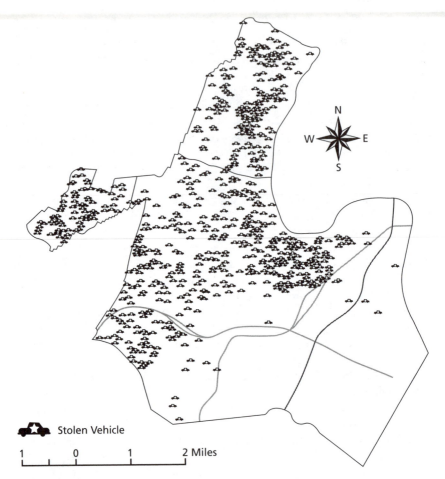

MAP 7.1 Pin Map of Auto Thefts in Newark
For clarity map shows a random selection of only
30% of stolen vehicles over a 6-month period.

Courtesy of Erika Poulsen, Rutgers—School of Criminal Justice.

GIS, focusing on the mapping of hot spots and the layering of sociodemo-
graphic characteristics that is possible using different geo-referenced databases.

As a preliminary step, the auto thefts in Newark were pin-mapped, verify-
ing that the distribution of these crimes was quite widespread throughout the
whole community (see Map 7.1). Density maps were then produced, which
showed a concentration of crimes in five primary areas. These areas, which accounted for 30 to 40 percent of all of the crimes that occurred in a 6-month
period, became the focal point of discussion for the class. Next, the police commanders were asked to describe these areas. One was a location that contained
a train station with a number of parking lots for New York–bound commuters.
The commanders said that these lots were likely not very well lit and that when
the lots were full, people parked their cars on the street. Of interest to the po-

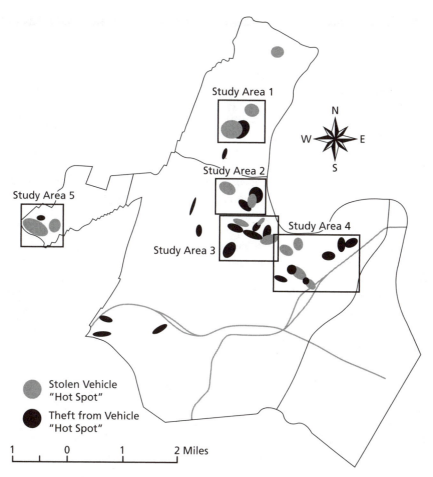

MAP 7.2 Study Areas of Auto Theft in Newark

Courtesy of Erika Poulsen, Rutgers—School of Criminal Justice.

lice was the location of the recovered car (about 50 percent were found in the city) and the time of the day of the offense. Time is important, because the vehicles are left parked in different areas at different times based on the activities of their owners—for example, commuting or visiting restaurants. The crime of auto theft clearly occurs over some period of time, especially because the car is taken someplace else. Determining the exact times that the car is both stolen and abandoned is of great difficulty for the police.

The study team was able to provide the time and location information from police records but encouraged the police to look more closely at the study areas to establish what factors might be contributing to this crime and to come up with solutions for stopping it. It was particularly interesting to compare the area around the train station (Study Area 3, Map 7.2) with a hot spot in a residential area where cars were routinely stolen from the street and from a large parking lot behind a row of high-rise apartments (Study Area 5, Map 7.2).

Whereas the thefts around the train station would be for reselling the cars or stealing their contents, the thefts from the neighborhood were more likely motivated by a desire to joyride or to travel to another part of the city. In other words, the locational factors were important for the crime occurrence. Knowing about what causes these crimes does not necessarily lead to implementing quick solutions to these problems. In discussing some possible remedies, the police felt that there was little they could do about changing important environmental factors, such as increased lighting and adding more security in private parking lots and so on. Strategies such as increased patrol were possible and were used from time to time but required resources not available to the police. The exercise made it clear that the attack on crime opportunities required coordinated efforts on the part of many agencies that can change the urban environment.

Police programs, such as Compstat, have provided a great deal of insight into the effectiveness of police strategies and have been important in holding police commanders accountable for their work. A negative aspect of this type of continuous review, which relies on statistical accounting of crime, is that the police are pressured to keep the crime rate going down. Because of the pressure, police may resort to aggressive tactics, such as pat-downs in minority neighborhoods. Such tactics have exacted a big price in police-community relations while having a questionable effect on overall crime numbers. Also, the pressure on commanders to fudge numbers to show their successes is extreme. A case reported in New York described a dramatic 19 percent increase in 1999 crime incidents for Fort Greene in Brooklyn at the time of an overall 8 percent drop for the rest of the city. It appears that in the previous year, the police commander for this precinct underreported serious crime in 1998, setting the stage for a sharp rise in 1999. Though the errors were attributed to sloppy record keeping, the police commissioner expressed suspicion that the commander kept reported crimes down in an effort to show successes in police efforts in this area (Forero, 2000). Interestingly enough, this area of Brooklyn was undergoing a real renaissance, partly because of the belief that crime was under control.

The flexibility of the Compstat data system is evident in the newfound uses for information that it provides. In an interview, a newly appointed commissioner of the New York Police Department said that he could improve police behavior and mend community police relations through the use of the key tool in fighting against crime—Compstat. As Herbert (2001) points out, the department has begun to look at civilian complaints: "Borough and precinct commanders will not just be quizzed at Compstat meetings about the robberies, rapes, murders, and other mayhem occurring in their areas. They will also be grilled about the complaints that local residents may be making about the officers under their command." This type of accountability shows the flexibility of the data management system, which tracks police work as well as the impact that the police are having on the community. Increasingly, the police have also begun cooperative activities with community groups in which crime mapping is part of their crime prevention strategies (Rich, 2001).

The police are realizing that crime control, by necessity, requires broadening their mandate once again to include order maintenance or compliance law enforcement (Greene, 1998). However, this notion is being resisted by police agencies that still regard law enforcement as their principal mandate. The internal workings of police organizations are such that peacekeeping and order maintenance functions are seen as residual matters (Bayley, 1994). Real policing, some argue, involves arrest. As Kelling (1999) notes, many people (including many police) view community policing as "soft" policing "comparable to community relations, or worse yet, social work" (Kelling, 1999: 10). However, Kelling notes, the styles of police work associated with crime fighting are inherently more conservative than community policing, which is inherently proactive. Thus, whereas traditional policing requires police to respond to citizen requests for assistance, community policing requires that officers scan for problems, diagnose and try to limit the damage, and restore victim–offender and community relations. The equation of community policing with soft policing, Kelling argues, is troublesome because it supports the view that "real" crime problems require "real" solutions and thus fails to appreciate how community policing styles can prove effective even when crime problems are serious.

CRIME PREVENTION
THROUGH SOCIAL DEVELOPMENT

Crime prevention through social development focuses not on the criminal act but on the serious, repeat offender. As we saw earlier, research suggests that a relatively small number of offenders are responsible for a disproportionately large number of crimes. These offenders begin their criminal careers early in life and end them (if at all) late in life. Over the course of their offending careers, they commit a wide variety of predatory offenses. The research also indicates that these individuals tend to come from disadvantaged backgrounds, that they abuse alcohol and other drugs, and that they have experienced serious family problems as well as school- and employment-related problems.

A range of social problems, from family victimization to poverty and racism, can provide a fertile breeding ground for crime. The building of communities is seen by advocates of the social development approach to be a comprehensive strategy that reduces crime by discouraging potential offenders while at the same time strengthening potential victims. The aim of crime prevention through social development is to correct the criminogenic social conditions that are assumed to be the root causes of crime. Oriented toward the achievement of long-range prevention, this approach seeks to eliminate the underclass from which serious, repeat offenders typically emerge.

Public policy in the area of health care suggests interesting parallels to the issue of crime prevention. One way society can deal with medical problems is to wait until people get sick and then make health care services available to them. Similarly, we can wait until people commit crimes and then use criminal justice resources to catch and then confine or treat them. The use of the word *rehabilitation* in reference to prison programs suggests a quite literal application of the medical model to our thinking about crime and punishment.

In the area of public health, however, most policy planners recognize the value of applying limited resources in a preventive rather than a reactive manner. If we can prevent illness, we won't need to treat it after the fact. For this reason, we are advised to get regular medical checkups, to exercise, and to watch our diets. We might view the problem of crime in a similar way. It is more sensible to take action before crimes occur than after harm has been done. Public health approaches to crime emphasize four basic elements (Anderson, Grandison, and Dyson, 1996; Durant, 1999; Potter and Saltzman, 2000):

- the identification of patterns and epidemics of violence
- epidemiological research on the causes of violence
- design and evaluation of prevention interventions
- implementation of prevention programs

Efforts have been made in the United States to focus on violent crime as one would focus on certain forms of disease (Meredith, 1984). For example, the Atlanta-based Centers for Disease Control and Prevention (CDC) studies violent crime as a form of life-threatening disease. James Mason, a former head of the CDC in Atlanta, has stated that public health measures have been successful in treating poverty-related problems (for example, venereal disease, lead poisoning, and tuberculosis) in the absence of attempts to alleviate the social ills associated with them. The campaign against smoking has been particularly successful. Warnings about the health hazards, the political activism of nonsmokers, demands for nonsmoking areas, and interest in public fitness are all factors that have forced smokers to reconsider their habits (Meredith, 1984).

According to Mason, we can do something about violence without first having to come up with solutions to poverty. Among his recommendations for reducing violence are developing programs that teach people how to handle conflict and restricting the availability of handguns (Meredith, 1984).

The gun control debate is highly contentious. It ranges from the facile observation that "guns don't kill people; people kill people" to evidence that gun control laws appear to have little effect on the amount of homicide by firearms that we see in the United States (Kleck and Patterson, 1989). Nonetheless, controlling guns is viewed by the CDC as a major factor in the successful eradication of violence in the United States.

Guns are the most popular means of committing homicide in the United States. In 1993, for example, 70 percent of homicides were perpetrated using some type of firearm (U.S. Department of Justice, 1994). Moreover, increasing numbers of young people now possess and use guns. The issue of gun control is complicated by those who argue that they have a right to use guns for sporting purposes or that the Second Amendment, which guarantees the right to bear arms, implies that no restrictions on the ownership of weapons are allowed under the Constitution of the United States. Despite such protests, guns provide a symbolic as well as a real threat to the well-being of crime-racked societies.

Under the direction of criminologist Terence Thornberry (Huizinga, Loeber, and Thornberry, 1994), the Rochester Youth Development Study tracked a large cohort of youths in Rochester, New York, over a 54-month period. In addition, data were collected from a variety of social agencies, including the schools, the police, and the courts. Overall, the study provides a thorough picture of adolescent development during the junior and senior high school years.

With respect to guns, the study found that by the ninth and tenth grades, more boys own illegal guns (7 percent) than own legal guns (3 percent). Of the boys who own illegal guns, about half of the whites and African Americans and nearly 90 percent of the Hispanics carry them on a regular basis. A strong relationship exists between owning illegal guns and delinquency. Among illegal gun owners, 74 percent commit street crimes, 24 percent commit gun crimes, and 41 percent use drugs. Boys who own legal guns, however, have much lower rates of delinquency and are even slightly less delinquent than nonowners of guns. The research also showed that socialization into gun ownership is vastly different for legal and illegal gun owners. Those who own legal guns have fathers who own guns for sport and hunting. On the other hand, illegal gun owners are more likely to be gang members.

Public opinion surveys in the United States suggest that many Americans are not opposed to increasing controls on the purchase of handguns. For example, a 1993 poll found that 76 percent of Americans favored stricter firearms control laws, 40 percent favored an outright ban on handguns, and 77 percent favored a ban on assault weapons (Thomas, 1995). Lawmakers have not always acted on these concerns of citizens, although some form of gun control is becoming more politically popular in the United States. For example, the Brady Bill (named for former White House press secretary James Brady, who was wounded in a 1981 assassination attempt on President Ronald Reagan) was passed by Congress in 1994 and provides for a mandatory five-day waiting period in the purchase of handguns. Proposals to ban (and alternatively, to prevent a ban on) a variety of assault, automatic, and semiautomatic weapons have been debated in the legislatures. Many states have also passed laws in recent years that limit the ease with which guns may be purchased. For example, in 1993 the Virginia Legislature approved a measure that limited citizens to the purchase of one gun per month (aimed at reducing or eliminating gunrunning in the state). A public health approach to reducing violence would emphasize educating citizens about the dangers associated with the improper use of firearms.

The notion that crime can be prevented by eliminating the social ills that breed crime (particularly teenage crime) is not new. There is a long history of social reformism that argues that we can best fight crime by fighting poverty, racism, unemployment, and other forms of social disadvantage (Graham, 1990; Rosenbaum, 1988). The social development approach differs from these older approaches in its more systematic efforts to identify and attack the root causes of crime.

Because predatory crime is part of a "tangle of pathologies" (Wilson, 1987) that characterizes the lives of the socially disadvantaged, our policies regarding crime prevention must extend beyond the criminal justice system into the areas of family, educational, housing, and health policy (Graham, 1990). One important theme emphasizes resource mobilization, which addresses crime issues in terms of whether the law helps people, especially the poor and power-less, protect themselves against victimization. Browne and Williams (1989) note that the enactment of domestic violence legislation (which makes arrest of offenders more likely), coupled with high levels of resource mobilization (including the provision of shelters for battered women), tended to reduce the rate of female-perpetrated homicide. That is, the more that women feel empowered to deal with violence directed against them, the less likely they are to react with fatal violence.

Browne and Williams admit that some issues remain unclear. They cannot establish the degree of awareness that individuals have of available resources. In addition, the researchers have no way of measuring the accessibility that individual women have to the mandated resources. Further, it is not clear how many people actually use the resources that are available or how effective these resources are in meeting individual needs. What is clear from this research, however, is that where these resources are available, criminal victimization from fatal assaults is lower. This finding provides a strong argument for the need to assess the extent to which society can provide alternatives to women that will enable them to avoid becoming victims.

Advocates of the social development approach see crime prevention not as the exclusive domain of any one social or governmental agency. Instead, they place considerable emphasis on the need to establish crime prevention councils at both the federal and the municipal levels. These councils would bring together those responsible for health, family, employment, and housing policies, as well as the police and voluntary agencies that are concerned with a broad range of social welfare issues. The idea behind such an arrangement is that, through shared ownership of the crime problem, more comprehensive solutions will be developed.

As the body of research relating to crime prevention through social development accumulates, it becomes clear that some important principles should guide such interventions, including the following (Prinz, 2000):

Intervene early. Research suggests that the risks of becoming delinquent develop early in childhood. For youths at greatest risk, waiting until adolescence to intervene may be too late.

Intervene in multiple settings. Interventions that simultaneously occur in schools, in the home, in the peer group, and in the neighborhood are preferred to interventions that occur in only one setting. For one thing, children will be more responsive to lessons that are reinforced across settings.

Move beyond the individual child, taking larger contexts into account. Children do not function in a vacuum. Family, peer, and classroom contexts are integrally related to a child's functioning.

Motivate children, teachers, and parents. Failure to reinforce the exhibition by parents and teachers of desired behaviors is a common reason for program failure.

Set and enforce appropriate limits. Programs must be prepared to sanction negative behavior as well as to reward positive behavior.

Use modeling as a positive influence. It is essential that children have adequate access to pro-social behaviors that can be modeled.

Involve the community. The level of violence in schools or in homes is related to the character and viability of the larger community. It is important therefore that prevention efforts take the community into account.

Provide adequate alternatives. Effective programming must provide positive alternatives to aggression and violence.

Although the social development approach has proven more popular in some European countries than in North America, it is clearly gaining momentum in North America. However, some advocates of opportunity reduction maintain that the social development strategy fails to recognize that crime is not a homogeneous event and that different crimes require different intervention strategies (Brantingham, 1989).

Other critics question whether we have the political will or are truly prepared to make the financial commitments that a comprehensive social development approach might entail. We might also ask if the linkages that social development advocates draw between factors such as family upbringing, employment, and school experience are as obvious and as straightforward as they are sometimes made out to be. The list of causative factors to which the social development approach draws our attention is long and unwieldy, and as we have seen, there is honest debate among criminologists about the relative importance of these factors (Graham, 1990).

Thus, although the tendency is to group together all "positive" interventions as likely to reduce crime, the empirical record suggests otherwise. For example, preschool and weekly home visits by teachers, and parent training about risk factors for delinquency, may reduce youthful engagement in crime, but subsidized work programs for at-risk youth may not (Sherman et al., 1998). Though all of these social development initiatives might have some merit and therefore be worthy of public support, it does not follow that they are equally likely to reduce crime.

For purposes of presentation, we have drawn a distinction between opportunity reduction and social development, but these two approaches are not in an inherent conflict. In the same way that we have borrowed from different theories to explain criminal events, we can borrow from these different perspectives to create an integrated approach to crime prevention. In fact, many policymakers have advocated a combination of these strategies, along with community policing, to form an integrated approach.

SUMMARY

One response to crime is to see it as a public health problem that is best addressed by removing some of the major instruments that bring about injury (for example, guns). A second view advocates the mobilization of social institutions and resources as a means of empowering victims to defend themselves against criminal attack. Given the already formidable challenges that public health institutions face in dealing with diseases and injuries that originate from non-crime sources, our heavy reliance on the police to confront the crime problem is unlikely to change, at least in the near future.

Prevention can include a number of elements, ranging from target hardening to increased surveillance. It can also set the targeting of violence as a priority and offer ways in which violence can be averted. Situational prevention is based on two main assumptions. The first is that crime is most effectively prevented when we attend to the particular characteristics of the type of crime in question. The second is that in most cases we are dealing with a rational offender, who calculates such things as risks, benefits, and ease of accomplishment before committing a crime. Thus it follows that raising the costs associated with crimes (which are largely opportunistic in nature) may reduce the frequency with which they occur. Neighborhood Watch and Block Watch programs assume that crime can be prevented by increasing surveillance and, by extension, increasing the risk of detection and apprehension, as it is perceived by the potential offender.

In contrast to the other prevention strategies, crime prevention through social development focuses on the serious, repeat offender. A relatively small number of offenders may be responsible for a disproportionately large number of crimes. These individuals tend to have in common many social and demographic characteristics. The aim of crime prevention through social development is to correct the criminogenic social conditions that are assumed to be important causes of crime. The focus of the social development approach is on long-range outcomes that enhance social security and reduce crime incidence.

The police are shifting their attention from crime fighting (that is, deterrence-based policing) to compliance policing, which is more directly integrated into the community. The principal objective of compliance law enforcement is to secure conformity with law through systems that encourage community participation in defining and solving problems. The former emphasis on the detection and punishment of violators has given way to an emphasis on the need to provide incentives to individuals as a means of encouraging them to comply with the law.

Compliance-based policing recognizes the need to include the public in controlling social disorder, beyond merely reporting crime to the police. Bringing together a number of services within the community, as well as community members, can help to form a multipronged attack on crime involving reeducation, mediation, opportunity removal, resource mobilization, the targeting of the roots of crime, and problem solving. Our success in controlling crime and diminishing the incidence of criminal events depends on our ability to understand where crime comes from and on our commitment to expend resources in broadening our responses to it.

References

Abbott, A. 1997. "Of Time and Space: The Contemporary Relevance of the Chicago School." *Social Forces* 75(4): 1149–1182.

Agnew, R. S. 1985. "A Revised Strain Theory of Delinquency." *Social Forces* 64(1): 151–167.

Agnew, R. S., and S. Huguley. 1989. "Adolescent Violence toward Parents." *Journal of Marriage and the Family* 51: 699–711.

Agnew, R. S., and D. M. Peterson. 1989. "Leisure and Delinquency." *Social Problems* 36(4): 332–350.

Akers, R. L. 1985. *Deviant Behavior: A Social Learning Approach*. Belmont, Calif.: Wadsworth.

Allan, E. A., and D. J. Steffensmeier. 1989. "Youth, Underemployment, and Property Crime: Differential Effects of Job Availability and Job Quality on Juvenile and Young Adult Arrest Rates." *American Sociological Review* 54: 107–123.

Amir, M. 1971. *Patterns of Forcible Rape*. Chicago: University of Chicago Press.

Anderson, J. F., T. Grandison, and L. Dyson. 1996. "Victims of Random Violence and the Public Health Implication: A Health Care or Criminal Justice Issue." *Journal of Criminal Justice* 24(5): 379–391.

Anselin, L., J. Cohen, D. Cook, W. Gorr, and G. Tita. 2000. "Spatial Analyses of Crime." In D. Duffee (ed.), *Measurement and Analysis of Crime and Justice*, vol. 4 of *Criminal Justice 2000*, pp. 213–262. Washington, D.C.: National Institute of Justice.

Arnold, B. L., and J. Hagan. 1992. "Careers of Misconduct: Prosecuted Professional Deviance among Lawyers." *American Sociological Review* 57(6): 771–780.

Barker, R., and P. Schoggen. 1973. *Qualities of Community Life*. San Francisco: Jossey-Bass.

Baron, S. 1997. "Risky Lifestyles and the Link between Offending and Victimization." *Studies on Crime and Crime Prevention* 6(1): 53–71.

———. 1989. "The Canadian West Coast Punk Subculture: A Field Study." *Canadian Journal of Sociology* 14(3): 289–316.

Baron, S., and L. W. Kennedy. 1998. "Deterrence and Homeless Male Street Youths." *Canadian Journal of Criminology* 40(1): 27–60.

Baumer, T. L. 1978. "Research on Fear of Crime in the United States." *Victimology* 3: 254–264.

Baunach, P. J. 1990. "State Prisons and Inmates: The Census and Survey." In D. L. Mackenzie, P. J. Baunach, and R. R. Roberg (eds.), *Measuring Crime: Large-Scale, Long-Range Efforts.* Albany: State University of New York Press.

Bayley, D. H. 1994. *Police for the Future.* New York: Oxford University Press.

———. 1988. "Community Policing: A Report from the Devil's Advocate." In J. R. Greene and D. Mastrofski (eds.), *Community Policing: Rhetoric or Reality?* New York: Praeger.

———. 1986. "The Tactical Choices of Police Patrol Officers." *Journal of Criminal Justice* 14: 329–348.

———. 1985. *Patterns of Policing: A Comparative International Analysis.* New Brunswick, N.J.: Rutgers University Press.

Beare, M. E. 1996. *Criminal Conspiracies.* Scarborough, Ont.: Nelson Canada.

Beck, A. J. 2000. *Prisoners in 1999.* Washington, D.C.: U.S. Department of Justice.

Becker, H. S. 1963. *Outsiders: Studies in the Sociology of Deviance.* New York: Free Press.

Bell, D. 1953. "Crime as an American Way of Life." *Antioch Review* 13 (June): 131–154.

Bell, D. J. 1987. "The Victim-Offender Relationship: A Determinant Factor in Police Domestic Dispute Dispositions." *Marriage and Family Review* 12(1–2): 87–102.

Bennett, T. 1989. "Burglar's Choice of Targets." In D. J. Evans and D. T. Herbert (eds.), *The Geography of Crime,* pp. 176-192. London: Routledge.

Bennett, T., and R. Wright. 1984. *Burglars on Burglary.* Brookfield, Vt.: Gower.

Benson, M. L. 1985. "Denying the Guilty Mind: Accounting for Involvement in a White-Collar Crime." *Criminology* 23(4): 583–607.

Benson, M. L., and E. Moore. 1992. "Are White-Collar and Common Offenders the Same? An Empirical and Theoretical Critique of a Recently Proposed General Theory of Crime." *Journal of Research in Crime and Delinquency* 29(3): 251–272.

Bernard, T. J. 1981. "The Distinction between Conflict and Radical Criminology." *Journal of Criminal Law and Criminology* 72(1): 362–379.

Best, J. 1999. *Random Violence: How We Talk about New Crimes and New Victims.* Berkeley and Los Angeles: University of California Press.

———. 1990. *Threatened Children.* Chicago: University of Chicago Press.

Birkbeck, C., and G. LaFree. 1993. "The Situational Analysis of Crime and Deviance." *Annual Review of Sociology* 19: 113–137.

Black, D. J. 1983. "Crime as Social Control." *American Sociological Review* 48 (February): 34–45.

———. 1980. *The Manners and Customs of the Police.* New York: Academic Press.

———. 1976. *The Behavior of Law.* New York: Academic Press.

———. 1970. "Production of Crime Rates." *American Sociological Review* 35: 733–747.

Block, C. R., and R. L. Block. 1984. "Crime Definition, Crime Measurement, and Victim Surveys." *Journal of Social Issues* 40(1): 137–160.

Block, R., M. Felson, and C. R. Block. 1984. "Crime Victimization Rates for Incumbents of 246 Occupations." *Sociology and Social Research* 69(3): 442–451.

Blumstein, A., and J. Wallman. 2000. *Crime Rate Drops.* New York: Cambridge University Press.

Blumstein, A., J. Cohen, and D. P. Farrington. 1988a. "Criminal Career Research: Its Value for Criminology." *Criminology* 26(1): 1–36.

———. 1988b. "Longitudinal and Criminal Career Research: Further Clarifications." *Criminology* 26(1): 57–74.

Blumstein, A., J. Cohen, and R. Rosenfeld. 1992. "The UCR-NCS Relationship Revisited: A Reply to Menard." *Criminology* 30(1): 115–124.

Bockman, L. S. 1991. "Interest, Ideology, and Claims-Making Activity." *Sociological Inquiry* 61(4): 452–470.

Box, S. 1981. *Deviance, Reality, and Society.* London: Holt, Rinehart & Winston.

Boyd, N. 2000. "Canadian Criminal Law." In R. A. Silverman, J. J. Teevan, and V. F. Sacco (eds.), *Crime in Canadian Society,* 6th ed., pp. 20–31. Toronto: Harcourt Brace.

Braithwaite, J. 1981. "The Myth of Social Class and Criminality Reconsidered." *American Sociological Review* 46 (February): 36–57.

Brantingham, P. L. 1989. "Crime Prevention: The North American Experience." In D. J. Evans and D. T. Herbert (eds.), *The Geography of Crime.* London: Routledge.

Brantingham, P., and P. Brantingham. 2001. "The Implications of a Criminal Event Model for Crime Prevention." In R. F. Meier, L. W. Kennedy, and V. F. Sacco (eds.) *The Process and Structure of Crime.* Volume 9 of Advances in Criminological Theory. Piscataway, N.J.: Transaction Press.

———. 1999. "A Theoretical Model of Crime Hot Spot Generation." *Studies on Crime and Crime Prevention* 8(1): 7–26.

———. 1990. "Situational Crime Prevention in Practice." *Canadian Journal of Criminology* 32(1): 17–40.

———. 1984. *Patterns in Crime.* New York: Macmillan.

Brantingham, P. J., and F. L. Faust. 1976. "A Conceptual Model of Crime Prevention." *Crime and Delinquency* 22: 284–296.

Browne, A., and K. Williams. 1989. "Exploring the Effect of Resource Availability and the Likelihood of Female-Perpetrated Homicides." *Law and Society Review* 23(1): 75–94.

Burgess, A. W., L. L. Holmstrom, and M. P. McCausland. 1977. "Child Sexual Assault by a Family Member: Decisions Following Disclosure." *Victimology* 2(2): 236–250.

Bursik, R. J., Jr., and H. G. Grasmick. 1993. *Neighborhoods and Crime: The Dimensions of Effective Community Control.* New York: Lexington Books.

Burt, M. R., and B. L. Katz. 1985. "Rape, Robbery, and Burglary: Responses to Actual and Feared Criminal Victimization with Special Focus on Women and the Elderly." *Victimology* 10: 325–358.

Calavita, K., and H. N. Pontell. 1991. "'Other People's Money' Revisited: Collective Embezzlement in the Savings and Loan Insurance Industries." *Social Problems* 38(1): 94–112.

Calhoun, T. C., and G. Weaver. 1996. "Rational Decision-Making among Male Street Prostitutes." *Deviant Behavior* 17: 209–227.

Campbell, G. 1990. "Women and Crime." *Juristat Service Bulletin* 10(20): 1–9. Ottawa: Canadian Centre for Justice Statistics.

Cantor, D., and K. C. Land. 1985. "Unemployment and Crime Rates in the Post–World War II United States: A Theoretical and Empirical Analysis." *American Sociological Review* 50 (June): 317–332.

Cater, J., and T. Jones. 1989. "Crime and Disorder." In J. Cater and T. Jones (eds.), *Social Geography—An Introduction to Contemporary Issues.* New York: Routledge, Chapman & Hall.

Centers for Disease Control and Prevention. 2001. Retrieved from http://www.cdc.gov/

Chaiken, J., and M. Chaiken. 1982. *Varieties of Criminal Behavior.* Rand Report r-2814-NIJ. Santa Monica, Calif.: Rand Corporation.

Chambliss, W. J. 1986. "On Lawmaking." In S. Brickey and E. Comack (eds.), *The Social Basis of Law.* Toronto: Garamond Press.

Chambliss, W. 1975. "On the Paucity of Original Research on Organized Crime: A Footnote to Gallihor and Cain." *American Sociologist* 10: 36–39.

Chiricos, T. G. 1987. "Rates of Crime and Unemployment: An Analysis of Aggregate Research Evidence." *Social Problems* 34(2): 187–242.

Clarke, R. V. 1992. "Introduction." In R. V. Clarke (ed.), *Situational Crime Prevention.* Albany, N.Y.: Harrow and Heston.

Clarke, R. V., and M. Felson. 1993. *Routine Activity and Rational Choice.* Vol. 5 of *Advances in Criminological Theory.* New Brunswick, N.J.: Transaction Publishers.

Cohen, L. E., and D. Cantor. 1981. "Residential Burglary in the United States: Lifestyle and Demographic Factors Associated with the Probability of Victimization." *Journal of Research in Crime and Delinquency* 18(1): 113–127.

Cohen, L. E., and M. Felson. 1979. "Social Change and Crime Rate Trends: A Routine Activity Approach." *American Sociological Review* 44 (August): 588–608.

Cohen, L. E., J. R. Kluegel, and K. C. Land. 1981. "Social Inequality and Predatory Criminal Victimization: An Exposition and Test of a Formal Theory." *American Sociological Review* 46 (October): 505–524.

Coleman, J. W. 1991. "Respectable Crime." In J. F. Sheley (ed.), *Criminology: A Contemporary Handbook.* Belmont, Calif.: Wadsworth.

———. 1987. "Toward an Integrated Theory of White-Collar Crime." *American Journal of Sociology* 93(2): 406–439.

Collins, J. J., B. G. Cox, and P. A. Langan. 1987. "Job Activities and Personal Crime Victimization: Implications for Theory." *Social Science Research* 16: 345–360.

Conklin, J. E. 1975. *The Impact of Crime.* New York: Macmillan.

Cornish, D. B., and R. V. Clarke. 1986. *The Reasoning Criminal.* New York: Springer-Verlag.

Cressey, D. R. 1969. *Theft of the Nation.* New York: Harper and Row.

Croall, H. 1987. "Who Is the White-Collar Criminal?" *British Journal of Criminology* 29(2): 157–174.

Cromwell, P. F., J. N. Olson, and D. W. Avary. 1991. *Breaking and Entering: An Ethnographic Analysis of Burglary.* Newbury Park, Calif.: Sage.

Currie, E. 1985. *Confronting Crime: An American Challenge.* New York: Pantheon.

Cusson, M. 1993. "Situational Deterrence: Fear during the Criminal Event." In R. V. Clarke (ed.), *Crime Prevention Studies,* vol. 1. Monsey, N.Y.: Criminal Justice Press.

Davis, P. W. 1991. "Stranger Intervention into Child Punishment in Public Places." *Social Problems* 38(2): 227–246.

DeKeseredy, W. S. 1988. *Woman Abuse in Dating Relationships: A Critical Evaluation of Research and Theory.* Toronto: Canadian Scholar's Press.

DeKeseredy, W. S., and R. Hinch. 1991. *Woman Abuse: Sociological Perspectives.* Ottawa: Thompson Educational Publishing.

Desroches, F. J. 1995. *Force and Fear: Robbery in Canada.* Toronto: Nelson Canada.

———. 1991. "Tearoom Trade: A Law Enforcement Problem." *Canadian Journal of Criminology* 33(1): 1–21.

"Driveby Shooting at Park Pool Leaves One Dead, Four Hurt in Cicero." 1993. *Chicago Tribune* (July 21), sec. 2, p. 2.

Dubow, F. E., E. McCabe, and G. Kaplan. 1979. *Reactions to Crime: A Critical Review of the Literature.* Washington, D.C.: U.S. Department of Justice.

Durant, T. J. 1999. "Violence as a Public Health Problem: Toward an Integrated Paradigm." *Sociological Spectrum* 19: 267–280.

Durkheim, É. 1933. *The Division of Labor in Society.* Trans. G. Simpson. Glencoe, Ill.: Free Press.

Dutton, D. G. 1987. "The Criminal Justice Response to Wife Assault." *Law and Human Behavior* 11(3): 189–206.

Eck, J. E. 2001. "Problem-Oriented Policing and Crime Event Concentration." In R. F. Meier, L. W. Kennedy, and V. F. Sacco (eds.), *The Process and Structure of Crime,* vol. 9 of *Advances in Criminological Theory.* Piscataway, N.J.: Transaction Press.

Eck, J., and D. Weisburd. 1995. *Crime and Place.* Monsey, N.Y.: Criminal Justice Press.

Eck, J., J. S. Gersh, and C. Taylor. 2000. "Finding Hot Spots through Repeat Address Mapping." In V. Goldsmith, P. G. McGuire, J. H. Mollenkopf, and T. A. Ross, *Analysing Crime Patterns: Frontiers of Practice,* pp. 49–63. Thousand Oaks, Calif.: Sage.

Ericson, R. V., and J. Haggerty. 1997. *Policing the Risk Society.* Toronto: University of Toronto Press.

Evans, D. J. 1989. "Geographical Analyses of Residential Burglary." In D. J. Evans and D. T. Herbert (eds.), *The Geography of Crime.* London: Routledge.

"Ex Bank Manager Gets Twenty-Four Years in Drug Money Case." 1993. *Los Angeles Times* (July 21), p. B2.

Fagan, J., and R. B. Freeman. 1999. "Crime and Work." *Crime and Justice* 25: 113–178.

Fagan, J., and S. Wexler. 1987. "Family Origins of Violent Delinquents." *Criminology* 25(4): 643–669.

Farberman, H. A. 1975. "A Criminogenic Market Structure: The Automobile Industry." *Sociological Quarterly* 16: 438–457.

Farrell, G. 1995. "Preventing Repeat Victimization." In M. Tonry and D. P. Farrington (eds.), *Building a Safer Society,* vol. 19 of *Crime and Justice.* Chicago: University of Chicago Press.

Farrell, G., C. Phillips, and K. Pease. 1995. "Like Taking Candy: Why Does Repeat Victimization Occur?" *British Journal of Criminology* 35(3): 384–399.

Farrington, D. P. 1989. "Implications of Longitudinal Studies for Social Prevention." *Canadian Journal of Criminology* 31(4): 453–463.

Fattah, E. A. 1991. *Understanding Criminal Victimization.* Scarborough, Ont.: Prentice-Hall.

Fattah, E. A., and V. F. Sacco. 1989. *Crime and Victimization of the Elderly.* New York: Springer-Verlag.

Federal Bureau of Investigation (FBI). 2000. *The Structure of Family Violence: An Analysis of Selected Incidents.* Washington, D.C.: FBI.

Feld, S. L., and M. A. Straus. 1990. "Escalation and Desistance from Wife Assault in Marriage." In M. A. Straus and R. J. Gelles (eds.), *Physical Violence in American Families: Risk Factors and Adaptations to Violence in 8,145 Families.* New Brunswick, N.J.: Transaction Publishers.

Felson, M. 1998. *Crime in Everyday Life,* 2d ed. Thousand Oaks, Calif.: Pine Forge Press.

———. 1992. "Routine Activities and Crime Prevention." *Studies in Crime and Crime Prevention Annual Review* 1(1): 30–34.

———. 1987. "Routine Activities and Crime Prevention in the Developing Metropolis." *Criminology* 25(4): 911–931.

Felson, M., and R. V. Clarke. 1998. "Opportunity Makes the Thief: Practical Theory for Crime Prevention." London: Home Office Police Research Series, Paper 98.

Ferraro, K. J., and J. M. Johnson. 1983. "How Women Experience Battering: The Process of Victimization." *Social Problems* 30: 325–335.

Figlio, R. M. 1990. "Measurement in Criminology and Criminal Justice: A Brief Twenty-Year Retrospective." In D. L. MacKenzie, D. J. Baunach, and R. R. Roberg (eds.), *Measuring Crime: Large-Scale, Long-Range Efforts.* Albany: State University of New York Press.

Finkelhor, D., G. T. Hotaling, and A. Sedlak. 1990. *Missing, Abducted, Runaway, and Thrownaway Children in America: First Report.* Washington, D.C.: Juvenile Justice Clearinghouse.

Fischer, C. S. 1981. "The Public and Private Worlds of City Life." *American Sociological Review* 46 (June): 306–316.

Fleisher, M. S. 1995. *Beggars and Thieves: Lives of Urban Street Criminals*. Madison: University of Wisconsin Press.

Flowers, R. B. 1989. *Demographics and Criminality: The Characteristics of Crime in America*. New York: Greenwood Press.

Forero, Juan. 2000. "Precinct's Rosy Crime Rate Was a Distortion, the Police Say." *New York Times* (January 7), p. B1.

Fox, J. A., and J. Levin. 2001. *The Will to Kill: Making Sense of Senseless Murder*. Boston: Allyn and Bacon.

Freudenheim, M. 1987. "Business and Health." *New York Times* (May 26).

Friedrichs, D. O. 1996. *Trusted Criminals*. Belmont, Calif.: Wadsworth.

Frieze, I. H., and A. Browne. 1989. "Violence in Marriage." In L. Ohlin and M. Tonry (eds.), *Family Violence*. Chicago: University of Chicago Press.

Furstenberg, F. 1971. "Public Reactions to Crime in the Streets." *American Scholar* 40: 601–610.

Gabor, T. 1990. "Crime Displacement and Situational Prevention: Toward the Development of Some Principles." *Canadian Journal of Criminology* 32(1): 41–73.

Garofalo, J., and M. McLeod. 1988. *Improving the Use and Effectiveness of Neighborhood Watch Programs*. Washington, D.C.: U.S. Department of Justice.

Garofalo, J., L. Siegel, and J. Laub. 1987. "School-Related Victimizations among Adolescents: An Analysis of National Crime Survey (NCS) Narratives." *Journal of Quantitative Criminology* 3(4): 321–338.

Gates, L. B., and W. M. Rohe. 1987. "Fear and Reactions to Crime: A Revised Model." *Urban Affairs Quarterly* 22: 425–453.

Gelles, R. J., and M. A. Straus. 1988. *Intimate Violence*. New York: Simon and Schuster.

Gill, Martin. 1994. *Crime at Work: Studies in Security and Crime Prevention*. Leicester, U.K.: Perpetuity Press.

Gilsinan, J. F. 1990. *Criminology and Public Policy: An Introduction*. Englewood Cliffs, N.J.: Prentice-Hall.

Giordano, P. C., S. A. Cernkovich, and M. D. Pugh. 1986. "Friendships and Delinquency." *American Journal of Sociology* 91(5): 1170–1202.

Goff, C., and N. Nason-Clark. 1989. "The Seriousness of Crime in Fredericton, New Brunswick: Perceptions toward White-Collar Crime." *Canadian Journal of Criminology* 31(1): 19–34.

Goffman, E. 1959. *The Presentation of Self in Everyday Life*. Garden City, N.J.: Doubleday.

Golant, S. M. 1984. "Factors Influencing the Nighttime Activity of Old Persons in Their Community." *Journal of Gerontology* 39: 485–491.

Goldstein, H. 1990. *Problem-Oriented Policing*. Philadelphia: Temple University Press.

Goodstein, L., and R. L. Shotland. 1982. "The Crime Causes Crime Model: A Critical Review of the Relationship between Fear of Crime, Bystander Surveillance, and Changes in the Crime Rate." *Victimology* 5(2–4): 133–151.

Gottfredson, M. R. 1984. *Victims of Crime: The Dimensions of Risk*. Home Office Research and Planning Unit Report. London: HMSO Books.

Gottfredson, M. R., and T. Hirschi. 1990. *A General Theory of Crime*. Stanford, Calif.: Stanford University Press.

Gould, L. C. 1989. "Crime, Criminality, and Criminal Events." Paper presented at the annual meeting of the American Society of Criminology, Reno, Nevada (November).

Gove, W. R., M. Hughes, and M. Geerken. 1985. "Are Uniform Crime Reports a Valid Indicator of the Index Crimes? An Affirmative Answer with Minor Modifications." *Criminology* 23(3): 451–501.

Graham, J. 1990. *Crime Prevention Strategies in Europe and North America.* Helsinki, Fin.: Helsinki Institute for Crime Prevention and Control.

Gramling, R., C. Forsyth, and J. Fewell. 1988. "Crime and Economic Activity: A Research Note." *Sociological Spectrum* 8: 187–195.

Grattet, R., V. Jenness, and T. R. Curry. 1998. "The Homogenization and Differentiation of Hate Crime Law in the United States, 1978 to 1995: Innovation and Diffusion in the Criminalization of Bigotry." *American Sociological Review* 63: 286–307.

Gray, H. 1989. "Popular Music as a Sound Problem: A Social History of the Claims against Popular Music." In J. Best (ed.), *Images of Issues.* New York: Aldine de Gruyter.

Greene, J. 1998. "Evaluating Planned Change Strategies in Modern Law Enforcement: Implementing Community-Based Policing." In J.-P. Brodeur (ed.), *How to Recognize Good Policing: Problems and Issues,* pp. 141–160. Thousand Oaks, Calif.: Sage.

Gurr, T. R. 1980. "Development and Decay: Their Impact on Public Order in Western History." In J. Inciardi and C. E. Faupel (eds.), *History and Crime.* Beverly Hills, Calif.: Sage.

Gusfield, J. 1989. "Constructing the Ownership of Social Problems: Fun and Profit in the Welfare State." *Social Problems* 36(5): 431–441.

Hagan, J. 1992. "White Collar and Corporate Crime." In R. Linden (ed.), *Criminology: A Canadian Perspective.* Toronto: Harcourt Brace Jovanovich.

———. 1985. *Modern Criminology.* New York: McGraw-Hill.

Hagan, J., A. R. Gillis, and J. H. Simpson. 1985. "The Class Structure of Gender and Delinquency: Toward a Power-Control Theory of Common Delinquent Behavior." *American Journal of Sociology* 90(6): 1151–1178.

Haller, M. H. 1992. "Bureaucracy and the Mafia: An Alternative View." *Journal of Contemporary Criminal Justice* 8: 1–10.

———. 1990. "Illegal Enterprise: A Theoretical and Historical Interpretation." *Criminology* 28(2): 207–235.

Hans, V. P., and D. Ermann. 1989. "Responses to Corporate versus Individual Wrongdoing." *Law and Human Behavior* 13(2): 151–166.

Harlow, C. W. 1991. *Female Victims of Violent Crime.* Washington, D.C.: U.S. Department of Justice.

Harries, K. 2000. "Filters, Fears, and Photos: Speculations and Explorations in the Geography of Crime." In V. Goldsmith, P. Maguire, and J. Mollenkopf (eds.), *Analyzing Crime Patterns,* 23–32. Thousand Oaks, Calif.: Sage.

Harris, D. A. 1999. *Driving While Black: Racial Profiling on Our Nation's Highways.* Washington, D.C.: American Civil Liberties Union.

Harris, M. K. 1991. "Moving into the New Millennium: Toward a Feminist Vision of Peace." In H. E. Pepinsky and R. Quinney (eds.), *Criminology as Peacemaking,* pp. 83–97. Bloomington: Indiana University Press.

Hartman, D. P., D. M. Gelfand, B. Page, and P. Walder. 1972. "Rates of Bystander Observation and Reporting of Contrived Shoplifting Incidents." *Criminology* 10(3): 247–267.

Hartnagel, T. F. 1992. "Correlates of Criminal Behaviour." In R. Linden (ed.), *Criminology: A Canadian Perspective.* Toronto: Harcourt Brace Jovanovich.

Hartnagel, T. F., and H. Krahn. 1989. "High School Dropouts, Labor Market Success, and Criminal Behavior." *Youth and Society* 20(4): 416–444.

Hasell, M. J., and F. D. Peatross. 1990. "Exploring Connections between Women's Changing Roles and House Forms." *Environment and Behavior* 22(1): 3–26.

"Helping to Eliminate Stress in the Workplace." 1994. *Business and Health* 12(4) (Depression Supplement): 28–31.

Hennigen, K. M., L. Heath, J. D. Wharton, M. L. Del Resario, T. D. Cook, and B. J. Calder. 1982. "Impact of the Introduction of Television on Crime in the United States: Empirical Findings and Theoretical Implications." *Journal of Personality and Social Psychology* 42(3): 461–477.

Herbert, D. 2001. "A Way to Find the Bad Cops." *New York Times* (March 19), p. A19.

Hindelang, M. J., M. R. Gottfredson, and J. Garofalo. 1978. *Victims of Personal Crime: An Empirical Foundation for a Theory of Personal Victimization.* Cambridge, Mass.: Ballinger.

Hindelang, M. J., T. Hirschi, and J. Weis. 1981. *Measuring Delinquency.* Beverly Hills, Calif.: Sage.

Hocker, Joyce L., and William W. Wilmot. 1985. *Interpersonal Conflict.* 2d ed. Dubuque, Iowa: William C. Brown.

Hope, T. 1995. "The Flux of Victimization." *British Journal of Criminology* 35(3): 327–342.

Hotaling, G. T., and M. A. Straus (with A. J. Lincoln). 1990. "Intrafamily Violence and Crime and Violence outside the Family." In M. A. Straus and R. J. Gelles (eds.), *Physical Violence in American Families: Risk Factors and Adaptations to Violence in 8,145 Families.* New Brunswick, N.J.: Transaction Publishers.

Hough, M. 1987. "Offenders' Choice of Target: Findings from Victim Surveys." *Journal of Quantitative Criminology* 3(4): 355–370.

Howitt, D. 1998. *Crime, the Media, and the Law.* New York: Wiley.

Huizinga D., R. Loeber, and T. P. Thornberry. 1994. *Urban Delinquency and Substance Abuse: Initial Findings.* Washington, D.C.: U.S. Department of Justice.

Ianni, F. A. J. 1971. "The Mafia and the Web of Kinship." *Public Interest* 16: 78–100.

Ianni, F. A. J., and E. Reuss-Ianni. 1972. *A Family Business: Kinship and Social Control in Organized Crime.* New York: Russell Sage Foundation.

Innes, C. A., and L. A. Greenfeld. 1990. *Violent State Prisoners and Their Victims.* Bureau of Justice Statistics Special Report. Washington, D.C.: U.S. Department of Justice.

Iso-Ahola, S. 1980. *The Social Psychology of Leisure and Recreation.* Dubuque, Iowa: William C. Brown.

Jackson, M. 1989. "The Clinical Assessment and Prediction of Violent Behaviour: Toward a Scientific Analysis." *Criminal Justice and Behavior* 16(1): 114–131.

Jackson, P. G. 1990. "Sources of Data." In K. L. Kempf (ed.), *Measurement Issues in Criminology.* New York: Springer-Verlag.

Jacobs, J. B. 1999. *Gotham Unbound: How New York Was Liberated from the Grip of Organized Crime.* New York: New York University Press.

Jang, S., and B. Johnson. 2001. "Neighborhood Disorder, Individual Religiosity, and Adolescent Use of Illicit Drugs: A Test of Multilevel Hypotheses." *Criminology* 39(1): 109–144.

Janoff-Bulman, R., and I. H. Frieze. 1983. "A Theoretical Perspective for Understanding Reactions to Victimization." *Journal of Social Issues* 39(2): 1–17.

Jensen, G. F., and D. Brownfield. 1986. "Gender, Lifestyles, and Victimization: Beyond Routine Activity." *Violence and Victims* 1(2): 85–99.

Johnson, I. M., and R. T. Sigler. 2000. "Public Perceptions: The Stability of the Public's Endorsements of the Definition and Criminalization of the Abuse of Women." *Journal of Criminal Justice* 28: 165–179.

Johnson, M., and K. Ferraro. 2000. "Research on Domestic Violence in the 1990s: Making Distinctions." *Journal of Marriage and the Family* 62(4): 948–963.

Johnson, S. D., K. Bowers, and A. Hirschfield. 1997. "New Insights into the Spatial and Temporal Distribution of Repeat Victimization." *British Journal of Criminology* 37: 224–241.

Jonassen, C. T. 1949. "A Re-evaluation and Critique of the Logic and Some Methods of Shaw and McKay." *American Sociological Review* 14 (October): 608–614.

Jupp, V. 1989. *Methods of Criminological Research.* London: Unwin Hyman.

Kantor, G. K., and M. A. Straus. 1987. "The Drunken Bum Theory of Wife Beating." *Social Problems* 34(2): 213–230.

Kappeler, V. E., M. Blumberg, and G. W. Potter. 2000. *The Mythology of Crime and Criminal Justice,* 3d ed. Prospect Heights, Ill.: Waveland Press.

Karasek, R., and T. Theorell. 1990. *Health Work.* New York: Basic Books.

Keane, C. 1991. "Corporate Crime." In R. A. Silverman, J. J. Teevan, and V. F. Sacco (eds.), *Crime in Canadian Society,* 4th ed.: 307–317. Toronto: Butterworths.

Kelling, G. L. 1999. *"Broken Windows" and Police Discretion.* National Institute of Justice Research Report. Washington, D.C.: Office of Justice Programs, National Institute of Justice.

Kelling, G. L., and C. M. Coles. 1996. *Fixing Broken Windows.* New York: Free Press.

Kempf, K. L. 1987. "Specialization and the Criminal Career." *Criminology* 25 (3): 399–420.

Kennedy, L. W., and S. Baron. 1993. "Routine Activities and A Subculture of Violence: A Study of Violence on the Street." *Journal of Research in Crime and Delinquency* 30(1): 88–112.

Kennedy, L. W., and D. Forde. 1998. *When Push Comes to Shove.* Albany: State University of New York Press.

———. 1990. "Routine Activities and Crime: An Analysis of Victimization in Canada." *Criminology* 28(1): 101–115.

Kennedy, L. W., and R. A. Silverman. 1990. "The Elderly Victim of Homicide: An Application of the Routine Activities Approach." *Sociological Quarterly* 31(2): 307–319.

Kennedy, R. 1998. *Race, the Police, and "Reasonable Suspicion."* Perspectives on Crime and Justice Lecture Series 1997–1998. Washington, D.C.: National Institute of Justice.

Klaus, P. A., and M. R. Rand. 1984. *Family Violence.* Washington, D.C.: Bureau of Justice Statistics.

Kleck, G., and B. Patterson. 1989. "The Impact of Gun Control and Gun Ownership Levels on City Violence Rates." Paper presented at the annual meeting of the American Society of Criminology, Reno, Nevada (November).

Kleck, G., and S. Sayles. 1990. "Rape and Resistance." *Social Problems* 37(2): 149–162.

Klockars, Carl B. 1985. *The Idea of Police.* Beverly Hills, Calif.: Sage.

Kornhauser, R. 1978. *Social Sources of Delinquency.* Chicago: University of Chicago Press.

Krahn, H., and Kennedy, L. W. 1985. "Producing Personal Safety: The Effects of Crime Rates, Police Force Size, and Fear of Crime." *Criminology* 23(4): 697–710.

Krupat, E., and P. Kubzansky. 1987. "Designing to Deter Crime." *Psychology Today* (October): 58–61.

Kurz, D. 1987. "Emergency Department Responses to Battered Women: Resistance to Medicalization." *Social Problems* 34(1): 69–81.

Lab, S. P. 1992. *Crime Prevention: Approaches, Practices, and Evaluations.* 2d ed. Cincinnati: Anderson.

LaGrange, R. L., K. F. Ferraro, and M. Supanic. 1992. "Perceived Risk and Fear of Crime: Role of Social and Physical Incivilities." *Journal of Research in Crime and Delinquency* 29: 311–334.

Langan, P., L. Greenfeld, S. Smith, M. Durose, and D. Levin. 2001. *Contacts between Police and the Public.* Washington, D.C.: Bureau of Justice Statistics.

Lasley J. 1998. *"Designing Out" Gang Homicides and Street Assaults.* National Institute of Justice, Research in Brief. Washington D.C.: U.S. Department of Justice.

Lasley, J. R., and J. L. Rosenbaum. 1988. "Routine Activities and Multiple Personal Victimization." *Sociology and Social Research* 73(1): 47–50.

Lauritsen, J. L., R. J. Sampson, and J. H. Laub. 1991. "The Link between Offending and Victimization among Adolescents." *Criminology* 29(2): 265–292.

Lawson, Paul E. 1982. *Solving Somebody Else's Blues*. Latham, Md.: University Press of America.

Leitzel, J. 2001. "Race and Policing." *Society* 38(3): 38–42.

Lejeune, R., and N. Alex. 1973. "On Being Mugged." *Urban Life and Culture* 2(3): 259–283.

Letkemann, P. 1973. *Crime as Work*. Englewood Cliffs, N.J.: Prentice-Hall.

Light, I. 1977. "The Ethnic Vice Industry, 1880–1944." *American Sociological Review* 42 (June): 464–479.

Lindner, C., and R. J. Koehler. 1992. "Probation Officer Victimization: An Emerging Concern." *Journal of Criminal Justice* 20(1): 52–62.

Liska, A. E., and W. Baccaglini. 1990. "Feeling Safe by Comparison: Crime in the Newspapers." *Social Problems* 37(3): 360–374.

Liska, A. E., and B. D. Warner. 1991. "Functions of Crime: A Paradoxical Process." *American Journal of Sociology* 6: 1441–1463.

Loftus, E. F. 1979. *Eyewitness Testimony*. Cambridge: Harvard University Press.

Loseke, D. R. 1989. "'Violence' Is 'Violence' . . . or Is It? The Social Construction of 'Wife Abuse' and Public Policy." In J. Best (ed.), *Images of Issues: Typifying Contemporary Social Problems*. New York: Aldine de Gruyter.

Luckenbill, D. F. 1984. "Murder and Assault." In R. F. Meier (ed.), *Major Forms of Crime*. Beverly Hills, Calif.: Sage.

———. 1977. "Criminal Homicide as a Situated Transaction." *Social Problems* 25(2): 176–186.

Luckenbill, D. F., and J. Best. 1981. "Careers in Deviance and Respectability: The Analogy's Limitation." *Social Problems* 29: 197–206.

Lurigio, A. J. 1987. "Are All Victims Alike? The Adverse, Generalized,

and Differential Impact of Crime." *Crime and Delinquency* 33: 452–467.

Lynch, J. P. 1987. "Routine Activity and Victimization at Work." *Journal of Quantitative Criminology* 3(4): 283–300.

Lynch, J. P., and D. Cantor. 1992. "Ecological and Behavioral Influences on Property Victimization at Home: Implications for Opportunity Theory." *Journal of Research in Crime and Delinquency* 29(3): 335–362.

Lyng, S. 1990. "Edgework: A Social Psychological Analysis of Voluntary Risk Taking." *American Journal of Sociology* 95(4): 851–886.

MacMillan, R. 1995. "Changes in the Structure of Life Courses and the Decline of Social Capital in Canadian Society: A Time Series Analysis of Property Crime Rates." *Canadian Journal of Sociology* 20(1): 51–79.

MacMillan, R., and R. Gartner. 1999. "When She Brings Home the Bacon: Labor Force Participation and the Risk of Spousal Violence against Women." *Journal of Marriage and the Family* 61(4): 947–958.

Madriz, E. 1996. "The Perception of Risk in the Workplace: A Test of Routine Activity Theory." *Journal of Criminal Justice* 24(5): 407–418.

Maguire, B., D. Sandage, and G. A. Weatherby. 2000. "Violence, Morality, and Television Commercials." *Sociological Spectrum* 20: 121–143.

Maguire, M. (with T. Bennett). 1982. *Burglary in a Dwelling: The Offence, the Offender, and the Victim*. London: Heinemann.

Malamuth, N. M. 1983. "Factors Associated with Rape as Predictors of Laboratory Aggression against Women." *Journal of Personality and Social Psychology* 45: 432–442.

Malamuth, N. M., and E. Donnerstein. 1984. *Pornography and Sexual Aggression*. Orlando, Fla.: Academic Press.

Martin, R., R. J. Mutchnick, and W. T. Austin. 1990. *Criminological Thought: Pioneers Past and Present*. New York: Macmillan.

Massey, J. L., M. D. Krohn, and L. M. Bonati. 1989. "Property Crime and the Routine Activities of Individuals." *Journal of Research in Crime and Delinquency* 26(4): 378–400.

Matza, D., and G. M. Sykes. 1961. "Juvenile Delinquency and Subterranean Values." *American Sociological Review* 26: 712–719.

Maxfield, M. G. 1999. "The National Incident-Based Reporting System: Research and Policy Implications." *Journal of Quantitative Criminology* 15(2): 119–149.

———. 1990. "Homicide Circumstances, 1976–1985: A Taxonomy Based on Supplementary Homicide Reports." *Criminology* 28: 671–695.

Mayhew, P., D. Elliott, and L. Dowds. 1989. *The 1988 British Crime Survey.* Home Office Research and Planning Unit Report. London: HMSO Books.

Mayhew, P., N. Maung, and C. Mirrlees-Black. 1993. *The 1992 British Crime Survey.* London: HMSO Books.

McCarthy, B., and J. Hagan. 1991. "Homelessness: A Criminogenic Situation?" *British Journal of Criminology* 31(4): 393–410.

McCord, J. 1991. "Family Relationships, Juvenile Delinquency, and Adult Criminality." *Criminology* 29(3): 397–417.

McIntosh, M. 1975. *The Organization of Crime.* London: Macmillan.

Menard, S., and H. C. Covey. 1988. "UCR and NCS: Comparisons over Space and Time." *Journal of Criminal Justice* 16: 371–384.

Meredith, N. 1984. "The Murder Epidemic." *Science* (December): 41–48.

Merry, S. E. 1981. *Urban Danger.* Philadelphia: Temple University Press.

Merton, R. K. 1938. "Social Structure and Anomie." *American Sociological Review* 3: 672–682.

Messner, S. F., and J. R. Blau. 1987. "Routine Leisure Activities and Rates of Crime: A Macro-Level Analysis." *Social Forces* 65: 1035–1051.

Michalowski, R. J., and E. W. Bohlander. 1976. "Repression and Criminal Justice in Capitalist America." *Sociological Inquiry* 46(2): 95–106.

Miethe, T. D., and G. R. Lee. 1990. "Fear of Crime among Older People: A Reassessment of the Predictive Power of Crime-Related Factors." *Sociological Quarterly* 25: 397–415.

Miethe, T. D., and R. F. Meier. 1990. "Opportunity, Choice, and Criminal Victimization: A Test of a Theoretical Model." *Journal of Research in Crime and Delinquency* 27(3): 243–266.

Miethe, T. D., and R. F. Meier. 1994. *Crime and Its Social Context: Toward an Integrated Theory of Offenders, Victims, and Situations.* Albany: State University of New York Press.

Miller, G. 1978. *Odd Jobs.* Englewood Cliffs, N.J.: Prentice-Hall.

Miller, L. J. 1990. "Violent Families and the Rhetoric of Harmony." *British Journal of Sociology* 41(2): 263–288.

Moeller, G. L. 1989. "Fear of Criminal Victimization: The Effects of Neighborhood Racial Composition." *Sociological Inquiry* 59: 208–221.

Monkkonen, Eric H. 1983. "The Organized Response to Crime in Nineteenth- and Twentieth-Century America." *Journal of Interdisciplinary History* 14(1): 113–128.

Newman, O. 1972. *Defensible Space: Crime Prevention through Urban Design.* New York: Macmillan.

Normandeau, A. 1987. "Crime on the Montreal Metro." *Sociology and Social Research* 71(4): 289–292.

O'Brien, R. M. 1985. *Crime and Victimization Data.* Vol. 4, Law and Criminal Justice Series. Beverly Hills, Calif.: Sage.

O'Kane, J. M. 1992. *Crooked Ladder: Gangsters, Ethnicity, and the American Dream.* New Brunswick, N.J.: Transaction Books.

Osgood, D. W., J. K. Wilson, P. M. O'Malley, J. G. Bachman, and L. D. Johnston. 1996. "Routine Activities and Individual Deviant Behaviour."

American Sociological Review 61: 635–655.

Packer, H. L. 1969. *The Limits of the Criminal Sanction.* Stanford, Calif.: Stanford University Press.

Pagelow, M. D. 1989. "The Incidence and Prevalence of Criminal Abuse of Other Family Members." In L. Ohlin and M. Tonry (eds.), *Family Violence,* pp. 263–313. Chicago: University of Chicago Press.

Palenski, J. E. 1984. "The Use of Mediation by Police." *Mediation Quarterly* 5: 31–38.

Patterson, G. R., and T. J. Dishion. 1985. "Contributions of Families and Peers to Delinquency." *Criminology* 23: 63–79.

Pease, K., and G. Laycock. 1996. *Revictimization: Reducing the Heat on Hot Victims.* Washington, D.C.: National Institute of Justice.

Peek, C. W., J. L. Fischer, and J. S. Kidwell. 1985. "Teenage Violence toward Parents: A Neglected Dimension of Family Violence." *Journal of Marriage and the Family* 47: 1051–1058.

Phillips, D. P. 1983. "The Impact of Mass Media Violence on U.S. Homicides." *American Sociological Review* 48 (August): 560–568.

Pillemer, K. A. 1985. "The Dangers of Dependency: New Findings on Domestic Violence against the Elderly." *Social Problems* 33: 146–158.

Pillemer, K. A., and D. Finkelhor. 1988. "The Prevalence of Elder Abuse: A Random Sample Survey." *Gerontologist* 28(1): 51–57.

Potter, R. H., and L. E. Saltzman. 2000. "Violence Prevention and Corrections-Related Activities of the Centers for Disease Control and Prevention." *Criminologist* 25(2): 1, 4–6.

Prinz R. 2000. "Research-Based Prevention of School Violence and Youth Antisocial Behavior: A Developmental and Education Perspective." In *Preventing School Violence: Plenary Papers of the 1999 Conference on Criminal Justice Research and Evaluation—Enhancing Policy and Practice through Research,*

vol. 2. Washington D.C.: U.S. Department of Justice.

Provenzo, E. F. 1991. *Video Kids: Making Sense of Nintendo.* Cambridge: Harvard University Press.

Quinn, M. J., and S. K. Tomita. 1986. *Elder Abuse and Neglect: Causes, Diagnosis, and Intervention Strategies.* New York: Springer-Verlag.

Rankin, J. H., and L. E. Wells. 1990. "The Effect of Parental Attachments and Direct Controls on Delinquency." *Journal of Research on Crime and Delinquency* 27(2): 140–165.

Reiman, J. H. 1998. *The Rich Get Richer and the Poor Get Prison,* 5th ed. New York: Macmillan.

———. 1990. *The Rich Get Richer and the Poor Get Prison,* 3d ed. New York: Macmillan.

Reiss, A. J., Jr. 1986a. "Official and Survey Crime Statistics." In E. A. Fattah (ed.), *From Crime Policy to Victim Policy—Reorienting the Justice System.* London: Macmillan.

———. 1986b. "Policy Implications of Crime Victim Surveys." In E. A. Fattah (ed.), *From Crime Policy to Victim Policy—Reorienting the Justice System.* London: Macmillan.

———. 1984. "Consequences of Compliance and Deterrence Models of Law Enforcement for the Exercise of Police Discretion." *Law and Contemporary Problems* 47(4): 83–122.

Rengert, G., and J. Wasilchick. 1985. *Suburban Burglary: A Time and a Place for Everything.* Springfield, Ill.: Charles C. Thomas.

Rennison, C. M. 2000. *Criminal Victimization 1999.* Washington, D.C.: Bureau of Justice Statistics.

Reppetto, T. 1974. *A Residential Crime.* Cambridge, Mass.: Ballinger.

Reppetto, T., and J. Lardner. 2000. *NYPD: A City and Its Police.* New York: Henry Holt and Company.

Reuter, P. 1995. "The Decline of the American Mafia." *Public Interest* 120: 88–89.

———. 1984. "The (Continued) Vitality of Mythical Numbers." *Public Interest* 75: 135–147.

Rich, T. 2001. *Crime Mapping and Analysis by Community Organizations in Hartford, Connecticut.* Washington, D.C.: National Institute of Justice, Research in Brief (March).

Richie, B. E. 2000. "Exploring the Link between Violence against Women and Women's Involvement in Illegal Activity." In *Research on Women and Girls in the Justice System,* vol. 3. Washington, D.C.: Office of Justice Programs, National Institute of Justice.

Riley, D. 1987. "Time and Crime: The Link between Teenager Lifestyle and Delinquency." *Journal of Quantitative Criminology* 3(4): 339–354.

Roncek, D. W. 1981. "Dangerous Places." *Social Forces* 60: 74–96.

Roncek, D. W., and P. A. Maier. 1991. "Bars, Blocks, and Crimes Revisited: Linking the Theory of Routine Activities to the Empiricism of 'Hot Spots.'" *Criminology* 29(4): 725–753.

Roncek, D. W., and M. A. Pravatiner. 1989. "Additional Evidence That Taverns Enhance Nearby Crime." *Sociology and Social Research* 73(4): 185–188.

Rosenbaum, D. P. 1988. "Community Crime Prevention: A Review and Synthesis of the Literature." *Justice Quarterly* 5(3): 323–395.

———. 1987. "The Theory and Research behind Neighborhood Watch: Is It a Sound Fear and Crime Reduction Strategy?" *Crime and Delinquency* 33(1): 103–134.

Rosenbaum, H. J., and P. C. Sederberg. 1976. "Vigilantism: An Analysis of Establishment Violence." In H. J. Rosenbaum and P. C. Sederberg (eds.), *Vigilante Politics.* Philadelphia: University of Pennsylvania Press.

Rosenfeld, R. 2000. In A. Blumstein and J. Wallman (eds.), *2000 Crime Rate Drops,* pp. 130–163. New York: Cambridge University Press.

Ruback, R. B., M. S. Greenberg, and D. R. Wescott. 1984. "Social Influence and Crime-Victim Decision Making." *Journal of Social Issues* 40(1): 51–76.

Rush, G. 1994. *The Dictionary of Criminal Justice,* 4th ed. Guilford, Conn.: Dushkin.

Sacco, V. F., and H. Johnson. 1990. *Patterns of Criminal Victimization in Canada.* Ottawa: Minister of Supply and Services.

Sacco, V. F., and R. A. Silverman. 1982. "Crime Prevention through Mass Media: Prospects and Problems." *Journal of Criminal Justice* 10: 257–269.

Sales, E., M. Baum, and B. Shore. 1984. "Victim Readjustment following Assault." *Journal of Social Issues* 40(1): 117–136.

Salinger, L. R., P. Jesilow, H. N. Pontell, and G. Geis. 1993. "Assaults against Airline Flight Attendants: A Victimization Study." In H. N. Pontell (ed.), *Social Deviance,* pp. 276–282. Englewood Cliffs, N.J.: Prentice-Hall.

Sampson, R. J. 1987. "Urban Black Violence: The Effect of Male Joblessness and Family Disruption." *American Journal of Sociology* 93(2): 348–382.

Sampson, R. J., and W. B. Groves. 1989. "Community Structure and Crime: Testing Social Disorganization Theory." *American Journal of Sociology* 94: 774–802.

Sampson, R. J., and J. H. Laub. 1990. "Crime and Deviance over the Life Course: The Salience of Adult Social Bonds." *American Sociological Review* 55: 609–627.

Sampson, R. J., and J. L. Lauritsen. 1990. "Deviant Lifestyles, Proximity Crime, and the Offender-Victim Link in Personal Violence." *Journal of Research in Crime and Delinquency* 27(2): 110–139.

Sampson, R., and S. Raudenbush. 1999. "Systematic Social Observations of Public Spaces: A New Look at Disorder in Urban Neighborhoods." *American Journal of Sociology* 105(3): 603–651.

Sampson, R., S. Raudenbush, and F. Earls. 1997. "Neighborhood and Violent Crime: A Multilevel Study of Collective Efficacy." *Science* 277(5328): 918–924.

Sanger, D. E. 1993. "How to Visit America and Get Out Alive." *Globe and Mail* (June 18), p. A9.

Saunders, D. G. 1989. "Who Hits First and Who Hurts Most? Evidence for the Greater Victimization of Women in Intimate Relationships." Paper presented at the annual meeting of the American Society of Criminology, Reno, Nevada (November).

Scheingold, Stuart A. 1984. *The Politics of Law and Order: Street Crime and Public Policy.* New York: Longman.

Schelling, T. C. 1967. "Economic Analysis of Organized Crime." In *President's Commission on Law Enforcement and Administration of Justice Task Force Report: Organized Crime, Annotations, and Consultant's Papers,* pp. 114–126. Washington, D.C.: U.S. Government Printing Office.

Scheppele, K. L., and P. B. Bart. 1983. "Through Women's Eyes: Defining Danger in the Wake of Sexual Assault." *Journal of Social Issues* 39: 63–81.

Schur, E. M. 1979. *Interpreting Deviance.* New York: Harper and Row.

Schwartz, M. D. 1988. "Ain't Got No Class: Universal Risk Theories of Battering." *Contemporary Crises* 12: 375–392.

Sedlak, A. J. 1988. "The Effects of Personal Experiences with Couple Violence on Calling It 'Battering' and Allocating Blame." In G. T. Hotaling, D. Finkelhor, J. T. Kirpatrick, and M. A. Straus (eds.), *Coping with Family Violence.* Newbury Park, Calif.: Sage.

Sellin, T. 1938. *Culture Conflict and Crime: A Report of the Subcommittee on Delinquency of the Committee on Personality and Culture.* Bulletin 41. New York: Social Science Research Council.

Shaffer, Evelyn B. 1980. *Community Policing.* London: Croom Helm.

Shaw, C. R., and H. D. McKay. 1942. *Juvenile Delinquency in Urban Areas.* Chicago: University of Chicago Press.

Shearing, C. D., and P. C. Stenning. 1983. "Private Security: Implications for Social Control." *Social Problems* 30: 493–506.

Sheley, J. F. 1991. "Conflict in Criminal Law." In J. F. Sheley (ed.), *Criminology: A Contemporary Handbook,* pp. 21–39. Belmont, Calif.: Wadsworth.

Sherman, L. 1992. *Policing Domestic Violence: Experiments and Dilemmas.* New York: Free Press.

Sherman, L., and R. Berk. 1984. "The Specific Deterrent Effects of Arrest for Domestic Assault." *American Sociological Review* 49: 261–272.

Sherman, L., P. R. Gartin, and M. E. Buerger. 1989. "Routine Activities and the Criminology of Place." *Criminology* 27(1): 27–55.

Sherman, L., D. C. Gottfredson, D. L. MacKenzie, J. Eck, P. Reuter, and S. D. Bushway. 1998. *Preventing Crime: What Works, What Doesn't, What's Promising.* National Institute of Justice, Research in Brief. Washington, D.C.: Office of Justice Programs, U.S. Department of Justice.

Sherman, L., J. Schmidt, D. Rogan, and C. DeRiso. 1991. "Predicting Domestic Homicide: Prior Police Contact and Gun Threats." In Michael Steinman (ed.), *Woman Battering: Policy Responses.* Cincinnati: Anderson.

Shotland, R. L., and L. I. Goodstein. 1984. "The Role of Bystanders in Crime Control." *Journal of Social Issues* 40(1): 9–26.

Shotland, R. L., and M. K. Straw. 1976. "Bystander Response to an Assault: When a Man Attacks a Woman." *Journal of Personality and Social Psychology* 34: 990–999.

Shover, N. 1983. "The Later Stages of Ordinary Property Offender Careers." *Social Problems* 30: 208–218.

———. 1973. "The Social Organization of Burglary." *Social Problems* 201 (Spring): 499–513.

Silverman, R. A., and L. Kennedy. 1993. *Deadly Deeds: Murder in Canada.* Scarborough, Ont.: Nelson Canada.

Silverman, R. A., and M. O. Nielsen. 1992. *Aboriginal Peoples and Canadian Criminal Justice.* Toronto: Butterworths.

Simon, D. R., and D. S. Eitzen. 1993. *Elite Deviance,* 4th ed. Boston: Allyn and Bacon.

Simpson, S. S., and C. S. Koper. 1992. "Deterring Corporate Crime." *Criminology* 30(3): 347–375.

Singer, S. I., and M. Levine. 1988. "Power-Control Theory, Gender, and Delinquency: A Partial Replication with Additional Evidence on the Effect of Peers." *Criminology* 26: 627–647.

Skogan, W. G. 1993. "The Various Meanings of Fear." In W. Bilsky, C. Pfeiffer, and P. Wetzels (eds.), *Fear of Crime and Criminal Victimization.* Stuttgart, Germany: Ferdinand Enke Verlag.

———. 1990a. *Disorder and Decline.* New York: Free Press.

———. 1990b. "The National Crime Survey Redesign." *Public Opinion Quarterly* 54: 256–272.

———. 1987. "The Impact of Victimization on Fear." *Crime and Delinquency* 33: 135–154.

———. 1986. "Methodological Issues in the Study of Victimization." In E. A. Fattah (ed.), *From Crime Policy to Victim Policy—Reorienting the Justice System.* London: Macmillan.

Skogan, W. G., and M. G. Maxfield. 1981. *Coping with Crime: Individual and Neighborhood Reactions.* Beverly Hills, Calif.: Sage.

Skogan, W. G., and M. A. Wycoff. 1987. "Some Unexpected Effects of a Police Service for Victims." *Crime and Delinquency* 33: 490–501.

Skolnick, J. 1966. *Justice without Trial.* New York: John Wiley.

Smith, D. A. 1987. "Police Response to Interpersonal Violence: Defining the Parameters of Legal Control." *Social Forces* 65(3): 767–782.

Smith, D. 1975. *The Mafia Mystique.* New York: Basic Books.

Smith, D. A., and G. R. Jarjoura. 1989. "Household Characteristics, Neighbourhood Composition, and Victimization Risk." *Social Forces* 68(2): 621–640.

Smith, R. S., S. G. Frazee, and E. L. Davison. 2000. "Furthering the Integration of Routine Activity and Social Disorganization Theories: Small Units of Analysis and the Study of Street Robbery as a Diffusion Process." *Criminology* 38(2): 489–524.

Smith, S. J. 1982. "Victimization in the Inner City." *British Journal of Criminology* 22: 386–401.

Snider, L. 1993. *Bad Business: Corporate Crime in Canada.* Scarborough, Ont.: Nelson Canada.

———. 1992. "Commercial Crime." In V. F. Sacco (ed.), *Deviance: Conformity and Control in Canadian Society,* 2d ed. Scarborough, Ont.: Prentice-Hall.

Snyder, H. 2000. *Sexual Assault of Young Children as Reported to Law Enforcement: Victim, Incident, and Offender Characteristics.* Washington, D.C: U.S. Department of Justice, Bureau of Justice Statistics.

Sourcebook of Criminal Justice Statistics. 1999. Albany: State University of New York.

Spelman, W., and J. Eck. 1995. "Sitting Ducks, Ravenous Wolves, and Helping Hands: New Approaches in Urban Policing." *Public Affairs Comment* 35: 1–9.

Stark, R. 1987. "Deviant Places: A Theory of the Ecology of Crime." *Criminology* 25(4): 893–909.

Steffensmeier, D. J., and E. Allen. 1991. "Gender, Age, and Crime." In J. F. Sheley (ed.), *Criminology: A Contemporary Handbook.* Belmont, Calif.: Wadsworth.

Steffensmeier, D. J., and R. H. Steffensmeier. 1973. "Who Reports Shoplifters? Research Continuities and Further Developments." *International Journal of Criminology and Penology* 3: 79–95.

Steinman, M. 1992. "Going beyond Arrest: Police Responses to Domestic Violence." Paper presented at the annual meeting of the American Society of Criminology, New Orleans, Louisiana.

Steinmetz, S. 1986. "The Violent Family." In M. Lystad (ed.), *Violence in the Home: Interdisciplinary Perspectives.* New York: Brunner/Mazel.

————. 1977–1978. "The Battered Husband Syndrome." *Victimology* 2: 499–509.

Stoddart, K. 1991. "It's Easier for the Bulls Now: Official Statistics and Social Change in a Canadian Heroin-Using Community." In R. A. Silverman, J. J. Teevan, and V. F. Sacco (eds.), *Crime in Canadian Society,* 4th ed., pp. 99–108. Toronto: Butterworths.

Straus, M. A. 1990. "Social Stress and Marital Violence in a National Sample of American Families." In M. A. Straus and R. J. Gelles (eds.), *Physical Violence in American Families: Risk Factors and Adaptations to Violence in 8,145 Families.* New Brunswick, N.J.: Transaction Publishers, pp. 181–202.

Straus, M. A., and R. J. Gelles. 1990. "How Violent Are American Families? Estimates from the National Family Violence Resurvey and Other Studies." In M. A. Straus and R. J. Gelles (eds.), *Physical Violence in American Families: Risk Factors and Adaptations to Violence in 8,145 Families,* pp. 95–112. New Brunswick, N.J.: Transaction Publishers.

Straus, M. A., and C. Smith. 1990. "Family Patterns and Child Abuse." In M. A. Straus and R. J. Gelles (eds.), *Physical Violence in American Families: Risk Factors and Adaptations to Violence in 8,145 Families,* pp. 245–262. New Brunswick, N.J.: Transaction.

Sullivan, M., and B. Miller. 1999. "Adolescent Violence, State Processes, and the Local Context of Moral Panic." In J. Heyman, *State and Illegal Practices,* pp. 261–283. New York: Oxford University Press.

Surette, R. 1992. *Media, Crime, and Criminal Justice: Images and Realities.* Pacific Grove, Calif.: Brooks/Cole.

Sutherland, E. H. 1940. "White-Collar Criminality." *American Sociological Review* 5: 1–12.

Suttles, G. 1972. *The Social Construction of Communities.* Chicago: University of Chicago Press.

Tanner, J. 2001. *Teenage Troubles,* 2d ed. Scarborough, Ont.: Nelson Canada.

Tanner, J., and H. Krahn. 1991. "Part-time Work and Deviance among High School Seniors." *Canadian Journal of Sociology* 16(3): 281–302.

Tate, E. D. 1998. "The Ontario Royal Commission on Violence in the Communications Industry: Twenty Years Later." *British Journal of Communication Studies* 13(1): 148–163.

Taylor, R. B., and S. Gottfredson. 1986. "Environmental Design and Prevention: An Examination of Community Dynamics." In A. J. Reiss, Jr., and M. Tonry (eds.), *Communities and Crime.* Chicago: University of Chicago Press.

Taylor, S. E., J. V. Wood, and R. R. Lichtman. 1983. "It Could Be Worse: Selective Evaluation as a Response to Victimization." *Journal of Social Issues* 39: 19–40.

Thomas, P. 1995 "Gun Control Will Decrease Crime." In P. A. Winters (ed.), *Crime and Criminals,* pp. 153–160. San Diego: Greenhaven Press.

Thompson, W. E. 1986. "Courtship Violence: Toward a Conceptual Understanding." *Youth and Society* 18(2): 162–176.

Thornberry, T. P. 1987. "Toward an Interactional Theory of Delinquency." *Criminology* 25(4): 863–892.

Timmer, D. A., and W. H. Norman. 1984. "The Ideology of Victim Precipitation." *Criminal Justice Review* 9: 63–68.

Tjaden, P., and N. Thoennes. 2000. "Full Report on the Prevalence, Incidence, and Consequences of Violence against Women." Washington, D.C.: National Institute of Justice.

Toby, J. 1983. *Violence in Schools.* National Institute of Justice, Research in Brief.

Washington, D.C.: U.S. Department of Justice.

———. 1974. "The Socialization and Control of Deviant Motivation." In D. Glaser (ed.), *Handbook of Criminology.* Chicago: Rand McNally.

Tremblay, M., and P. Tremblay. 1998. "Social Structure, Integration Opportunities, and the Direction of Violent Offenses." *Journal of Research in Crime and Delinquency* 35(3): 295–315.

Tunnell, K. D. 1992. *Choosing Crime: The Criminal Calculus of Property Offenders.* Chicago: Nelson-Hall.

Uggen, C. 2000. "Work as a Turning Point in the Life Course of Criminals: A Duration Model of Age, Employment, and Recidivism." *American Sociological Review* 65(4): 529–546.

Unger, D. G., and A. Wandersman. 1985. "The Importance of Neighbors: The Social, Cognitive, and Affective Components of Neighboring." *American Journal of Community Psychology* 13(2): 139–169.

U.S. Department of Justice. 2000. *Criminal Victimization in the United States: 1998 Statistical Tables.* Washington, D.C.

———. 1998. *First Annual Report on School Safety: 1998.* Washington, D.C.

———. 1994a. *Criminal Victimization in the United States, 1992.* Washington D.C.: U.S. Government Printing Office.

———. 1994b. *Sourcebook of Criminal Justice Statistics, 1993.* NCJ-148211. Washington D.C.: Bureau of Justice Statistics.

———. 1993. *Felony Defendants in Large Urban Counties, 1990.* NCJ-141872. Washington D.C: Bureau of Justice Statistics.

Van den Haag, E. 1975. *Punishing Criminals: Concerning a Very Old and Painful Question.* New York: Basic Books.

van Dijk, J. J. M., and J. de Waard. 1991. "A Two-Dimensional Typology of Crime Prevention Projects with a Bibliography." *Criminal Justice Abstracts* (September).

Visher, C. A. 1991. "Career Offenders and Selective Incapacitation." In J. F. Sheley (ed.), *Criminology: A Contemporary Handbook.* Belmont, Calif.: Wadsworth.

Wachs, E. 1988. *Crime-Victim Stories: New York City's Urban Folklore.* Bloomington: Indiana University Press.

Walklate, S. 1989. *Victimology: The Victim and the Criminal Justice System.* London: Unwin Hyman.

Waller, I., and N. Okihiro. 1978. *Burglary: The Victim and the Public.* Toronto: University of Toronto Press.

Walsh, W. F., and E. J. Donovan. 1989. "Private Security and Community Policing: Evaluation and Comment." *Journal of Criminal Justice* 17: 187–197.

Warchol, G. 1998. *Workplace Violence, 1992–1996.* National Crime Victimization Survey; Bureau of Justice Statistics Special Report. Washington, D.C.: U.S. Department of Justice.

Warr, M. 1998. "Life-Course Transitions and Desistance from Crime." *Criminology* 36(2): 183–215.

———. 1988. "Rape, Burglary, and Opportunity." *Journal of Quantitative Criminology* 4(3): 275–288.

Warr, M., and C. Ellison. 2000. "Rethinking Social Reactions to Crime: Personal and Altruistic Fear in Family Households." *American Journal of Sociology* 106(3): 551–578.

Weis, J. G. 1989. "Family Violence Research Methodology and Design." In L. Ohlin and M. Tonry (eds.), *Family Violence, Crime, and Justice—A Review of Research,* vol. 11. Chicago: University of Chicago Press.

Wellford, C. F. 1997. "Victimization Rates for Domestic Travelers." *Journal of Criminal Justice* 3: 205–210.

West, D. J., and D. P. Farrington. 1977. *The Delinquent Way of Life.* London: Heinemann.

"Westray Charges Thrown Out." 1993. *Globe and Mail* (July 21), p. A1.

Whitaker, C. J., and L. D. Bastian. 1991. *Teenage Victims.* National Crime Survey Report. Washington, D.C.: U.S. Department of Justice.

Widom, C. S. 1995. "Victimization of Childhood Sexual Abuse—Later Criminal Consequences." Washington, D.C.: U.S. Department of Justice.

Williams, K. R., and R. L. Flewelling. 1988. "The Social Production of Criminal Homicide: A Comparative Study of Disaggregated Rates in American Cities." *American Sociological Review* 53: 421–431.

Williams, K. R., and R. Hawkins. 1986. "Perceptual Research on General Deterrence: A Critical Review." *Law and Society Review* 20: 545–572.

Wilson, J. 1980. "Sociology of Leisure." *Annual Review of Sociology* 6: 21–40.

Wilson, J. Q. 1983. *Thinking about Crime.* New York: Vintage.

Wilson, J. Q., and R. J. Herrnstein. 1985. *Crime and Human Nature.* New York: Simon and Schuster.

Wilson, J. Q., and G. L. Kelling. 1982. "Broken Windows." *Atlantic Monthly* (March): 29–38.

Wilson, W. J. 1987. *The Truly Disadvantaged: The Inner City, The Underclass, and Public Policy.* Chicago: University of Chicago Press.

Wirth, L. 1938. "Urbanism as a Way of Life." *American Journal of Sociology* 44: 3–24.

Wirtz, P. W., and A. V. Harrell. 1987. "Police and Victims of Physical Assault." *Criminal Justice and Behavior* 14: 81–92.

Wittebrood, K., and P. Nieuwbeerta. 2000. "Criminal Victimization during One's Life Course: The Effects of Previous Victimization and Patterns of Routine Activities." *Journal of Research in Crime and Delinquency* 37(1): 91–122.

Wolff, D. 1991. *The Rebels: A Brotherhood of Outlaw Bikers.* Toronto: University of Toronto Press.

Wolfgang, M. 1958. *Patterns in Criminal Homicide.* Philadelphia: University of Pennsylvania Press.

Wolfgang, M., R. M. Figlio, and T. Sellin. 1972. *Delinquency in a Birth Cohort.* Chicago: University of Chicago Press.

Wright, J. D., and P. Rossi. 1986. *Armed and Considered Dangerous: A Survey of Felons and Their Firearms.* Hawthorne, N.Y.: Aldine de Gruyter.

Wright, J. P., and F. T. Cullen. 2000. "Juvenile Involvement in Occupational Delinquency." *Criminology* 38(3): 863–896.

Wright, R., and T. Bennett. 1990. "Exploring the Offender's Perspective: Observing and Interviewing Criminals." In K. L. Kempf (ed.), *Measurement Issues in Criminology.* New York: Springer-Verlag.

Zawitz, M. W., P. A. Klaus, R. Bachman, L. D. Bastian, M. M. DeBerry, Jr., M. R. Rand, and B. M. Tayler. 1993. *Highlights from Twenty Years of Surveying Crime Vic\tims.* Washington, D.C.: Bureau of Justice Statistics.

Ziegenhagen, E. A., and D. Brosnan. 1985. "Victims Responses to Robbery and Crime Control Policy." *Criminology* 23: 675–695.

Index

Abbott, A., 60–61, 75
acquaintance rapes, 16
actus reus, 3
African Americans, 43, 48, 52, 151
aftermath of criminal events: and crime prevention, 138; as criminal event component, 11, 16–19; and criminal justice system, 8–9; and data collection, 28; and employment, 103–104; and enterprise crime, 115–116; and family violence, 85–88; and leisure settings, 128–129; and property crime, 91–93; and tourism, 131; and victim-offender relationship, 26; and work-related crime, 110–111
age: and conceptualization of crime, 4; and criminal career, 40; and data collection, 25–26; and property crime, 88; and type of crime, 36; and victims, 43. *See also* children; elderly; juvenile delinquency; teenagers
Agnew, R. S., 46
Akers, R. L., 105
alcohol: and conflict, 127; and crime prevention, 19; and dating violence, 83; and employment, 102; and enterprise crime, 112; and family violence, 84, 85; and leisure settings, 124; and lifestyle exposure theory, 71; and offenders, 36, 149; and precursors of criminal events, 12–13; and property crime, 92; and transactions of criminal events, 14; and zero-tolerance policies, 99
Alex, N., 47
American National Crime Survey, 103

Amir, M., 13
Anselin, L., 55
authority relations, 23
avoidance behavior, 79

Barker, R., 10
Baron, S., 71–72, 124, 125, 126, 128
bars: as criminal event domains, 19–20; and employees as crime victims, 97; as leisure settings, 119, 123–124, 127, 128, 132; and lifestyle exposure theory, 64; and precursors of criminal events, 12; and routine conflict theory, 70
battered-woman syndrome, 4
Bayley, D. H., 142
Beare, M. E., 112
Beck, A. J., 48
Bell, Daniel, 114
Benson, M. L., 109
Berk, R., 52
Best, Joel, 9, 41
Black, D. J., 51, 143
Blau, J. R., 123
Block, C. R., 97–98
Block, R., 97–98
Box, Steven, 6
Brady, James, 151
Brady Bill, 151
Brantingham, Patricia, 135–136
Brantingham, Paul, 135–136